Santa Fe's history is more than words on paper.
It is an epic story on a human scale.
Engaged, energetic people are the pulse of this enchanting
place, and that means you, the friends and partners,
the readers and customers of *The Santa Fe New Mexican*.
Please accept this book as a gift, a symbol of our shared
and enduring civic pride and community spirit.

Robin McKinney Martin
Editor and Publisher

SANTA FE ❋
NEW MEXICAN

Santa Fe

Its 400th Year

Exploring the Past, Defining the Future

Santa Fe

Its 400th Year

Exploring the Past, Defining the Future

Rob Dean, Editor

A
SANTA FE ✧
NEW MEXICAN
Book From

SUNSTONE
PRESS
SANTA FE

Sunstone books may be purchased for educational, business, or sales promotional use.
For information please write: Special Markets Department, Sunstone Press,
P.O. Box 2321, Santa Fe, New Mexico 87504-2321.

Book and Cover design › Vicki Ahl
Body typeface › Adobe Garamond Pro and Expressa
Printed on acid free paper

Library of Congress Cataloging-in-Publication Data

Santa Fe : its 400th year : exploring the past, defining the future / Rob Dean, editor.
p. cm.
Includes bibliographical references and index.
ISBN 978-0-86534-795-3 (hardcover : alk. paper) -- ISBN 978-0-86534-796-0 (softcover : alk. paper)
1. Santa Fe (N.M.)--History. 2. Santa Fe (N.M.)--Anniversaries, etc. 3. Santa Fe (N.M.)--Social life
and customs. 4. Santa Fe (N.M.)--Biography. I. Dean, Rob, 1954-
F804.S257S25 2010
978.9'56--dc22
                                        2010045871

Published in

WWW.SUNSTONEPRESS.COM
SUNSTONE PRESS / POST OFFICE BOX 2321 / SANTA FE, NM 87504-2321 /USA
(505) 988-4418 / ORDERS ONLY (800) 243-5644 / FAX (505) 988-1025

…What is history?
And we say: *Listen. Turn around. Turn ahead.*

—from "Listen" by Valerie Martínez,
Santa Fe Poet Laureate 2008–2010

Contents

11: Warriors / 285

12: Family / 313

Contributors / 345

Foreword

by
Carmella Padilla

In his classic 1959 book, *Santa Fe: The Autobiography of a Southwestern Town*, Oliver La Farge sifts through the social history of this storied city between 1849 and 1953. By then, Santa Fe had survived as the capital of New Mexico under Spanish, Mexican and American rule to arrive at the venerable old age of 349. Rather than detailing three-and-a-half centuries of the city's ever-changing story, La Farge focuses his narrative on a much tighter, though no less telling, period between the mid-nineteenth and mid-twentieth centuries.

By definition, as autobiography, the reader has every reason to expect La Farge's chronicle of Santa Fe to be couched within the author's story of himself. The prolific Pulitzer Prize-winning writer, noted anthropologist and champion of Indian rights made Santa Fe his permanent home from 1941 until his death in 1963. His personal story is tightly woven into the literary and cultural fabric of twentieth-century Santa Fe and the American Southwest. But instead of pointing his pen at himself, La Farge chose a decidedly different point of view from which to reflect on the city's life and times. In this case, the author cedes the literary front seat to the city's then 94-year-old newspaper, *The Santa Fe New Mexican.*

La Farge's approach was more than a clever twist on the art of autobiography. By examining Santa Fe's history and ongoing story of change in the mirror of its long-running newspaper, he gave journalism an elevated place in the realm of storytelling. More important, he brought the often romanticized, oversized story of Santa Fe down to earth, cutting it down to the everyday size of its residents, in whose narrow, winding streets life is worked and lived in all its glory and contradiction. Through their collective experience and personal voice, as documented in the pages of *The Santa Fe New Mexican*, La Farge enabled the city to speak for itself, to share its own inspiring, imperfect, incredible tale. Despite his national literary stature, La Farge counts himself as just another voice in the telling, the voice of a husband and father, a participant and observer, an ordinary character in the extraordinary Santa Fe human parade.

Of course, La Farge was no ordinary Santa Fean. Born in New York City, the Harvard-educated anthropologist had been propelled to the pinnacle of literary success by the time he was 30, winning the 1930 Pulitzer for his first novel, *Laughing Boy*. Set in 1915, the Navajo love story was inspired by the author's early work and travels on the Navajo reservation, which also inspired his deep love of the Southwest and lifelong commitment to Indian rights. After *Laughing Boy*, he wrote a string of fiction, nonfiction and scholarly works, including several books about the history and contemporary life of Native Americans. His memoir, *Raw Material*, was published in 1945. There and in other works, we begin to feel La Farge's love for the Old World charm, unpretentious style and multicultural milieu of Santa Fe. His 1956 *Behind the Mountains*, about the old Hispano life and culture of New Mexico, reflects his love of his second wife, Consuelo Baca of Rociada, whom he married in 1939.

In 1948, La Farge signed on as a weekly columnist for *The Santa Fe New Mexican*. From the perch of his post as "The Santa Fe Bird Watcher," La Farge commented upon and critiqued the comings, goings and doings of Santa Fe and Santa Feans. Alternately referring to his subject as "The City Different" and "The City Difficult," he called out the city's complexities and eccentricities, passionately describing and defending its qualities and quirks alike. La Farge was known to rail against any gesture by city leaders toward crass commercialism or modernity as a stake in the city's historic heart. He was active in the Old Santa Fe Association, founded in 1926 to preserve the best of the city's cultural traditions and to guide its future growth and development through the lens of history. He was a major player in the creation of the city's 1957 Historic Styles Ordinance, which strictly regulated architectural styles in designated historic zones.

For all La Farge's words and work in Santa Fe, he largely limits his authorial voice in the city's autobiography to the book's brief preface and a few select personal columns. More than anything, his words serve to help move the reader through the collection with a running commentary that illuminates local issues and personalities, notes factual and grammatical inaccuracies, and tracks the revolving door of *Santa Fe New Mexican* editors and owners through time. La Farge stays true to original news articles and editorials, allowing their diverse subject matter and often formal, but always colorful, language to open the window to the world of Santa Fe.

In using journalism to convey the city's realism, La Farge not only penned an autobiography of Santa Fe, he wrote an autobiography of *The Santa Fe New Mexican's* first one hundred years. He began at the newspaper's earliest documented appearance as a weekly publication, on November 28, 1849. With the Treaty of Guadalupe Hidalgo signed one year earlier, the terms were set for New Mexico's designation as a U.S. Territory, making Santa Fe the territorial capital. In their inaugural issue, *Santa Fe New Mexican* editors proposed a publication "devoted to the interests of the Territory of New Mexico," vowing "strict neutrality" in issues of politics and religion, and attention to "the advancement of Literature, the Arts and Sciences, and Agriculture." The issue was comprised of two pages in Spanish and two in English. The price to subscribe: $7 a month, $4 for six months, and $2.50 for three months.

As the voice of the territory, the newspaper's interests were not strictly limited to the affairs of Santa Fe, and newspapers were distributed throughout the sprawling New Mexico landscape. The paper's debut noted the perilous conditions of traveling in the far-flung territory, when robberies and murders by roving Apache, Navajo and Ute Indians were at a peak. Murders and other criminal affairs of the day were also recorded. From that first issue forward, as documented in *The Santa Fe New Mexican*, Santa Fe's unique place in western history and individual story as a city begin to unwind through the century.

The paper, according to La Farge, probably appeared irregularly until 1863. In 1864, we are reading about the Long Walk and incarceration of the Navajo at the Bosque Redondo and the arrival of the French cleric Jean Baptiste Lamy, who will become New Mexico's first archbishop. In 1865, with the assassination of President Abraham Lincoln, we see how Santa Feans mourned their leader: "the dark drapery on every house, betokened too plainly, that some awful and terrible calamity had befallen our nation." In 1867, editors grieved the death of Archbishop Lamy's fiercest opponent, Padre José Antonio Martínez of Taos, whom they described as "universally beloved by all who knew him." At the end of the decade, editors applauded the arrival of the railroad and the telegraph in the territory under the headline, "Steps Forward," declaring these signs of progress would allow New Mexico to "shine as brightly and potently in the national galaxy as any of her now more favored sisters."

Not every entry includes a headline, though with the 1880 arrest of Billy the Kid, the paper happily reported "The Kid and Two of His Gang in Limbo—They Now Roost in Santa Fe Jail." Despite their ongoing coverage of such territorial characters as The Kid and Kit Carson, editors in 1900 scolded parents for allowing their children to read "literature of the blood and thunder kind," including "dime novels and wild, wooly west stories." In 1902, they scolded proponents of a proposal to change New Mexico's name. While conceding that readers overwhelmingly favored a name change, they declared their reasons to be mistakenly "founded upon the expressions of ignorant persons in the east who have vague ideas about New Mexico just as they probably have about Oregon or Montana."

Editors were frequently willing to go to the national mat for New Mexico, particularly in the decades-long quest for statehood. In 1906, they even endorsed a proposal of joint statehood for New Mexico and Arizona, though the measure was voted down by Arizonans. Finally, with the 1912 proclamation of statehood by President William Howard Taft, the headline in the new state capital blared "Santa Fe is Wild With Joy." Statehood brought a flood of new visitors from the east, including artists, writers, archaeologists and cultural patrons who set down roots in Santa Fe. With the city's rise as an art colony and cultural mecca, *The Santa Fe New Mexican* established itself as a staunch supporter of arts and culture, printing news of area artists and writers, cultural patrons and preservationists, museum exhibitions and other cultural affairs. Readers were now as likely to be perusing poetry by poet-painter Marsden Hartley or articles by writer-preservationist Ina Sizer Cassidy as they were to be reading about Prohibition or the nationwide "Red Scare."

The city's earliest art controversies made banner news. Among these were a 1926 Chamber of Commerce plan for wealthy female Texas patrons to establish a "cultural colony" near Sun Mountain and a 1927 proposal by the Daughters of the American Revolution to erect a statue named "Pioneer Woman" at the end of the Santa Fe Trail. Local artists and patrons banded together to vehemently oppose both projects on the basis of overt commercialism and cultural insensitivity, claiming both failed to accurately reflect the city's deep-seated history and living cultures.

Both issues made national news. So did the 1950 controversy surrounding a terracotta, bas relief sculpture titled *Earth* that was slated for display on the exterior of the new state Capitol. Cast in the buxom figure of a female nude, the sculpture was created as a symbol of fertility, but a group of local Baptist ministers decried the piece as too suggestive for public display. Governor T. J. Mabry, who initially approved the sculpture, first ordered its removal. But after local artists hotly accused him and the Baptists of censorship and artistic ignorance, he gave the architect the final say in the matter. The ministers prevailed.

The most egregious but unspoken case of censorship, however, was imposed on *The Santa Fe New Mexican* itself. Between 1943 and 1945, the U.S. military instructed editors that they were not to print a word about the mysterious government site in nearby Los Alamos. Auto accidents and other incidents in the town could only be reported as "somewhere north of Santa Fe." Rumors and whispers were rife about the strange city on the hill, yet for two years, *The Santa Fe New Mexican* obediently ignored the story. Finally, on August 6, 1945, when the secret of the atomic bomb was revealed to the country by President Harry Truman, *The Santa Fe New Mexican* reported with relief: "Santa Fe learned officially today of a city of 6,000 in its own front yard."

By now, *The Santa Fe New Mexican* appeared daily and reporters' and editors' bylines frequently appeared on its pages. E. Dana Johnson. Will Shuster. Will Harrison. William McNulty. Calla Hay. John Maguire. Art Morgan. Oliver La Farge. The names are just a sprinkling of the countless voices that have steered readers through the issues and opinions of the day; indeed, most entries appear anonymously written. Taken as a whole, the writing ranges from independent to partisan to pompous, straightforward to eccentric, sentimental to sensational, wry to whimsical. La Farge notes occasions when the writing is overtly conservative or "less steeped in the Santa Fe tradition." The best writing, however, is unabashedly steeped in local atmosphere.

Consider the entry of August 4, 1866: "Otto Buchman will accept the thanks of the *New Mexican* employees for the supply of beer left at our office on Thursday." Mr. Buchman, presumably, complied.

E. Dana Johnson's March 2, 1914, editorial, "Bury It," addresses an issue that revealed Santa Fe's raw frontier nature, even after statehood. Johnson's topic is a dead rooster that has lain at the corner of Palace and Lincoln Avenues for three days. Despite the seriousness of the unsanitary matter, Johnson approaches it with humor: "There is no doubt about that rooster's death. No physician's certificate is required, as the passerby may testify. He has passed away.... Every rooster removed and buried makes Santa Fe one rooster the cleaner, one rooster the brighter and more attractive. Let us let no dead rooster escape."

One of the most powerful examples of editorial writing came from William McNulty in 1945 on the occasion of the nation's newfound knowledge of Los Alamos. Much of the piece is laced with sarcasm regarding the chain of secrecy around the Manhattan Project as McNulty's long-simmering anger over the blatantly successful censorship of his newspaper boils over. Yet he also manages to capture the eerie reality of knowing that the world's most dangerous weapon was built in silence, and less than an hour away from Santa Fe: "The taboo on the mention of Los Alamos was final, complete and until today, irrevocable and not susceptible to any exceptions whatsoever. A whole social world existed in nowhere in which people were married and babies were born nowhere. People died in a vacuum, autos and trucks crashed in a vacuum and the MP's baseball team materialized out of a vacuum, trained in a vacuum and after their games at Fort Marcy Park returned to the vacuum."

December 1948 marked the beginning of *The Santa Fe New Mexican's* current legacy of ownership with the late Robert McKinney's purchase of the paper. Under prior ownership, the paper had been conservative but lively, capturing the unique feel of Santa Fe. Will Harrison, editor since 1940, remained editor under McKinney, who gave him leeway to give the paper a more Democratic slant. The paper's first Sunday page was devoted to the arts, with La Farge and the renowned artist Will Shuster named as columnists. The addition of "poor man's editorials" invited all staff members to submit their own reflections on Santa Fe. Among the most memorable is Society Editor Calla Hay's 1950 rant on the improper but oh-so-local tradition of what she dubs "bilingual slanguage," commonly known as Spanglish today.

La Farge's autobiography of Santa Fe ends with a chapter that, he writes, is intended to illustrate "the special oomph, the oddity, and the liveliness of Santa Fe," as well as the uniquely intimate and informal relationship of *The Santa Fe New Mexican* to its community of readers. He calls the chapter "Just the Other Day."

Cattle rustlers and the Navajo Nation are still headline news a full century after the topics appeared in the paper's early editions. Politics are also at the fore, with stories of missing ballots and other electoral shenanigans, as well as questions about the future of the "Spanish-Anglo" political balance.

Crime and criminals still get their fair share of space in the paper. In 1951, we read about a riotous band of "I Am" cult members who descended on *The Santa Fe New Mexican* offices to claim libel over a recent news article about their president. By the time police arrived to take the vigilantes away, editors, writers and office furniture had all been assaulted.

Two final stories show how much and how little Santa Fe and New Mexico had changed since the newspaper began churning out the local news. In one report, a posse of Santa Fe women on horseback rode into the bar of La Fonda for some Fiesta cheer. In another, the owner of a New Mexico mortuary asked that license plates for his hearses be issued without the "Land of Enchantment" slogan of the state. Editor Will Harrison used the occasion to make one more case for the quality of life in New Mexico, reporting that the hearse drivers often transport their cargo to "such less enchanting places as Texas and California."

In the preface to *Santa Fe: The Autobiography of a Southwestern Town*, La Farge concedes that while historians may turn to *The Santa Fe New Mexican* for items of local fact and interest, the newspaper "on the whole, its material uncorrected, is a poor source of history." And yet, in its scope of issues, voice and vision, La Farge would surely agree that it's difficult to find a more representative or comprehensive history than the archives of a city newspaper. Indeed, in compiling what he called Santa Fe's "social history," La Farge understood that the city's story has less to do with its most prominent dates than its sense of place.

The same is true of *The Santa Fe New Mexican* writers and editors who have compiled the anthology that follows. *Santa Fe, Its 400th Year: Exploring the Past, Defining the Future* continues in the same spirit of imagination and documentation that La Farge brought to his earlier work. In this case, Santa Fe's story is based on a year's worth of reportage—from January to December 2010—by some of the modern-day *New Mexican's* finest chroniclers and storytellers. Just as La Farge chose the birth of *The Santa Fe New Mexican* as his narrative launching point, this book was born in the 400th anniversary year of Santa Fe. As a once-in-a-lifetime opportunity for commemoration and reflection, the now 161-year-old *New Mexican* tells the city's story with creativity and gusto. History's passage is clearly the point of reference, but the finished product is a story for today.

This book, then, is also an autobiography. Viewed through the lens of 400 years, but interpreted through the eyes and voices of contemporary Santa Feans, we are presented with a living, breathing portrait of the city in 2010. In these pages, and every day in *The Santa Fe New Mexican*, we meet people whose lives and experiences take shape on our own narrow, winding streets. Many cling fiercely to the power of Santa Fe's past, but all are acutely aware of the power of its future.

In the writing of *New Mexican* staffers, we discover many recurring themes that come with living in Santa Fe. Issues of politics and religion, power and faith, still dominate the daily scene. Questions about cultural preservation continue to fuel passionate debate about modernity, antiquity, authenticity. Residents' relationships to the land, and to one another, are often tense with questions about race, rights and who was here first. Art controversies abound, as do questions about the direction of the city's development. How much nudity is too much? How fast, how far, should our city move and grow? And onward goes the Santa Fe human parade.

By their nature, newspapers inspire controversy and contradiction. At their best, they encourage connection to one another, to a community, to a common place. In an age when newspapers are on the decline, a time of over-whelming global reach and progress, the local news still has the most intimate and immediate impact on our daily lives. Thanks to the long, committed work of *The Santa Fe New Mexican*, this is perhaps most true in Santa Fe.

There is comfort in Santa Fe's long story, and in our place within it. As long as the city endures, the story goes on. So sit down, relax, read, listen. The city speaks.

Oliver La Farge Books for Further Reading:

Behind the Mountains. Santa Fe: Sunstone Press, 2008.

The Enemy Gods. Santa Fe: Sunstone Press, 2010

Laughing Boy, A Navajo Love Story. New York: Mariner Books / Houghton Mifflin Company, 2004.

The Man With the Calabash Pipe, (Articles from *The Santa Fe New Mexican*). Santa Fe: Sunstone Press, 2011.

A Pause in the Desert. Santa Fe: Sunstone Press, 2009.

Raw Material. Santa Fe: Sunstone Press, 2009.

Santa Fe: The Autobiography of a Southwestern Town. Norman: University of Oklahoma Press, 1981.

Preface

by
Rob Dean, Editor

T his book had a modest beginning but has arrived at a proud end. It began as a series of newspaper stories, based on a promise from *The Santa Fe New Mexican*, the West's oldest newspaper, to honor 400 years of Santa Fe history. Those stories are now *Santa Fe, Its 400th Year: Exploring the Past, Defining the Future*, the publication of which came as 2010 drew to an end and helped close the 400th anniversary commemoration with a flourish.

This is a book for the present time, not about yesterday. Yes, it looks back at 400 years of history but always turns its eye forward toward Santa Fe's future. The stories in this book happened because skilled journalists searched to explain life as they found it in 2010 and to spot clues about what may come for their community. Their journalism created a coherent narrative that put the people of Santa Fe in the midst of a story both layered and thrilling, and a community both familiar and invigorating.

It is important to stress that this is not the history of gray-haired leading men. This is the story of a people—the young and old, the women and men, the founders and latecomers. What paths did they follow? What impulses drove them? What hopes and fears guided them once they arrived? What values propel them into the future? Those questions ask Santa Feans to look back at the same time that the challenge compels them to imagine tomorrow. Turn around. Look ahead. Historians do that. So do journalists, the creators of the rough draft of history.

Santa Fe's story arcs brightly across time, from the talking drums of the pueblos to the pioneering work on complex systems at the Santa Fe Institute. The historian views it all from on high, like a cameraman in a news chopper. The journalist is on the ground in the crowd. The ground-level images from the swirl of excitement might be tilted or grainy, but they are of life close up in real time. So it is with this book.

In these pages, the contextual depth of history got a fresh telling because of the journalists' earnest effort to represent—to stand in for—regular folks who can't be everywhere the journalist goes. Picture the reporter, and imagine her as researcher sifting through stacks of archival material, or see him interviewing the witness to history and the heir to ways gone by. Imagine, too, that standing behind the journalist are the spirits of a thousand people, all virtual observers and news consumers who are equally curious to know what the journalist is finding.

This book arose from that shared commitment of journalists to turn history into public history—knowledge for the masses.

That commitment also lives in the offices of Sunstone Press. This project could not have happened without the guidance and encouragement of Jim Smith and his able staff at Sunstone. They are unsung heroes in preserving New Mexico's heritage in general and in memorializing the Santa Fe 400th in particular.

This book has twelve parts, each a selection of original writings organized around a unifying theme. In the lead piece of the first part, Sandra Baltazar Martínez details how Native, Spanish and Anglo histories are intertwined and how, in the words of historian Estevan Rael-Gálvez, cultural interaction was the basic force in shaping and reshaping communities.

The next chapter is by Dennis Carroll, who describes Santa Fe as a commercial and cultural crossroads. It was the destination for Native, Spanish and American settlers who followed dusty trails to the base of the Sangre de Cristos. Later, the railroads, the highways and the airplanes all brought newcomers who came and went and routinely made established residents feel under siege.

Reporter Robert Nott, the author of three books, moves the story along by honoring the cherished tradition of storytelling in New Mexico. From creation myths to conquistadors to pioneers of all sorts, Santa Fe is rich with truths and legends that are worth retelling. Nott focuses on the efforts of many people to keep the art of storytelling alive.

Any conversation about Santa Fe past or present must include religion. Editor and writer Anne Constable says that not only is faith part of the city's name, but religious diversity also is a good measure of what makes the community so different from other places. Religion both defines and binds people. A young man comfortable in two cultures said it well when he explained that both of his religions "stress taking care of one another and loving each other."

The sense of place starts with natural surroundings. Reporter Staci Matlock offers a perspective on the fact that the Santa Fe basin landscape changed ever so slowly across millions of years only to go through rapid change since man arrived along with his urge to develop the land. The pace of man's impact also has led to new efforts to pull back and to protect water supplies and sustain land-based cultures for generations to come.

The chapter framed by veteran Santa Fe observer Steve Terrell recounts episodes of bad behavior in our local and regional history. Writers and filmmakers long have been drawn to Santa Fe rogues. Some were more colorful than criminal. Some were brutal and cruel. All of them added an element that makes the Santa Fe story riveting, if sometimes unsettling.

Santa Fe's image is the topic of a piece by reporter Tom Sharpe. More than most communities, Santa Fe has moved to the rhythms of cultural celebrations and debates over history. Historical preservation is code, and some say heavy-handed. At any rate, Sharpe writes, it is safe to say that Santa Fe is uncommonly self-aware when it comes to what image it protects, what history it embraces and what values it projects.

And what is that image? Art historian Douglas Fairfield provides an answer. Imagine Santa Fe without its galleries, museums, lowriders, markets, performances and descansos. It would be a city without a pulse, Fairfield concludes. Santa Fe is Santa Fe because, as one authority states matter-of-factly, it fosters creative activity and thought.

As much as anyone, students and teachers feel shifts in the community and the sense of community. Against a backdrop of computers and smart devices, reporter Robert Nott honors the constant in education—the teachers, roughly 1,000 dedicated and innovative leaders who inspire the love of learning.

Next, public-affairs reporter Julie Ann Grimm describes a political city that for 400 years has been the meeting place for conventions, rallies and protests, and has been at the intersection of money and influence. But it would be too easy to see only a capital city defined in terms of political power. As one person who knows put it, "I think it's more of a testament to the values that families have about public service and the obligation that we have to it more than an accumulation of power."

Reporter Kate Nash explores power of another sort. The military presence and sense of duty is a signature feature of Santa Fe. From the Spanish *cuadrilla* that founded Santa Fe to the Native bands that led the Pueblo Revolt, from the Presidio cavalry to the Great War foot soldiers, Santa Fe residents have responded when called to fight. And many others gave us examples of unsung heroism behind the scenes.

The book closes with writer Phaedra Haywood's recognition of family and celebration of community. For more than 400 years, Santa Fe has been an active, colorful place. It is the people and their customs, talents and varied passions that have made it so. Although Santa Fe offers the close-knit comfort of community and family, reality shows that Santa Fe sometimes falls short in keeping children and families safe and well.

Together, stories are meant to connect people living today to the currents of history and expectations for the future. But let us also acknowledge how challenging, perhaps impossible, it is to look forward with any measure of certainty. For that very reason, each of us in our own way tries to understand where we are today as a community. Thus, conveniently, we circle back to where this project started.

In one of the first interviews for this book, Native American artist Bob Haozous expressed high hopes for the events that would mark Santa Fe's 400th anniversary. He said we should remember, first, that the people of Santa Fe are a rich blend of blood and cultures. We should remember, he said wisely, the words of his old Spanish friend who said that "We have all been here four hundred years together, that we are all brothers."

First Contact

The procession from the Cathedral Basilica of St. Francis of Assisi to the Shrine of Our Lady of Guadalupe in December 2009. Our Lady of Guadalupe Parish was saved from shutting down when Mexican immigrants began arriving. Photograph by Natalie Guillén.

Spanish and Native Peoples Gave Santa Fe Its Unique Identity

by
Sandra Baltazar Martínez

The procession of La Conquistadora happens every September in Santa Fe, but the 1962 celebration in particular marked a turning point in young Jerome Martínez y Alire's life. That year, as he stood before the virgin's altar, the 12-year-old boy felt the calling to priesthood.

Today he is Monsignor Jerome Martínez y Alire, a worldly man who became rector of the Cathedral Basilica of St. Francis of Assisi in Santa Fe a decade ago. His mission constantly exposes him to the ethnically diverse population of his church and his city, and occasionally what he finds is friction. To illustrate, he says, "When some come and the Mass is in Spanish, they say, 'I thought we were American.' My response is, 'I thought we were all Catholic first.'"

With those words, the monsignor was in effect stating his strongest case to parishioners about bridging differences, about understanding each other and sharing each other's life stories: One person must measure another by what burns inside, not by appearances on the outside.

In important ways, including that lofty call to his congregation, Martínez y Alire exemplifies the melting pot of Santa Fe's cultural history. On a personal level, he is the heir to a family heritage that blends Indian and Spanish. In a broader sense, he presides over Masses that welcome native New Mexicans, Anglos, American Indians, recent Latino immigrants, the faithful from all races and many backgrounds—the blend of people that founded and settled Santa Fe and propelled it forward over four centuries.

During the city's yearlong cuartocentenario celebration, filled with seminars, lectures and performances, it was important to highlight the significance of Santa Fe's cultural formation.

The contact between the Spanish and Natives—made concrete by the establishment of Santa Fe—"reshaped both communities in profound ways," said Estevan Rael-Gálvez, executive director of the National Hispanic Cultural Center in Albuquerque, New Mexico, and former New Mexico state historian. He said it's important for people in each community to sit together, share each other's stories and realize how intertwined their histories are. "The complexity of who we are today is shaped by that point of contact," Rael-Gálvez said. "It's tragic and beautiful, binary and everything in between."

Monsignor Jerome Martínez y Alire, rector of the Cathedral Basilica of St. Francis of Assisi, celebrates Christmas Eve Mass. Martínez y Alire's mission exposes him to the ethnically diverse population of Santa Fe, and occasionally what he finds is friction. Photograph by Natalie Guillén.

Voice in the Community

Santa Fe's story has many chapters—a place settled by Pueblo Indians, a city founded by the Spanish, an outpost once conquered and occupied by the American army.

The brush of one culture against another is as old as Santa Fe but as fresh as today in the life and work of Martínez y Alire. Forty-seven years ago, the tug of the priesthood came to him in the same moment he set aside to celebrate the Spanish reconquest of Santa Fe. Today the monsignor is both a product of and voice for a community defined by its diversity and harmony, but also marked by cultural clashes that flare up even today. One of his ancestors was a Tano Indian who married Hernán Martín Serrano, one of the Spanish soldiers who arrived in Santa Fe with the Juan de Oñate expedition in the late 1500s.

The demands of a multicultural city are a daily reality for Martínez y Alire. On any one day, he might use his time visiting the sick in the hospital, advising a disenfranchised teen, counseling married couples, helping immigrant families find their way through a system that's completely new.

And during Masses, he chooses his words carefully to get his message across. During an evening Mass on Christmas Eve, Martínez y Alire told the story of a group of animals—prey and predators—who in a cold winter night looked for shelter in a stable. The dogs, cats and mice decided though to overlook their differences and overcome their anxiety. By the time Joseph and Mary walked in, the animals were ready to receive baby Jesus.

"They all welcomed him into the warmth of the stable," Martínez y Alire instructed. "If you make room for others in your heart, you make room for Jesus."

Parishioners take part in a procession from the Cathedral Basilica of St. Francis of Assisi to the Shrine of Our Lady of Guadalupe. Photograph by Natalie Guillén.

Identity

Santa Fe's 400th celebration was an opportunity for people in the city to remember that history shaped what Santa Fe is today and to talk openly and frankly about what all that means, historian Rael-Gálvez said.

The conflicts that arose from each interaction—Spanish, Indian, Anglo and most recently with immigrants—always have been triggered by misunderstandings and misconceptions, he said. "It's based largely on fear, fear of taking the job, fear of the unknown." In New Mexico, we have these older *Hispano* families, and there too, there is a misunderstanding, a division between us and them. It's false consciousness. It's failure to recognize, to see how real connected we are to Mexico."

That type of mentality is what triggers conflict even for the younger generation. In Santa Fe, some youth have created rival gangs, the Westsiders—native New Mexicans—and Southsiders—Mexicans. During a shooting incident last June, a 16-year-old Santa Fe boy shot and killed another teen, a Mexican immigrant. The main motive for the killing: hatred because the immigrant wasn't a native New Mexican.

"The need for communication, for a better way to sit and share each others' stories is needed, that way each community will recognize the fusion of their histories," Rael-Gálvez said. With that goal in mind, Somos un Pueblo Unido, the pro-immigrant rights organization in Santa Fe, launched a Somos Primos (We are Cousins) campaign in the early part of 2009 to promote similarities in both communities.

Contact between peoples for all of its 400 years—sometimes gruesome, sometimes magnificent—has given Santa Fe a unique identity.

Robert J. Baca, president of the New Mexico Genealogical Society in Albuquerque, said it's important for people to know about their ancestors in order to appreciate their identity today. "A lot of people in New Mexico want to identify with Spanish heritage [only] because it was important in New Mexico to be that. The Spanish in New Mexico were the highest cast, Indians were at the bottom. And people still want to be that."

Nonetheless, the concept of being a descendant from a pure Spanish lineage is nothing but a myth, said Laura E. Gómez, professor of law and American studies at The University of New Mexico. "The reality of this notion that Hispanics in New Mexico are Spanish … is a much more complex story. Pueblos were in a unique position because they made accommodations for the Spanish and then the

Mexicans.… It also meant an exchange and interaction, exchange and mixture of all kinds: religious, sexual, cultural."

Emelda María Martínez y Alire, Monsignor Jerome Martínez y Alire's sister, stands near a 1920s picture of her father, Gregorio Martínez, left, and her uncle, Santiago Martínez. Photograph by Luis Sánchez Saturno.

Throughout time, Emelda María Martínez y Alire, Monsignor Jerome Martínez y Alire's sister, has learned to feel proud of their heritage. Knowing her Indian ancestor only helps fortify their identity, she said.

According to Henrietta Martínez Christmas, a genealogist and member of the Hispanic Genealogy Research Center in Albuquerque, the desire to have an identity has led many New Mexican residents to participate in the New Mexico DNA project. So far, the results have only helped strengthen the state's cultural foundation.

DNA results on 1,085 men who have participated in the project throughout the past five years, have found that 80 percent of them were descendants of a European male and 20 percent from a Native American male. Results for the nearly 500 women who have participated, though, have shown that 90 percent of them were descendants of a Native American female and 10 percent from a European woman.

"This only proves that we're a *mestizaje*," Christmas said. "The ship didn't land here directly. We certainly are a mixed race. In a hundred years, race won't look like it does today."

Newcomers

The arrival of immigrants is not a new story. El Camino Real settlers from different origins came and went, many of them establishing homes along the way. Four hundred years ago, the unfounded stories of gold mines in this area lured the Spaniards north from Mexico. That same hope—economic prosperity—is the main reason that generations of British, Italians and most recently, Chinese and Mexicans, have flocked to the United States.

Those early immigrants who arrived in New Mexico did not find the gold they anticipated; instead they found arid lands. Yet, settlers such as Hernán Martín Serrano, the monsignor's ancestor, stayed and contributed to the formation of New Mexico and, in turn, of Santa Fe.

Population numbers in Santa Fe have grown steadily. U.S. Census Bureau data indicate that in 1850 Santa Fe had just over 4,500 residents. By 1930 it registered about 11,000 residents, and by 1960 it had grown to more than 34,600 residents. In the 1960s—when race was classified only as white and non-white—Santa Fe County had nearly 45,000 residents, and about 43,800 classified themselves as white.

By the 1990 census, Santa Fe for the first time became a majority white city, as the self-identified white population surpassed the number of residents who identified themselves as Hispanic. By 2000, though, the counts had reversed. Currently, Santa Fe Hispanics account for 47.7 percent of its residents, and the state reports a 45 percent Hispanic population, compared to 41 percent white.

In 2007, the nation's Hispanic population reached a record 45.5 million, equivalent to 15 percent of the total 301 million residents. Latinos are in fact the fastest-growing minority. That's why for the 2010 count, census officials pushed to have a more accurate count of the immigrant population. For the first time in the history of the census, a questionnaire in Spanish arrived in the mail to residents of largely Hispanic-populated towns. Immigrants have the potential of affecting every level of this country's strata. Locally, they have helped redeem towns, city leaders say.

Española Mayor Joseph Maestas, for example, acknowledged that Mexican immigrants and the businesses they established revived the city's downtown. In

Santa Fe, Martínez y Alire and other church officials recognize that Our Lady of Guadalupe Parish was saved from shutting down when the Mexican immigrants started arriving. The church was scheduled to close its doors because of low attendance. Now hundreds of children participate in religious education courses and its members have grown to 1,800 families, the second largest congregation from Santa Fe churches.

Jon Feere, a legal policy analyst with the Center for Immigration Studies in Washington, DC, said that over the past 20 years, immigration pools have become less diverse due to policies the United States has in place. Most of the immigrants who have arrived to this country over the past 20 years have been Latino and Spanish speaking, primarily Mexicans, Feere said.

Reports compiled by the center indicate that immigrants account for one in eight U.S. residents, compared to one in 16 in 1980 and one in 13 in 1990. When it comes to immigration numbers, New Mexico ranks 29th on the list of most popular states for immigrants. A 2007 Center for Immigration Studies report, titled *Immigrants in the United States, 2007: A Profile of America's Foreign-Born Population*, indicates that New Mexico had 179,000 immigrants, 68,000 of whom arrived between 2000 and 2007.

Studies from 2007 showed that about 1.6 million legal and illegal immigrants settle in the United States each year. At that rate, the country's population will grow to a projected 468 million in 2060. Immigrants and their descendants will account for 105 million of the residents.

Santa Feans celebrate Fiesta in front of the Palace of the Governors in September 1919. The Palace of the Governors, with its thick adobe walls built for defense, was one of the first buildings constructed in the city. Photograph William H. Roberts, Courtesy Palace of the Governors Photo Archives (NMHM/DCA), #149982.

The Founding of Santa Fe

by
Jason Strykowski

When Juan de Oñate first came to New Mexico, he was under strict instructions from Spain to establish a new capital in an uninhabited area. For its abundance of water and dearth of indigenous people, Oñate selected a site just below the Sangre de Cristo Mountains. The exact plot of land that would become Santa Fe likely attracted the attention of Captain Juan Martinez de Montoya for its relatively mild weather and fertile fields. Wood in the area was plentiful, and water from the mountains filled the streams. The area was rich in fish and game.

Although the area was uninhabited when the Spanish came to colonize in 1610, archaeology suggests that Tewas established a small settlement in the area earlier, from which they migrated long before the Spanish arrived. Perhaps they even networked with the pueblos built in the foothills of the nearby mountains. Partial ruins of these communities still exist.

In a way, the footprint left by the Tewas is more definitive than that left by the first Spaniards. Even the name "Santa Fe" is something of a mystery. Perhaps, the New Mexican capital was named after a city in Spain. Santa Fe de Granada was built as a massive stone guard to keep Queen Isabel safe. The stronghold was so impressive that it struck fear into the Moors and helped convince them to surrender to the Spanish. The city of "Holy Faith" in Spain stood as a reminder that Christendom could not be conquered.

The new citizens of Santa Fe in New Mexico perhaps saw themselves as champions of the cross fighting against heathen Natives, just as their forebears had campaigned against the Moors.

Pedro de Peralta established the capital at Santa Fe. Under vice-regal directions he established six districts and marked one square block for public offices. The land settled, Peralta instructed the region's settlers to elect a handful of representatives who would serve for some 30 years each and apportion the running of the village to themselves and a few others of their choosing.

A diverse little town, Santa Fe was ringed by a Mexican Indian settlement. The native Mexicans named their barrio using the Nahuatl (language spoken by the Aztecs) for "the other side of the river," Analco. South of Analco were fields watered by an acequia madre, which had likely been dug by Natives under forced labor. In the center of town stood a fort manned by armed sentries. From their post, sentries likely had a clear view in all four directions.

Early construction also included the Palace of the Governors, with its thick adobe walls built for defense. Other details of the town's layout remain somewhat mysterious. No maps of the hamlet predate the 1700s. But clearly, adobe homes surrounded by small farms sprang up around the walled capital at the center of town.

That said, the most important infrastructure in town was the establishment of a social network. The *encomienda* system truly ran Santa Fe. Loyal Spanish citizens who stayed with the crown for five years would receive partial dominion or acquire local Native Americans as bondservants. These Natives were required to pay tribute to their Spanish *encomenderos*. For their part, the *encomenderos* paid fealty to the crown with military service.

New Mexicans sent surplus goods to central Mexico on wagons. Many of the goods were produced by the pueblos and included pine nuts, wool, sheep and blankets. In return, the *encomenderos* received swords, daggers, armor and other goods often imported from Spain. Although they were relatively few in number, some of these *encomenderos* made a significant profit from their positions in New Mexico.

Aside from the elected council and the *encomenderos*, power in the colony resided most strongly in the Catholic Church.

Controversy over an El Paso statue of Juan de Oñate resulted in its being named *The Equestrian*. Photograph courtesy of XII Travelers of the Southwest Project.

Oñate's Contentious Legacy

by
Jason Strykowski

Despite the fact that he has not stepped foot in New Mexico for 400 years, Juan de Oñate remains controversial. Under his watch, the people of Acoma Pueblo received brutal punishment simply for defending their liberty. Oñate also oversaw the first Spanish capital at San Gabriel, and, by default, led the way for a colony to be established at Santa Fe.

A child of the New World, Oñate grew up accustomed to military campaigns waged against native populations. In Mexico, he gained a reputation as a soldier, and the Spanish crown put him in charge of a company of settlers to colonize New Mexico. The 500 some people who set out from Santa Barbara in New Spain with Oñate undertook a serious financial risk, but stood to gain a great deal if they succeeded in New Mexico. Oñate himself staked much of his financial fortunes on the success of the mission.

Oñate and the intrepid settlers entered New Mexico in 1597 and reached the Tewa village of Okhe by 1598. Almost immediately, Oñate confronted a rebellion—from his own people. A number of mutineers, likely tired of travel and harsh conditions, turned against their leader. Despite Oñate's quick and decided response, soldiers continued to desert the colony. A more serious revolt, however, brewed farther south.

Less than a year later the people of Acoma rebelled against Spanish control under Juan de Zaldivar. Perhaps reacting to the death of Zaldivar, his nephew, Oñate reacted swiftly with force. Despite the physical defenses of Acoma's freestanding mesa, the townspeople could not overcome Spanish cannon fire and surrendered to Oñate's forces after his battalion killed 800 residents of the pueblo. Oñate punished the survivors harshly for insurrection. Males over the age of 25 lost their feet and were sentenced to several decades of slavery. Oñate's actions drew criticism from both the people of Acoma and royal authorities. They also failed to convince other Natives in New Mexico to fear Spanish power.

Many colonists felt New Mexico was unsafe and found the dry terrain difficult. The sparse population waned progressively as many left the small colony.

Oñate had no response to this mounting challenge, and instead of focusing on the strife in the colony, he sought his fortune throughout North America. He courted rumors that he had located the Northwest Passage. Despite the failure of his forebears to find Quivira, the city of gold, he did not end his search despite the fact that he never found a valuable mine. And, while Oñate combed the continent for gold, his colony suffered.

Aware of these struggles and his unjust treatment of Natives, the Spanish crown decided to remove Oñate from his position. Officially, they recalled him in 1606, but he had already resigned and left his office at the capital in San Gabriel a year earlier. As he left, the capital was all but abandoned, populated by only a handful of Spaniards. Oñate's 12-year career in New Mexico stained an otherwise promising résumé. He devoted much of the next 20 years of his life defending himself and lobbying for the restoration of his status. He even traveled to Spain shortly before his death and succeeded in regaining some of his wealth and status, but remained banished from New Mexico for the rest of his life.

Even after his death, though, Oñate remains on trial. In 1998, unknown vandals sabotaged a bronze statue of Oñate. They removed the left foot of the statue, recalling Oñate's harsh treatment of the Acomans. Several years later, debate erupted in El Paso over a huge statue of Oñate that in the end was named simply, *The Equestrian*.

Personalities: Women of History

by
Sandra Baltazar Martínez

The tapestry of cultures that makes New Mexico such a unique place has been woven with the help of many personalities. Women, many in their own unassuming ways, have left permanent marks throughout history. Meet some of them:

Doña Inés

Doña Inés (no last name found) was a Tano Indian woman who gave birth to the first recorded child of mixed parents. She married Hernán Martín Serrano. History indicates that Doña Inés was taken by Spaniards when she was a child from the Tano Pueblo of San Cristóbal in 1591. She was raised with Spanish customs and returned to New Mexico with the Juan de Oñate expedition. It is said that she was expected to serve as an interpreter, as La Malinche did for Hernán Cortés in Mexico some eight decades before.

Source: *La Herencia.*

Doña Tules

Born around the 1800s in Sonora, Mexico, María Gertrudis Barceló's history is often debated. She came to Santa Fe at some point in the early to mid 1800s and opened a gambling and prostitution hall along Burro Alley. Her gambling hall and persona—faulty in the eyes of many—connected the locals, the church and the military. She contributed money to the construction of what's now known as Cathedral Basilica of St. Francis of Assisi, and historians say she paid Archbishop Jean-Baptiste Lamy $1,200 to be buried on the cathedral property. Records do not show she had any descendants.

Doña Tules.

Source: New Mexico History Museum and *The Santa Fe New Mexican* archives; engraving made in 1854, two years after her death, for *Harper's Weekly*.

Rosario Romero

Rosario Romero's real name was *Ated-Bah-Hozhoni* (Happy Girl), a Navajo slave who with her daughter, Soledad, was captured and sold into slavery after her husband and two boys were killed. They were sold for 150 pesos to serve Padre Antonio José Martínez in Taos. Rosario tried to escape several times, but was captured and returned to Martínez's possession. Census records indicate that she and her daughter lived in Taos by 1870, but left to Ocaté once Martínez died. Romero left with Soledad and Martínez's son, George Romero. George Romero's mother was Teodora Romero, Martínez's "housekeeper."

Source: Estevan Rael-Gálvez, National Hispanic Cultural Center executive director.

Josefa López Zambrano de Grijalva

Josefa López Zambrano de Grijalva is notorious for her brave rescue of La Conquistadora when Pueblo Indians attacked the local church on August 10, 1680, during the Pueblo Revolt. Zambrano de Grijalva was a *sacristana*, or lay woman, at the time.

Source: New Mexico State Library research database.

Jesusita Aragón

Jesusita Aragón became a *partera*, a midwife, at age 14 in Trujillo, New Mexico. She was born in 1908; by 1980 she had delivered more than 12,000 babies. Many times she worked with doctors, teaching them what she had learned through her years of experience as a *partera*. She also became the first in her family to attend school and learn English. Her bilingual skills led her to become the town's interpreter. In 1952 she moved to Las Vegas, New Mexico, with her two children, Ernesto and Dolores. In Las Vegas she built her own home while she worked at a parachute factory and continued her work as a midwife.

Jesusita Aragón.

Source: *More than Petticoats: Remarkable New Mexico Women* by Beverly West. Photograph Courtesy Santa Fe Living Treasures.

Susan Shelby Magoffin.

Susan Shelby Magoffin

Susan Shelby Magoffin was one of the few women who traveled along the Santa Fe Trail along with her husband, Samuel Magoffin, an expert trader in Santa Fe. She was an 18-year-old newlywed who kept detailed journal entries of her trip from Missouri to Mexico, beginning in 1846. Her diary became an important part of this region's history not only because she was a woman, but because she witnessed two important events: trade and the start of the war with Mexico. She was also recording during the period when then-President James K. Polk had won the presidency because of his expansionism ideals.

Source: *Down the Santa Fe Trail and into Mexico* by Susan Magoffin, edited by Stella M. Drumm. Photograph Courtesy of the Missouri Historical Society, St. Louis.

Ramona Sakiestewa

Ramona Sakiestewa (in 2010) is of Hopi ancestry whose work involves paper, tapestry and architectural design. She is a self-taught weaver who later became the first Native American director of the Southwestern Association on Indian Affairs. She was born in Albuquerque and graduated from the Santa Fe Preparatory School in 1966. She draws inspiration from early Pueblo, Navajo and Hispanic textiles. Sakiestewa's love for art has taken her to many countries, including Mexico, Peru and Japan.

Source: *A Tribute to the Women of Santa Fe* by William Constandse and www.ramonasakiestewa.com (active at time of publication).

Lily Gonzales

Lily Gonzales was the first female police officer to join the Santa Fe Police Department, in 1964. She worked in many positions, from dispatcher to detective. She also worked as the department's community relations expert, a job that took her into the community to speak to schools, women's organizations and neighborhood associations. Gonzales later served as county probate judge from 1986 to 1998.

Source: *A Tribute to the Women of Santa Fe* by William Constandse.

Lily Gonzales.

Laura E. Gómez.

Laura E. Gómez

Laura E. Gómez (in 2010) is a law professor at The University of New Mexico. Although Santa Fe is not her home, she focuses on issues vital to the community. She is a lecturer and an author; her most recent book is *Manifest Destinies: The Making of the Mexican American Race*, where she focuses on what she calls the "mythical" racial identity many Northern New Mexicans ground themselves in. In 1994, she obtained her doctorate degree from Stanford University and is active in national scholarly organizations such as the Law and Society Association. She has won several residential fellowships and serves as the associate editor for the *Law & Society Review*. Gómez was born in Roswell and raised in Albuquerque.

Source: Interview and The University of New Mexico Law School biography.

Evaline Myers and Luna Leopold at Fiesta de Santa Fe in the mid-1930s.

Timeline

1200 – 1500s: Pueblo Indians establish villages.

1598: Oñate establishes Spanish settlement to the north.

1680: Pueblo Indians revolt.

1693: Don Diego de Vargas retakes Santa Fe.
1821: Santa Fe Trail opens.
1846: U.S. Army enters Santa Fe; U.S. annexes New
    Mexico.
1848: Treaty of Guadalupe Hidalgo ends U.S.-Mexican
    War; New Mexico a territory, not a state.

1851: Bishop Jean Baptiste Lamy arrives, sets up schools
    and hospitals.

1878: Railroad opens migration from east.

1912: New Mexico becomes a state.

1942 – 1945: In World War II, state's soldiers endure
    Bataan Death March, Navajo Code Talkers help end
    war, and Los Alamos develops atomic bomb.
1948: Native Americans win right to vote.

Suggested Books

Bohnaker, Joseph J. *Of Arms I Sing*. Santa Fe: Sunstone Press, 1990.

Bullock, Alice. *Loretto and the Miraculous Staircase*. Santa Fe: Sunstone Press, 1978.

Brooks, James. *Captives & Cousins: Slavery, Kinship, and Community in the Southwest Borderlands*. Chapel Hill [u.a.]: University of North Carolina Press, 2002.

Chávez, Fray Angélico. *La Conquistadora*. Santa Fe: Sunstone Press, 1975; Revised Edition, 1983.

Chávez, Fray Angélico. *Our Lady of the Conquest*. Santa Fe: Sunstone Press, 2010.

Chevalier, Jaima. *La Conquistadora, Unveiling the History of Santa Fe's Six Hundred Year Old Religious Icon*. Santa Fe: Sunstone Press, 2010.

Cook, Mary J. Straw. *Doña Tules, Santa Fe's Courtesan and Gambler*. Albuquerque: The University of New Mexico Press, 2007.

Burroughs, Jean M. *Bride of the Santa Fe Trail*. Santa Fe: Sunstone Press, 1984.

Gómez, Laura E. *Manifest Destinies: The Making of the Mexican American Race*. New York: New York University, 2007.

Grant, Blanche Chloe. *Doña Lona, A Novel Based on the Life of Doña Tules*. Santa Fe: Sunstone Press, 2007.

Gutierrez, Ramón A. *When Jesus Came, the Corn Mothers Went Away: Marriage, Sexuality, and Power in New Mexico, 1500-1846*. Stanford: Stanford University Press, 1991.

Keleher, William A. *Turmoil in New Mexico, 1846 – 1868*. Santa Fe: Sunstone Press, 2008

Kessell, John L. *Spain in the Southwest: A Narrative History of Colonial New Mexico, Arizona, Texas, and California*. Norman: University of Oklahoma Press, 2002.

Lamadrid, Enrique R. *Hermanitos Comanchitos: Indo-Hispano Rituals of Captivity and Redemption*. Paso por aquí series. Albuquerque: The University of New Mexico Press, 2003.

Laughlin, Ruth. *Caballeros, The Romance of Santa Fe and the Southwest*. Santa Fe: Sunstone Press, 2007.

Lavash, Donald R. *A Journey Through New Mexico History*. Santa Fe: Sunstone Press, 2006.

Melzer, Richard. *Buried Treasures, Famous and Unusual Gravesites in New Mexico History*. Santa Fe: Sunstone Press, 2007.

Morand, Sheila. *Santa Fe Then and Now*. Santa Fe: Sunstone Press, 1998.

Ortega, Pedro Ribera. *Christmas in Old Santa Fe*. Santa Fe: Sunstone Press, 1973.

Nusbaum, Rosemary. *The City Different and the Palace*. Santa Fe: Sunstone Press, 1978.

Riley, Carroll L. *The Kachina and the Cross: Indians and Spaniards in the Early Southwest*. Salt Lake City: University of Utah Press, 1999.

Romero, Orlando, ed. *All Trails Lead to Santa Fe*. Santa Fe: Sunstone Press, 2010.

Sanchez, Richard, ed. *White Shell Water Place*. Santa Fe: Sunstone Press, 2010.

Sando, Joe S. *Pueblo Indians of North America*. New York: Holt, Rinehart and Winston, 1970.

Sheppard, Carl. *The Saint Francis Murals of Santa Fe*. Santa Fe: Sunstone Press, 1989.

Simmons, Marc. *Yesterday in Santa Fe, Episodes in a Turbulent History*. Santa Fe: Sunstone Press, 1989.

Simmons, Marc. *The Last Conquistador: Juan de Oñate and the Settling of the Far Southwest*. Norman: University of Oklahoma Press, 1991.

Twitchell, Ralph Emerson. *The History of the Military Occupation of the Territory of New Mexico from 1846 to 1851*. Santa Fe: Sunstone Press, 2007.

Twitchell, Ralph Emerson. *Old Santa Fe, The Story of New Mexico's Ancient Capital.* Santa Fe: Sunstone Press, 2007.

Twitchell, Ralph Emerson. *The Spanish Archives of New Mexico,* Two Volumes. Santa Fe: Sunstone Press, 2008.

Weber, David J. *The Spanish Frontier in North America.* New Haven: Yale University Press, 1992.

Weigle, Marta, ed. *Telling New Mexico, A New History.* Santa Fe: Museum of New Mexico Press, 2009.

Yoder, Walter D. *The Santa Fe Trail Activity Book.* Santa Fe: Sunstone Press, 1994.

Suggested Websites

(active at time of publication)

Founding families of Santa Fe: www.santafenm.gov/index.aspx?nid=1231
400 years of Santa Fe history and culture: www.psantafe400th.com/index.
    php?page=culture history
Office of the State Historian: www.newmexicohistory.org/

2

Pathways

Charles Lindbergh, center, landed his Spirit of St. Louis in Santa Fe, pictured above, in 1927 on an airstrip south of where present-day St. Michael's Drive meets Cerrillos Road. Photograph courtesy of the Palace of the Governors Photo Archives (NMHM/DCA), #168501.

Spirit of Santa Fe: A Crossroads for Adventurers, Not All Welcome

by
Dennis J. Carroll

ucky Lindy wanted to open Santa Feans' eyes to the promise of air travel but instead left them gasping for breath.

As he made his approach over La Bajada that September day in 1927, Charles Lindbergh, flying his famous Spirit of St. Louis, "spied a row of autos buzzing along the road, swooped down to a few feet above the ground and crow-hopped over one after the other," a news report said. "[He] shot like an arrow over to the landing field, a tumbleweed dangling from his tail skid."

Lindbergh, only four months from his historic nonstop flight across the Atlantic, was headed for Santa Fe as part of his nationwide flyover to promote air travel and commerce. After landing on an airstrip south of where present-day St. Michael's Drive meets Cerrillos Road, Lindbergh went to the statehouse to give a speech. Thousands cheered as Lindbergh climbed the steps to declare that air travel was the future and that Santa Fe would have the same opportunities for air development as any other city, thanks to new aircraft engines that could conquer the city's high altitude. Santa Feans forged an instant connection with Lindbergh. For generations, after all, their pioneer spirit had blazed many a trail.

The story of Santa Fe, which celebrated its 400 years of history in 2010, has always been linked to one trail or another. Native, Spanish and American settlers followed dusty paths to open space, water and wildlife at the foot of the Sangre de Cristos. Traders, often following the vestiges of centuries-old pathways, carved out wider and more well-defined trails for their wagons. Eventually, the railroads, the highways and the airplanes all raced through town.

Santa Fe's story always has been about newcomers who came and went and natives who often resisted, feeling as though their long-established communities and traditions were under siege.

"Everybody who came here was an outsider totally convinced that the people here were subhuman and that the land was free," said Bob Haozous, a prominent Chiricahua Apache artist and son of the late Allan Houser, the famous sculptor.

Bill Sauter holds up a photograph that his father, Harry, made in 1927 of Charles Lindbergh's Spirit of St. Louis at what was then a landing strip near the Toney Anaya Building on Cerrillos Road. Harry Sauter first met Lindbergh in New York and years later guarded his room at La Fonda. Photograph by Jane Phillips.

Adventurers Meet Pioneers

Lindbergh was the most famous flier to visit Santa Fe but not the first. Nine years before Lindbergh, a mail plane had landed on an airstrip that a gang of prison inmates hastily scratched into the dirt. Townspeople rushed to the edge of town to see, partly because they had something in common with the aviators. Like the young pilots, the folks of 1927 Santa Fe knew about adventure. They came from the men and women who rode El Camino Real and the Santa Fe Trail.

From its beginning, Santa Fe was a destination. In the late-1500s, Juan de Oñate led a four-mile-long caravan of soldiers, settlers and livestock on a grueling 1,700-mile journey on El Camino Real from Mexico City to New Mexico. "The day-to-day dangers encountered were the unknown perils posed by the terrain, the weather and potentially hostile Indians," read a vivid account published in the fall 2005 *La Herencia* by New Mexico Highlands historian Maurilio E. Vigil. "The greatest fear, however, was of starvation and the scarcity of water."

As the main link between the Spanish provinces to the south with New Mexico, the trail became the pathway for much of what would compose the tapestry of the New Mexico territory. "It was the route along which all the elements of culture, everything from music to furniture making to religious practices, were brought into New Mexico," said historian Tom Merlan of Santa Fe. "If you are Hispanic and you live in New Mexico, then one or more of your forebears came up or used the Camino Real."

Starting in 1821, Santa Fe's door opened to the east via 1,200 miles of plains, desert and mountains called the Santa Fe Trail. Wagon trains heading north and west met in Santa Fe to sell silver, furs and other natural resources or swap them for tools, weapons and manufactured goods from the east.

John Barker gets what motivated the Santa Fe Trail pioneers. Barker, whose family today runs the Old Santa Fe Inn, is the great-great-grandson of one of those pioneers, N.B. Laughlin. "He had been a Confederate soldier," Barker said. "And if you had fought for the South, the only thing to do was head west." The trail carried more traders than settlers, but Laughlin, who eventually rose to a seat on the territorial Supreme Court, represented the disenfranchised travelers looking for a new start. "It was always about making money, and everybody made a lot of money both ways," Barker said.

Railroads Changed the Game

Rails replaced the trails in 1880s, because trains were faster, more comfortable and in the long run cheaper than wagon trains. Railroads, competing for the lucrative markets and settlement opportunities, were in fierce competition with each other, and as quickly as one went under or merged with a competitor, another would spring up.

Fred Friedman, longtime head of the rail division of the Department of Transportation, figures that nearly 145 rail lines have operated in New Mexico at one time or another. From 1880 to the present, five rail lines have served Santa Fe County alone. They left tracks, literally and figuratively, Friedman said, "in the form of tracks and depots, built-up alignments, and a confusing paper trail of mergers, leases, sales, purchases, abandonments, bankruptcies and acquisitions."

The companies often stuck local communities with worthless bonds and other public debts spent on construction and expansion of rail lines. The anti-donation clause of the state Constitution stands today to shield taxpayers from the bungling, corruption and greed of the railroad era. The law prohibiting use of state money to build rail lines has modern-day implications.

The anti-donation clause, which bars state appropriations from going to private interests, remains a contentious political issue today as the state, counties and cities wrestle with intermodal transportation financing, Friedman said.

Open Road Opened Worlds

The automobile gave the freedom of travel and relocation to the masses. Once again, Santa Fe would watch people come and go. When highway engineers in 1926 first laid out U.S. Route 66, it passed through Santa Fe, encouraging motels, restaurants and other travel-related businesses along the way.

"For the Route 66 traveler coming from back east it was as if they had entered another country," said one description of the highway. "The fascinating Native American and Spanish cultures encountered along New Mexico Route 66 opened up new worlds never dreamed of by [the motorists]."

Wide-eyed travelers gave Route 66 its purpose. Political shenanigans took it all away. After 12 years, in 1938, Route 66 was rerouted to sidestep Santa Fe.

The state's governor, Arthur Hannett, stinging from a re-election defeat, saw to it that a new stretch of the highway directly connected Santa Rosa to

Albuquerque, according to The Road Wanderer Web site. The new road that bypassed Santa Fe also saved drivers almost four hours. The hard climb to 7,000 feet had convinced the railroads to bypass Santa Fe and helped Albuquerque boom. Airlines made the same choice.

Lindbergh's Vision Now

The promise of air travel never matched the grand vision Lindbergh outlined years ago on the statehouse steps, but an increase in commercial flights has been one of the biggest business stories in Santa Fe in recent years.

Regional airline American Eagle added daily flights to Dallas in 2009, as well as a direct flight to Los Angeles later that year. Santa Fe travelers, as of 2010, took 240,000 to 250,000 commercial flights each year, statistics showed. Jim Montman, director of the Santa Fe Municipal Airport, said he expects no more than 30 percent of those flights in the future to originate in Santa Fe. The rest will fly out of the regional airport in Albuquerque. The current local airport, established by the military in 1941 and at roughly its present size since the 1950s, is the latest of four defined airfields in Santa Fe.

Historically, mergers and business failures cursed the airlines, as they did the railroads of an earlier era. Continental, Pioneer, Texas International, Zia Airlines, Mountain Air, Trans-America and Air Midwest—one by one, they left Santa Fe, citing the companies' financial woes, poor runway conditions and lack of sustained support from the city.

Carry on, But How?

Transportation is a hot topic again, because of the Rail Runner Express, which in December 2008 connected Santa Fe and Albuquerque by commuter rail. Matters of coming and going and memories of boom and bust are on the public agenda in a new way. Planners are looking once and for all for a sustainable regional transportation system.

In August 2008, the state Department of Transportation and the New Mexico Association of Regional Councils convened a statewide meeting. Good transportation systems strengthen the economy and improve quality of life, the people in attendance quickly agreed. But how do communities maintain

The railroad depot in Santa Fe—pictured around 1912—has seen plenty of action: From 1880 to the present, five rail lines have served Santa Fe County alone. Today another train has pulled up to the station, the Rail Runner Express, which began commuter service between Albuquerque and Santa Fe in December 2008. Historical photograph courtesy of the Palace of the Governors Photo Archives (NMHM/DCA), #66658. Recent photograph by Clyde Mueller.

safe roads and bikeways, control congestion, minimize pollution, promote fuel conservation, provide mobility for disabled people and senior citizens, and make it all affordable for taxpayers?

In the 20 years after 2010, the study produced from the meeting concluded, New Mexico will need $22 billion in highways, bridges and interchanges but will have just $5 billion to spend. Public funding has not kept pace with the cost of transportation projects, and that explained the funding gap.

To fight that trend, the report recommended that:

- Transportation and community planners get people involved to help draft an integrated, public-spirited vision for good roads, rails and runways.
- State and local governments coordinate efforts to make projects efficient and affordable.
- The state spend transportation revenue only on transportation, adjust revenue for inflation and create a permanent trust fund.

Brothers at End of the Trail

While officials looked toward a sustainable transportation future built on the shoulders of the past, native artist Bob Haozous urged celebrants of Santa Fe's 400th anniversary in 2010 to remember the past but not to distort it with revisionist history. Haozous, 67 at the time, whose maternal ancestors passed through the hands of Abiquiú slave traders, said the anniversary should be more a time of accurate historical education, rather than glorification of economic, commercial invasions that dispossessed indigenous people. "They came and took away our religion, took away our language, took away our laws and our philosophical concepts," Haozous said.

He hoped that Santa Fe 400th celebrants, while honoring exploration and trade that led to prosperity, would also mourn the murders and hangings of Native Americans on the Plaza.

Now, Haozous said, Santa Feans—descendants of the Spanish, the genetic mix of Anglo Americans and the people already here hundreds of years before the Camino Real, Santa Fe Trail or Lindbergh's airplane—are a blended people.

"There's an old [Spanish] guy up on Upper Canyon Road whom I sit and talk with," Haozous said. "He says we have all been here four hundred years together, that we are all brothers."

Bob Haozous, a prominent Chiricahua Apache artist and son of the late Allan Houser, stands next to his sculpture honoring extinct tribes in front of the Capitol in January, 2010. Photograph by Jane Phillips.

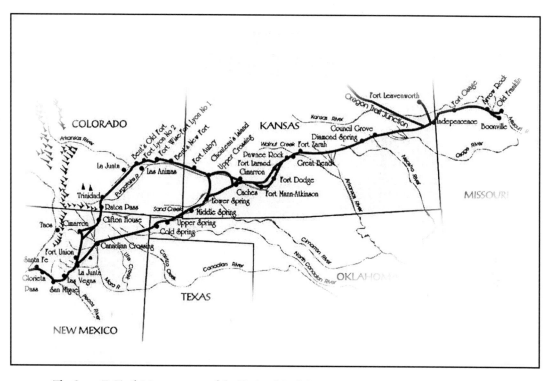

The Santa Fe Trail. Map courtesy of the National Park Service.

The Santa Fe Trail Today: Accepting the Challenge, Minus the Hardships

by
Robin Martin

In 1848, a Canadian-born trader, Francis X. Aubry, made a bet that he could travel the trail from Santa Fe to Independence, Missouri., in six days. Along the way he changed mounts often, having ridden the horses until they dropped. He tied himself to his saddle, so as not to fall off if he dozed.

Near Point of Rocks, Kansas, he found the man who was supposed to provide him with fresh mounts, dead and scalped, with the horses run off. He rode another 200 miles on his already exhausted horse, until he could borrow a fresh one from a passing wagon train. Farther east in Kansas—after an exhausted mount died under him—he walked and ran more than 20 miles to Fort Mann.

Aubry won the bet and fame at both ends of the trail, having ridden and walked the route in five days and 16 hours. He also made three round trips on the trail in one year, and delivered mail relatively rapidly. But he didn't enjoy prosperity and fame into old age. In 1854, at 28, he was knifed to death on Santa Fe's Plaza.

Times have changed, but time on the trail, not so much.

In the fall of 2009, my husband, Meade, and I followed the Santa Fe Trail from Missouri to the Santa Fe Plaza. Along the way, we stopped to look for ruts left by the wagons, visit parks and museums, tour restored forts that once guarded the traders who traveled the trail, and take plenty of photographs. It took us four days.

Trade on the Santa Fe Trail was active for 60 years, from Mexican independence from Spain in 1821 to the year the railroad came to Santa Fe in 1880. Although the route was less than 1,000 miles long, typically it took traders, with loaded ox-drawn or mule-drawn wagons, about two months to traverse. The trains averaged about 15 miles a day. Each trading trip was a risk. A creek in Kansas is named after New Mexican trader Don Antonio José Chavez, who, after being caught in a snowstorm during the 1840s, was murdered by the bandit John McDaniels.

Most traders waited until spring to travel, but any trip could be perilous due to lack of water, violent storms and disease—in 1867, my great-great-uncle, Frank Moody, died of cholera along the trail. As the years passed, traders suffered increasing attacks from the native tribes who were being pushed out of their ancestral homes by American expansion. A St. Louis newspaper reported that in 1847, 47 Americans were killed along the way, 6,500 animals stolen and 330 wagons destroyed.

On our 2009 trip, Meade and I spent our evenings in safe and comfortable hotel rooms where I read David Dary's *The Santa Fe Trail: Its History, Legends and Lore*, from which I learned this information.

In spite of the dangers, trade could be enormously profitable. We ate dinner one night at the Hays Tavern in Council Grove, Kansas, which was operated as a store and saloon during trail days. A sign under the old porch said that in 1857 some $40 million worth of freight went past the front door.

When William Becknell completed the first wagon trip from Franklin, Missouri, to Santa Fe in 1822, he had used three farm wagons. At the end of the trail's life, traders were hauling wagons that could carry 6,000 pounds.

Until U.S. annexation of New Mexico in 1848, the international border between the United States and Mexico was at the Arkansas River.

Even today, the two ends of the trail seem like different countries. Missouri and eastern Kansas are well populated, full of sprawling suburbs and tidy small towns. The rectangular farms of central Kansas continue the orderly march of civilization. Inhabitants there have German, Scandinavian and British names.

But across the Arkansas in western Kansas and beyond, the horizons open. Towns become less symmetrical. Antelope, deer and even a few bison graze near the highway. Snowy mountains appear on the horizon. The descendants of native tribes and Mexican settlers live on the land.

Unlike a modern highway, the trail followed more than one track. Traders chose routes according to their fears of waterless camps or Indian attacks or dangerous river crossings.

In the years before the Civil War, as river boats became more sophisticated and were able to travel farther upstream on the Missouri, the eastern terminus migrated from Franklin, west to Independence, then to Westport, Missouri. After the war, as new railroad track expanded west, the trail became even shorter, with the wagons taking up freight at each year's new railhead.

Trade items shipped from St. Louis were unloaded from steamboats and barges on the Missouri River near Old Franklin, Missouri, where the Santa Fe Trail began, to continue their journey west by wagon. Photograph by Meade Martin.

The trail was not only a connection between Santa Fe and Missouri. Goods of European manufacture crossed the Atlantic, were shipped up the Mississippi, to St. Louis, then on the Missouri River to the trailhead. Manufactured American items came from the East Coast on the Erie Canal, and then to St. Louis. Furs brought by trappers from the Rocky Mountains, and buffalo hides collected by native tribes, went east. American luxuries found their way south from Santa Fe along the Chihuahua trail.

Finally, transcontinental railroad replaced the lumbering wagons, teams of mules and oxen. Today, the wagon ruts are faintly visible, and only in scattered locations. But many rail lines also lie idle. The interstate highways and air corridors carry most traffic.

One morning I stood on the highway bridge near Franklin, Missouri, near where Becknell started his first trip on the trail. I sent a photograph of the Missouri River to my children by iPhone. The methods of communication and transportation continue to change. What hasn't changed is the need for trade and information sharing.

Freighters on the Santa Fe Trail, from left, Bernard Seligman, Zadoc Staab, Lehman Spiegelberg and Kiowa Indian scouts. Photograph courtesy Palace of the Governors Photo Archives (NMHM/DCA), #7890.

The Rise and Decline
of the Santa Fe Trail

by
Jason Strykowski

On November 13, 1821, Don Pedro Ignacio Gallego, the alcalde of Abiquiú, New Mexico, and his small militia chanced upon a handful of Americans near Las Vegas, New Mexico. Probably no more than a dozen men, this little group must have looked weary and starved from several months on the trail.

By accident, Don Gallego witnessed the first crossing of the Santa Fe Trail. He might have liked to congratulate these adventurers, but neither he nor any of his men spoke English. As it happened though, one of the Americans spoke French as did a member of Gallego's militia. With pigeon French and Native American sign language, the New Mexicans welcomed the Americans and informed them that the terminus of the Santa Fe Trail and the rest of New Mexico had come under Mexican sovereignty.

For the leader of this rag-tag bunch of Americans, William Becknell, this came as great news. In the summer of 1821, Becknell organized the trip out of sheer financial desperation. A resident of the city of Franklin, Missouri, Becknell had garnered little success as an entrepreneur, but he found the courage, and the money, for one more gamble.

He planned to lead a small, well-fortified and armed group of men into Spanish territory in the hopes of inaugurating trade. Americans knew that Spanish citizens had little in the way of cheap manufactured goods.

Becknell had correctly reasoned that these people could be a source of immense profit for agile and clever traders. No longer ruled by the Spanish government, the New Mexicans welcomed this commerce. Soon other traders reached the same conclusion that Becknell reached and chanced the long road to Santa Fe in the hopes of earning great fortunes.

The golden period of the Santa Fe Trail was under way.

From 1821 to 1880, the dirt road stretched from Missouri to New Mexico across Kansas, Oklahoma and Colorado. Enterprising traders not intimidated by dry, bumpy stretches of land and Native American raiders stood to reap great financial gain by trading sundry goods. Those goods included razors, scissors, linens, gloves, axes and alcohol. When they returned, traders brought their rewards mostly as currency, but sometimes they bargained for furs and mules.

Even as the trail grew more well-worn, it hardly evolved past a set of rough wagon ruts along the plains. Typically, the journey began each spring in Independence, Missouri. Traders would fill the little town and purchase their necessary provisions before taking the trail.

Those courageous enough to take the trip could expect to encounter hostile Native American tribes, American bison and grizzly bears. Each night, to protect themselves, travelers would "circle the wagons" and assign sentries to stand guard holding guns. The constant threats of starvation and dehydration plagued the travelers as well. The trip could take three months.

The trade route became so effective that some Americans opted to spend a little more time in Santa Fe. The Santa Fe Trail and trade provided some of the inspiration that led the United States to war with Mexico, even though the value of the trade rarely soared and Mexico actually halted all exchange in 1844.

Trade along the trail continued after the United States took possession of New Mexico in 1848 but began to decline along with the fur trade and the era of the mountain man. Later, the Civil War diverted resources from the forts along the route that protected travelers and created business for suppliers.

The hardy souls who took the route set an example of exploration and survival for latter pioneers to follow. In time, though, the railroads after 1880 would change the rules completely and usher in an era of faster commerce and tourism.

Telegraph: The First Information Superhighway

by
Rob Dean

B y the mid-1800s, traders were moving in and out of Santa Fe in growing numbers. U.S. soldiers had arrived. The feds ruled the territory. Settlers were coming in from the south and the east. Along their pathways sprouted telegraph lines, the original information highway and a key instrument of America's push into the Southwest.

Santa Fe was the regional headquarters of the Signal Corps, the branch of the U.S. Army that built and operated the nation's telegraph lines. From Santa Fe, the telegraph line stretched south to El Paso and west across a wide swath of desert to Phoenix. Soldiers in the Signal Corps considered theirs a plum assignment. They saw themselves as an elite corps and tended to make long careers of the Army.

Propelled by Manifest Destiny, America's self-endowed claim on the West, the Signal Corps took control of the telegraph in 1867 and strung lines that speeded communications between army commanders and government officials in the East and their outposts across the West. The men who made the wires talk had a sense that their mission was big. The telegraph served as "a helper to the people without the distinction of persons" and delivered information "on terms that will barely pay for compiling and transmitting it," boasted a Santa Fe-based Signal Corps officer.

The telegraph line running south from Santa Fe was the picture of left-brain precision. Among the Signal Corps' awestruck neighbors was a correspondent for *The Santa Fe New Mexican*. "The telegraph lines [are] a fine piece of work, symmetrical and durable," William Dawson wrote. "The poles are all of uniform size and height and numbering precisely 25 to the mile all along the line."

Reporters and soldiers may have been amazed by the network of floating wires, but the power of the telegraph didn't impress everyone. Vandals, it seemed, couldn't resist pulling down the wires or smashing the glass insulators. The telegraph line was a frequent target in the late-1860s and 1870s of people bent on destruction.

Why? Was it one person's desire to tear down what someone else built, or was it sabotage as an act of resistance against American expansionism? Decades later, writer Oliver La Farge speculated that the motive was not so sinister, not so calculated. "Maybe," he wrote, "a man cut down the wire simply because he needed it to fix his wagon."

Personalities: Trail Blazers

by
Rob Dean

Miguel Antonio Otero Jr.

Miguel Antonio Otero Jr., born in St. Louis to a family with deep New Mexico roots, rode the Santa Fe Trail back to his parents' home territory, where he distinguished himself in banking, politics and letters. He studied at Notre Dame University, then joined his family in banking and worked as a court official. He was one of the last territorial governors before serving as U.S. marshal of the Panama Canal Zone. Otero County in Southern New Mexico was named for his family. He founded a newspaper in Las Vegas, New Mexico, and wrote a widely read three-volume memoir about life on the frontier and in politics.

Source: Otero autobiography, *My Life on the Frontier, 1864 – 1882.*

Miguel A. Otero Jr. Santa Fe, 1906. Photograph by Prince Studio, courtesy Palace of the Governors Photo Archives (NMHM/ DCA), # 50609.

Rufus J. Palen

Rufus J. Palen typified the merchant and professional who arrived on the Santa Fe Trail. Born in New York and trained in law at the University of Michigan, Palen served as a Union officer in the Civil War. He traveled to Santa Fe after his father, Joseph, was named to the territorial supreme court. The younger Palen founded the Santa Fe Board of Trade and served many years as president of the First National Bank of Santa Fe. Palen and his associates were a virtual who's who of Santa Fe Trail pioneer families, including L. Bradford Prince, a future governor; Abraham Staab, trader and government contractor; the Seligmans, a family of merchants and political leaders; A.F. Spiegelberg, mercantile owner; Enos Andrews, dentist, silversmith and a founder of the city water company; Charles H. Gildersleeve, a lawyer and leader of the Democratic Party; and Thomas B. Catron, lawyer and Republican politician.

Source: Primarily Corinne P. Sze's *History of Fairview Cemetery*.

Nina Otero-Warren

Born in 1881, Nina Otero-Warren saw firsthand the changes in civic life that accompanied immigrants from the East. She witnessed the transformation of New Mexico from a place of Hispano-run sheep and cattle ranches to a state ruled increasingly by Anglo newcomers. Her own father was murdered in a dispute over the family's land. She married an Anglo man, divorced him and kept his last name. The hyphenated name of Otero-Warren opened doors for her in both cultures. She was a leader of women's suffrage and served as one of New Mexico's first female public officials, as Santa Fe school superintendent and as chairwoman of the Board of Health. Later she lost a Republican bid for Congress.

Nina Otero-Warren.

Source: Charlotte Whaley's *Nina Otero-Warren of Santa Fe*.

Reynaldo "Sonny" Rivera's massive bronze sculpture, *Journey's End*, at the entrance to Museum Hill off Old Santa Fe Trail. Photograph by Leigh Fagerstrom.

Reynaldo "Sonny" Rivera

In 2002, Reynaldo "Sonny" Rivera planted *Journey's End*, above, his massive bronze sculpture, at the entrance to Museum Hill off Old Santa Fe Trail. Since then, the captivating sculpture has transported modern-day museum visitors back in time to walk among the characters frozen in the era of the wagon trains. Rivera, who lives in Albuquerque, collaborated with landscape architect Richard Borkovetz on *Journey's End*, which depicts a Santa Fe Trail caravan as it nears Santa Fe complete with mules, a wagon, a Pueblo woman, and a boy and his dog. Rivera, a native New Mexican known for tributes to his Hispanic heritage, also has created a sculpture honoring the Spanish colonizers and a monumental bronze sculpture of acclaimed author Rudolfo Anaya.

Source: Santa Fe Trail Association.

Mother Magdalen

When Mother Magdalen and the Sisters of Loretto arrived in 1852, they followed what would become a familiar journey to Santa Fe. At first, they were strangers, but soon they felt at home in the city. "I was deeply conscious of my utter loneliness in this strange land," she wrote to her sister, but she quickly stopped complaining and went to work. The sisters' mission was education, and a girls school and Loretto Chapel became their legacy.

Source: Beverly West's *More than Petticoats: Remarkable New Mexico Women*.

José Leandro Perea

Native New Mexicans as well as easterners grew wealthy hauling freight on the Santa Fe and Mexican trails. For instance, José Leandro Perea of Santa Fe became one of the richest men in New Mexico by capitalizing on the trade routes that linked the United States and Mexico. Perea and other New Mexican traders went east to buy wholesale, returning to Santa Fe to sell goods in a favorable market. As Mexican citizens who paid low import duties, the New Mexicans were able to undercut prices offered by American merchants.

Source: Historian Marc Simmons.

Susan E. Wallace

In 1878, Susan E. Wallace arrived in Santa Fe in a buckboard along with her husband, territorial Governor Lew Wallace, who later gained fame as the author of *Ben-Hur*. She was a writer and poet in her own right. Susan Wallace was noteworthy as a Santa Fe newcomer from the East who looked down her nose at her new home. She wrote in a book that Santa Fe was "the sleepiest place in the world," a dusty town that retained "the charm of foreign flavor" and "some portion of the grace which lingers about … the spot where Spain has held rule for centuries, and the soft syllables of the Spanish language are yet heard."

Source: Susan Wallace's *The Land of the Pueblos*.

Susan E. Wallace. Photograph courtesy Polyglot Press.

Timeline

1598: El Camino Real de Tierra Adentro connects Mexico and New Mexico.

1743: French trappers reach Santa Fe and begin limited trade with the Spanish.

1807: Zebulon Pike leads first Anglo expedition into New Mexico and publishes account of way of life upon return to U.S.

1821: Mexico declares independence from Spain at the same time Santa Fe Trail opens to international trade.

1828: First major gold discovery in Western U.S. made in Ortiz Mountains south of Santa Fe.

1846: Mexican-American War begins. Stephen Watts Kearny annexes New Mexico to the U.S.

1878: The railroad arrives in New Mexico, opening full-scale trade and migration from the East and Midwest.

1918: First plane lands in Santa Fe at an airstrip built by penitentiary inmates, 10 years before Charles Lindbergh flew into town.

1927 – 1937: Route 66 runs through Santa Fe, but later a new Santa Rosa-to-Albuquerque leg bypassed city.

2008: Rail Runner begins commuter-rail service between Santa Fe and Albuquerque.

—Adapted from *New Mexico Blue Book*, 2007/2008 Edition

Suggested Books

Boyle, Susan Calafate. *Los Capitalistas: Hispano Merchants and the Santa Fe Trade*. Albuquerque: The University of New Mexico Press, 2000.

Burroughs, Jean M. *Bride of the Santa Fe Trail*. Santa Fe: Sunstone Press, 1984

Dary, David. *The Santa Fe Trail: Its History, Legends, and Lore*. New York: A.A. Knopf, 2001.

Greever, William S. *Arid Domain: The Santa Fe Railway and Its Western Land Grant*. Stanford: Stanford University Press, 1954.

Lamar, Howard R. *The Far Southwest, 1846 – 1912: A Territorial History*. New Haven: Yale University Press, 1966.

Magoffin, Susan Shelby. *Down the Santa Fe Trail and into Mexico: The Diary of Susan Shelby Magoffin, 1846 – 1847*. New Haven: Yale University Press, 1962.

Moorhead, Max L. *New Mexico's Royal Road*. Norman: University of Oklahoma Press, 1958.

Otero, Miguel Antonio. *My Life on the Frontier, 1864 – 1882*. Santa Fe: Sunstone Press, 2007.

Otero, Miguel Antonio. *My Life on the Frontier, 1882 – 1897*. Santa Fe: Sunstone Press, 2007.

Otero, Miguel Antonio. *My Nine Years as Governor of the Territory of New Mexico, 1897 – 1906*. Santa Fe: Sunstone Press, 2007.

Otero-Warren, Nina. *Old Spain in Our Southwest*. Santa Fe: Sunstone Press, 2006.

Palmer, Gabrielle G., June-el Piper, and LouAnn Jacobson. *El Camino Real De Tierra Adentro*, vols. 1 and 2. Santa Fe: Bureau of Land Management, 1993 and 1999.

Perrigo, Lynn I. *Hispanos, Historic Leaders in New Mexico*. Santa Fe: Sunstone Press, 1985.

Rittenhouse, Jack D. *The Santa Fe Trail, A Historical Bibliography*. Albuquerque: The University of New Mexico Press, 1971.

Sides, Hampton. *Blood and Thunder: An Epic of the American West*. New York: Doubleday, 2006.

Simmons, Marc. *On the Santa Fe Trail*. Lawrence: University Press of Kansas, 1986.

Torrez, Robert J. *New Mexico in 1876 – 1877: A Newspaperman's View, the Travels and Reports of William D. Dawson*. Los Ranchos de Albuquerque: Rio Grande Books, 2007.

Wallace, Susan E. *The Land of the Pueblos*. Santa Fe: Sunstone Press, 2006.

Whaley, Charlotte. *Nina Otero-Warren of Santa Fe*. Santa Fe: Sunstone Press, 2008.

Yoder, Walter D. *The Santa Fe Trail Activity Book*. Santa Fe: Sunstone Press, 1994

Suggested Websites

(active at time of publication)

El Camino Real de Tierra Adentro: http://reta.nmsu.edu/camino
Santa Fe Trail Association: www.santafetrail.org
New Mexico Route 66 Association: www.national66.com
Fairview Cemetery: www.newmexicohistory.org/filedetails.php?fileID=9948
Atcheson, Topeka and Santa Fe Railway: www.atsfry.com/index1.htm

3

Storytelling

Making movies at Tesuque Pueblo, circa 1920. Photograph courtesy of the Palace of the Governors Photo Archives (NMHM/DCA), #004821.

Carrying Our Story: Face-to-Face Style Keeps Storytelling Tradition Alive

by
Robert Nott

New Mexico storytelling: It started with a creation myth and will likely end with the apocalypse. Yes, that's a fiery, exaggerated statement designed to get your attention. But isn't that what all good storytellers do?

New Mexico can nonetheless claim to be home to stories that provide a narrative arc for the history of the world. The Pueblo natives have creation myths detailing how people first came to this land. The story of the conquistadors is ours, as is the tale of the Pueblo Revolt. We've got stories of the Santa Fe Trail, of the railroad, of famous outlaws (who needs Jesse James when we have Billy the Kid?) and famous pioneers (forget Daniel Boone—New Mexico has Kit Carson!), of New Deal artists, of Los Alamos and the creation of the atomic bomb (hence the apocalyptic suggestion), of the Harvey Girls and Route 66 and Geronimo and the Civil War and ghosts galore.

Most of these tales are based on real-life incidents, giving them elements of historical truth that make them worth retelling. And as the city celebrated its 400th anniversary in 2010, it could look back to the past and forward to the future as many of its people keep the art of storytelling alive.

"I see storytelling as a multipurpose genre," said Nasario García, author of more than 20 books, most on the poems, cultural customs, myths and tales of this part of the state. "First of all, it is to entertain. In the past, when you were sitting around the pot-belly stove on a winter night, you didn't have to worry about weeding corn, so you would tell a story."

"Second, you tell stories to educate. You inculcate an awareness of cultural traditions … [and] so many stories have a moral underpinning."

García has collected many personal stories from those who live or lived in the Santa Fe region. Yet he worries that the tradition of oral storytelling is dying.

Nasario García tells a story about witches while speaking at the Santa Fe Main Library in 2006. Photograph by Shih Fa Kao.

What's Past is Present

"People in the hinterland had no radio, no television, nothing, so the oral word was key," García said. "When they told stories, people were knowingly— and perhaps unknowingly—preserving culture. But all that has pretty much gone by the wayside as the old-timers die. And technology is affecting young kids, teenagers today. The elders have no one to pass the torch to because children and grandchildren are not interested. Their kids are more interested in Nintendo."

That's not stopping García from carrying on the tradition. He has stories galore: of men cursed to go legless because they disrespected their parents, wailing *brujas* seeking vengeance, strong Hispanic women who prove their power in unexpected ways, and mischievous children whose pranks backfire with humorous results. For García, who still reads to his grandchildren at bedtime, the notion of a professional storyteller keeping the tradition of tales going is alive and well.

And that sort of baffles Joe Hayes, one of Santa Fe's most famous storytellers. He has told tales for more than 25 years at museums and schools, and has published roughly 25 books of stories.

Joe Hayes. Photograph by Kathy De La Torre.

"People doing what I do, declaring themselves to be a storyteller and putting on a formal performance, that's a real new phenomena," Hayes said. "Because traditional storytelling, within families, within the community, is nowhere near as strong as it used to be."

Hayes keeps the tradition going by connecting every story he tells—be it about a gum-chewing rattler or the day it snowed tortillas—back to this region. He thinks it's vital to project sincerity, so listeners "realize that this is important to the person who is sharing this with them; it's not something they memorized just to do a performance."

Magic of Humor

Hayes strikes a chord with children who remain eager vessels for stories—
one reason Mary Ellen Gonzales, a Santa Fe school board member, takes her
talent to the classroom. She's been doing it since 1992, offering bilingual takes on
traditional tales, and she's a member of Storytellers of New Mexico, a nonprofit
organization headquartered in Albuquerque. Her advice to would-be storytellers:
use humor, make them short, and have as many ghost stories as possible on hand
to keep things lively.

Mary Ellen Gonzales. Photograph by Amiran White.

She's lived the stories of the Southwest, including a stint cooking for
cowboys on a ranch. She first told stories while washing dishes with her sister—a
nod to García's notion that stories were shared during the work day. Gonzales'
face lights up with animation, and her arms and hands start gesturing when she
tells stories. It's a completely different mask than the more subdued, somber one
she puts on for SFPS board meetings. "You can't talk about storytelling without
talking about education," she explained. "To me they are one and the same."

Young listeners will develop not only their own visuals for a story, but build their own moral lessons into it. When Gonzales tells the tale of La Llorona—the weeping woman of the arroyo who still mourns the death of her children (reportedly by her own hand)—she quickly sees how the piece affects students of different ages. The very young see it as a cautionary tale not to get lost (especially down by the river at night). Preteens may view it as a warning to avoid getting abducted by strangers. And for teen girls in particular, the moral here is clear: Don't get pregnant.

But Gonzales' main character is the community where she lives. She figures 75 percent of her stories are New Mexico-based. She'll borrow from other storytellers, including Hayes, but try to turn the tale around to make it her own. She reaches into the past to inform the present.

Voice to Ancestors

As does storyteller Eva Torres Aschenbrener. When she gathers a group of some two dozen visitors to her home for a morning of storytelling, she promises to not only entertain and educate, but to draw a story out of every one of her guests. Aschenbrener believes that everyone has a story to tell—which doesn't mean everyone can tell a story well—and to her the tradition is a great way to rub elbows and learn about other people.

Like Hayes, she is a professional storyteller, and her family members are the main characters of her stories: her kind, thoughtful and ingenious mother; her father, the late judge J. Frank Torres, who overcame racism and strove to be fair to everyone; and a number of other characters, including a naughty aunt—the "Scarlett O'Hara of the family"—who had a yen for using her fan to flirt with married men.

One of Aschenbrener's antecedents knew Kit Carson, Governor Charles Bent, Archbishop Jean Baptiste Lamy and other famous New Mexicans. "Wouldn't you like to have her here?" Aschenbrener asks, smiling.

Aschenbrener uses a self-deprecating sense of humor and a ton of heart to connect to young people. What young, insecure teen today could not relate to Aschenbrener's story of not being asked to the school dance? Her mother urged her to pray to St. Anthony, the saint of lost causes (and, apparently, suitors). Moments later Eva encountered the captain of the school's football team, a handsome bloke who asked her to the dance. Eva was in heaven, until, years later, she ran into the guy again.

"I really liked your mom," he told Eva. "And she paid me real well."

Aschenbrener involves her audience, and insists that, "My endeavor is to get people to understand and respect one another. Stories help us do that."

And you realize Aschenbrener is right: In telling stories of our ancestors, we relate the history of the righteous, the rogues and the rascals, the fallen women—and the men who helped them fall. They're with us still. In some cases, they are us.

Storyteller Eva Torres Aschenbrener entertains guests at her home with stories of her father in February 2010. Photograph by Luis Sánchez Saturno.

400 More Years

While most storytellers look back to inform their listeners, Santa Fe's poet laureate, Valerie Martínez, looked ahead. In her poem commemorating 400 years of Santa Fe, she asked that readers both turn around and turn ahead with wonder:

And the child walks carefully into blue air,
into the light silver with sun,
into the city's steady murmuring:
what will come, what will come?

A native New Mexican, Martínez was responsible for the book and corresponding exhibition, *Lines and Circles: A Celebration of Santa Fe Families*. The project relied on first-person accounts, poems, mixed-media art, and religious, cultural and personal items to tell the story of several generations of 11 families in Santa Fe.

"My priority is the present," Martínez said.

"As poet laureate, people come to me and tell me their stories, and often they talk about how they feel about Santa Fe. They're concerned about the divisions in the community, and how, geographically, things have changed, and they also say they're tired about fighting over the past."

Instead of celebrating the 400 years behind us, she urged Santa Feans to look at the next 400 years. "When you say the word *story*, it sparks in people's minds what went past," she said. "But my poem is actually a meditation on how history is actually a step we need to take—forward."

New Mexico in Film

by
Robert Nott

In movie making, New Mexico prides itself on being ahead of the pack—both now, with lucrative film incentives drawing filmmakers such as the Coen Brothers, who filmed a remake of *True Grit* here—and in the past, when filmmakers came here to take advantage of the beautiful locale. Since the Edison Motion Pictures company set up shop here in 1898 to film *Indian Day School* at Isleta Pueblo, the state has served as the backdrop for well over 500 films, according to Jon Bowman's book *100 Years of Filmmaking in New Mexico* and the New Mexico Film Office website.

Not all of these films deal with New Mexico stories. Here's a list of some that do:

Redskin (1929): Richard Dix is a Navajo trying to build a life between his own nation and the "white" world against a backdrop of racism and culture clash at an Indian boarding school. Shot in and around Acoma Pueblo.

Ace in the Hole (1951): Billy Wilder's incisive autopsy of a once-good newspaper man gone bad (played by Kirk Douglas) who takes advantage of a tragedy involving a trapped miner. The film features great shots of the Albuquerque and Gallup region.

Salt of the Earth (1953): Shot in and around Silver City, this drama was made by blacklisted film artists and (mostly) amateur actors and was based on the real-life union struggle between exploited miners and Empire Zinc. It's required viewing for any student of New Mexico filmmaking.

Lonely Are the Brave (1962): Kirk Douglas is the last cowboy (in New Mexico), vainly trying to outrun progress in this hard-hitting drama based on Edward Abbey's *The Brave Cowboy*.

Red Sky at Morning, **filmed in 1971 in New Mexico, starred Richard Thomas, right, and Catherine Burns. Photograph courtesy Universal Pictures.**

Red Sky at Morning (1971): Beautiful coming-of-age story set in Northern New Mexico, based on Richard Bradford's novel and featuring a stellar cast including Richard Thomas, Catherine Burns and Desi Arnaz Jr.

Billy Jack (1971): This one seemed really good back in 1971, when it played in the local drive-in. Now, it seems dated and dull. It still has moments, especially when Tom Laughlin beats up bad guys who bully Indian students. Great locale shooting in Santa Fe and Northern New Mexico.

Powwow Highway (1989): Insightful and quite funny road-trip movie directed by Jonathan Wacks (former chairman of the film department at the College of Santa Fe) and featuring strong ensemble work by Gary Farmer, Graham Greene, Wes Studi and others.

Gas, Food, Lodging (1992): Allison Anders' low-key drama about a woman (Brooke Adams) trying to make a life for herself and her two daughters in a desert town in New Mexico (Deming).

The Hi Lo Country (1997): Passionate adaptation of Max Evans' book spotlights the challenges faced by the state's cowboys as World War II and trucks took the place of range wars and horses.

Tortilla Heaven (2007): An image of Jesus shows up in a tortilla in a small New Mexican village. Antics, inspired by the devil, ensue. It's not perfect, but it will give you a sense of what life is like in a sleepy New Mexican hamlet (it was shot in Dixon).

When News Was A Participatory Sport

by
Rob Dean

Santa Fe newsman E. Dana Johnson had quite a story to tell—in this case about what happened to him, not about what he covered. Johnson was the editor in 1917 when *The Santa Fe New Mexican* uncovered malfeasance by the prison warden who doubled as the political boss of Socorro.

The boss bit back, using a home-field advantage to get the Socorro prosecutor to file criminal libel charges in the court of a friendly judge. When Johnson violated a gag order, the judge jailed him for contempt of court. In time, Johnson beat the contempt and libel charges, but the whole affair stood as proof that rivals in New Mexico's combative politics often slugged it out using the press and the courts as their own.

Johnson stood up to a bully, obeyed principle under threat of jail and clung to faith in final justice, but not without feeling the sting of a political machine willing to punish its enemies in the pursuit of power and profit. Not that Johnson was some timid weakling. He was the outspoken editor working for Bronson Cutting, the rich owner of *The Santa Fe New Mexican* who rode his paper's influence all the way to the U.S. Senate.

Through the territorial period of the late-1800s and early-1900s, writers often blurred the line between journalism done to inform and journalism meant to persuade, and in the early days after statehood in 1912, remnants of that head-knocking style led to Johnson's jailing.

Johnson later guaranteed his fame by helping Will Shuster think up Zozobra. But outside Santa Fe, his legal fight became one of the last chapters in the colorful era of Santa Fe newspapering that continued past World War II.

Colorful aptly described reporters' work from the time they began telling Santa Fe stories in 1834. A rich piece of history was the Spanish-language press that protected the Hispanic culture and language against the Anglo invasion from the east, according to historian Doris Meyer. Three editors who left an imprint on Santa Fe were Enrique Salazar, Hilario Ortiz and Nestor Montoya, all sharing a newspaper pedigree—*La Voz del Pueblo* founded in 1888.

Salazar, a Santa Fe native and the stepson of a newspaper owner, made his paper an influential voice for liberal causes and statehood. He later was a federal land administrator. Ortiz, too, was born in Santa Fe and started Spanish newspapers in Socorro and Albuquerque. After journalism, he worked in education and practiced criminal law. Montoya left *La Voz* after two years and returned to his native Albuquerque to enter public service and participate in the constitutional convention.

One of the first crusading Anglo journalists was Charles Greene, whose *Santa Fe New Mexican* pushed land development. He later moved south to promote mining and irrigation.

At the turn of the century, one of the loudest voices in Santa Fe belonged to publisher Max Frost, soldier, lawyer, political broker and protector of the Ring that used legal tricks to gain title to blocks of land.

Newspaper editor Will Harrison patrolled Santa Fe as its watchdog in the 1940s and '50s. He had a nose for scandal and a hunger to tell all, but also kept the secrets of Los Alamos before Hiroshima. Reputed to carry printers' lead wrapped in a handkerchief for protection, Harrison made enemies by fingering an attorney general who pocketed corporate legal fees on the side, by exposing a politician who misused the highway department to pave his private road and by carrying on a feud with a governor Harrison dismissed as a pawn of the bosses.

Tony Hillerman, a decorated World War II veteran and Oklahoma-trained newspaper man, was editor of *The Santa Fe New Mexican* and later a journalism professor. Before his 2008 death, he wrote widely read mysteries set in Navajo country.

Richard McCord inspired award-winning reporting at the *Santa Fe Reporter*, promoted independent journalism and published an influential book in 2001 on the monopolistic practices of Gannett, the largest U.S. newspaper chain that tried to capture Santa Fe in the 1970s.

The editorial staff of *The Santa Fe New Mexican* around the turn of the century included editor and publisher Max Frost, seated second from right. Photograph courtesy Palace of the Governors Photo Archive (NMHM/DCA), #15275.

Ben-Hur Creator Was No Hero in New Mexico

by
Jason Strykowski

One hundred thirty years ago, the governor of New Mexico took a most unusual personal leave. He had to travel to New York to oversee the publication of his novel. Although the trip interrupted a troubled tenure, *Ben-Hur: A Tale of the Christ* would become a big success, a best-seller second only to the Bible.

For General Lew Wallace, however, the road to success had been a bumpy one. Literally.

Wallace arrived in Santa Fe in fall 1878 at the behest of President Rutherford B. Hayes. The railroad had yet to reach the capital city, and Wallace was forced to take a carriage ride on a buckboard road. He compared the experience to torture. Wallace's first days in Santa Fe provided little more comfort than the carriage. The Santa Fe Ring, at the height of its power, showed little affection for Wallace, who had replaced one of their own, Samuel Axtell, as territorial governor.

Like the men who ran the ring, Wallace emerged from the Civil War hoping to profit from a reunited nation. After serving on the Lincoln assassination tribunal and failing in repeated attempts at federal office, Wallace returned to his native Indiana to practice law. The attorney's life was a poor fit for the adventurous Wallace.

Former governor of New Mexico, Lew Wallace. Etching from *Harper's Weekly,* **March 6, 1886.**

On the strength of his military career, Wallace was the president's pick to govern the territory of New Mexico. Washington hoped he could use his military experience to quell the violence in Lincoln County that by 1878 had become a national embarrassment. The violence that became known as the Lincoln County War had arisen several years earlier as an enterprising Briton, John Tunstall, moved to Lincoln and attempted to gain a foothold in the trade-goods market. Economic competition spawned physical warfare.

Wallace chose to stop the fighting by issuing a general pardon to the men who had participated in the violence. While the pardon did little to end the war, it inadvertently brought about the last days of a young ranch hand known as William H. Bonney, Billy the Kid. Bonney, finding himself the only Lincoln County warrior not excused by the pardon, still faced charges for crimes committed during the fighting.

Bonney tried to cut a deal with Wallace in the hopes that his record would be erased. What began as a simple offer of help in a solitary letter soon evolved into a lengthened correspondence and bred the oddest set of pen pals in the history of the United States.

Up until his death in 1881, Bonney continued to write Wallace in the hopes that the governor might eventually make good on the agreed terms. For his part, Bonney had met with Wallace and informed on other criminals operating in the Lincoln County area. He had also agreed to testify in court.

But, rather than grant the promised pardon, Wallace decided to put a bounty on Bonney's head. By the time Pat Garrett finally got Bonney in Fort Sumner, Wallace was far from Santa Fe in Paris, where he and his wife had stopped on their way to his diplomatic post in Turkey.

The ambassadorship came to Wallace, in fact, as something of a pardon. Wallace hated the nearly three years he spent in New Mexico. He arrived with hopes of mining profits and of quick completion of his novel. The book took him longer than expected as he slaved away into the night at the Palace of the Governors. His mines produced little. Fortunately, *Ben-Hur* was a gold strike.

President James Garfield viewed the book as fit reason to send Wallace to Turkey. Fame and riches eventually followed as the novel climbed the best-seller lists.

Variations on the novel appeared soon on the stage in New York, where directors used live horses on stage to recreate the pivotal chariot race. The action drew crowds. The new medium of film offered entrepreneurs an opportunity to cash in on the popularity of the novel. Three films based on Wallace's novel were produced, including the Charlton Heston blockbuster made over a half century ago.

Although Santa Fe has been home to more than its fair share of notable authors, Lew Wallace remains one of its most successful. Unfortunately, when Wallace used his powers of the pen to describe the capital city, he could only write: "Every calculation based on experience elsewhere fails in New Mexico."

Personalities: Storytellers

by
Rob Dean

Here is a small selection of the writers and historians, the filmmakers and photographers who keep Santa Fe's story alive.

Carmella Padilla, right, with her mother, Zenaida Padilla. Photograph by Katharine Kimball.

Carmella Padilla

Carmella Padilla has written, "The history of Northern New Mexico is a complex chronicle of resilience and resourcefulness, shaped by individuals with the same stalwart qualities." That belief propels the work of Padilla, a Santa Fe native devoted to telling the stories of her hometown. Her books celebrate the state's chile industry, El Rancho de las Golondrinas and lowriding. Her devotion to arts and culture serves the Spanish Colonial Art Society, the Railyard Park and the International Folk Art Market. In 2009, her work earned a Governor's Award for Excellence in the Arts.

Evelina Zuni Lucero

Evelina Zuni Lucero.

Stanford-educated Evelina Zuni Lucero teaches, at the time of publication of this book, creative writing at the Institute of American Indian Arts in Santa Fe. Drawing on her roots in the Isleta Pueblo and Ohkay Owingeh communities, she worked as a news reporter, earned a master's degree in English and won praise in 2000 for the novel *Night Sky, Morning Star*. Lucero used the story to deal with 500 years of trauma for American Indians and developed the characters—a Native political activist jailed for a crime he did not commit and a Pueblo potter—to "illustrate the unresolved pasts shoved into the closet." She has expanded her work as a storyteller to include cultural events that combine music, poetry and oral storytelling.

Source: Institute of American Indian Arts.

Myra Ellen Jenkins

From 1960 to 1980, Myra Ellen Jenkins served as state archivist and state historian, earning her place as the final authority on New Mexico history. Known for scrupulous research and devastating wit, Jenkins rescued and protected many of the state's historical documents. Her efforts brought order to the long-neglected archives. She was state historian from 1967, when the Legislature re-established the position, to her retirement, elevating in the public mind the historian's role in society. Her successors included Stanley Hordes, Robert Torrez, Estevan Rael-Gálvez, and Rick Hendricks. Jenkins died in 1993.

Source: Santa Fe Living Treasures and Office of the State Historian.

George C' de Baca

George C' de Baca learned early to be the family storyteller. As a boy in the 1940s, he ran errands by walking three miles from his grandparents' home in La Cienega to his relatives' farm in remote La Cieneguilla. "Since they were so isolated they were curious to know what was going on," recalled C' de Baca. "I told them what little I knew." From that modest start, C' de Baca has taken family history to the limit, and why not? His family tree has deep roots in the Santa Fe area. His book, *The Eden of La Cienega*, published in 1998, tells of early life in that representative Hispanic village of Northern New Mexico.

Source: *Mora Family Stories* by George C' de Baca.

Leonora F. Curtin Paloheimo

The sights and sounds of the Spanish Colonial period come to life at El Rancho de las Golondrinas thanks to Leonora F. Curtin Paloheimo. Her family bought the La Cienega property in the 1930s, and she and her husband started a living museum replicating colonial village life and authentic old structures. The museum welcomes teachers and students for tours and workshops. Before transforming the ranch into the museum, Leonora Curtin Paloheimo, a California native, worked to preserve Native languages and revive Spanish Colonial arts and crafts.

Source: El Rancho de las Golondrinas.

Leonora F. Curtin Paloheimo.

Tom Chávez

Tom Chávez, historian and writer, was for 20 years the director of the Palace of the Governors and then director of the National Hispanic Cultural Center in Albuquerque. He drew inspiration from his uncle, Fray Angélico Chávez, distinguished priest, historian, poet and artist who died in 1996. Tom Chávez described the essence of the historian as storyteller in the introduction to his book of New Mexico history: "an opportunity to view, and learn from, our predecessors, our ancestors."

Tom Chávez.

Alice Corbin Henderson

Tuberculosis brought poet Alice Corbin Henderson from Chicago in 1916, and she became the leader of writers and artists in the early 20th century. Recognized as a poet before moving to Santa Fe, Corbin was co-founder of a magazine that popularized the new poetry of Carl Sandburg, Ezra Pound and Witter Bynner. Corbin died in 1949. Her contemporaries included three distinguished writers who lived into the 1960s: Ina Cassidy, who supported the arts and cultural preservation through her writing; Sara Woolfolk McComb, an advocate for American Indian rights and host of an annual Poets' Roundup; and native Santa Fean Ruth Laughlin Barker Alexander, a journalist specializing in nonfiction and historical fiction.

Source: Fairview Cemetery history by Corinne Sze.

Fantasia Lonjose

Majestic and inspiring described Fantasia Lonjose's work in 2007, as she competed in the national finals of a poetry recitation and interpretation competition. Lonjose's accomplishment came as a member of the Santa Fe Indian School Spoken Word Club. Under the direction of teacher Jim McLaughlin, club members found a modern way to honor their ancestors' tradition of storytelling. The students tell stories of their ancestors and ceremonies and give voice to the forces in their worlds. The young storytellers have attracted the attention of *The New York Times*, a documentary filmmaker for HBO and the organizer of a cultural exchange in Latvia, Estonia and Lithuania.

Fantasia Lonjose competes in the national finals of a poetry recitation and interpretation competition in 2007. Photograph courtesy of James Kegley.

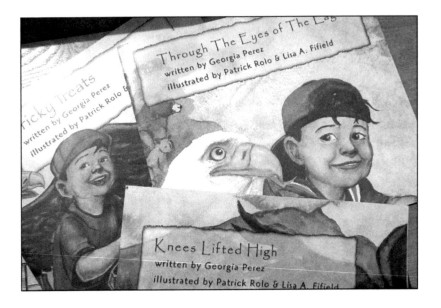

Georgia Perez

A dream inspired Georgia Perez, and an eagle circling in the sky showed her the way. Perez, a member of Nambé Pueblo, wrote four books promoting healthy living for children. The four books tell the story of an American Indian boy who learns the keys to living a healthy life from a bald eagle. Perez began writing the Eagle Books series in 2002 after a vision came to her as she slept. "In my dream, the eagle was showing me how life for Native Americans used to be and some things that Native people should do to be healthy once again," Perez said. Soon after, an eagle actually appeared in the high sky, and Perez realized that an eagle, if given a voice in her writing, could effectively get through to children.

Georgia Perez.
Photographs by Natalie Guillén.

Joe Sando

Joe Sando of Jemez Pueblo is a historian, teacher and writer who has spent his career educating all people about Pueblo culture and history. His books include *Pueblo Nations: Eight Centuries of Pueblo Indian History* and *Pueblo Profiles: Cultural Identity through Centuries of Change.* He and Herman Agoyo co-authored *Po'pay: Leader of the First American Revolution.* Sando was the longtime director of the Institute of Pueblo Study and Research at the Indian Pueblo Cultural Center in Albuquerque.

Source: Museum of Indian Arts and Culture.

Joe Sando. Photograph by Clyde Mueller.

Marc Simmons.

Marc Simmons

Marc Simmons never stops trying to make history a delight. For nearly 50 years, he has told New Mexico's story by wrapping doctorate-level research inside an easy, narrative style. Working at a manual typewriter in a house he built off the beaten path, Simmons churns out history for the masses, more than 40 books and hundreds of articles. Over the years, he has written a weekly column for *The Santa Fe New Mexican* and has several children's books to his credit. His expertise is wide-ranging—from the Spanish archives to Billy the Kid.

Timeline

1609 – 1610: De Villagra publishes epic on founding New Mexico, first book in modern United States.

1712: Governor proclaims duty to maintain public records.

1807: Zebulon Pike publishes account of New Mexico life.

1834: First newspaper in Spanish followed by the first English paper in 1847.

1835: First school text printed by Padre Martinez.

1846 – 1847: Susan Magoffin journal tells of Santa Fe Trail.

1891: After years of neglect, Legislature okays money to catalog Spanish and Mexican archives.

1898: First film made in New Mexico, Edison's Indian Day School.

1909: Legislature creates Museum of New Mexico.

1917 – 1918: Writers' colonies form in Santa Fe and Taos.

1930 – 1943: New Deal funds Depression-era writers' projects.

1945: Office of the State Historian established.

Suggested Books

Aragon, Ray John de. *The Legend of La Llorona*. Santa Fe: Sunstone Press, 2006.

Austin, Mary. *The American Rhythm: Studies and Re-expressions of Amerindian Songs*. Sante Fe: Sunstone Press, 2007.

Baca, Jimmy Santiago. *A Place to Stand: The Making of a Poet*. New York: Grove Press, 2001.

Beatty, Judith S, ed. *La Llorona, Encounters with the Weeping Woman*. Santa Fe: Sunstone Press, 2004

C' de Baca, George. *The Eden of La Cienega*. Kearney: Morris Publishing, 1998.

Chávez, Angélico. *Chávez: A Distinctive American Clan of New Mexico*. Santa Fe: Sunstone Press, 2009.

Cargo, David Francis. *Lonesome Dave, The Story of New Mexico Governor David Francis Cargo*. Santa Fe: Sunstone Press, 2010.

Cline, Donald. *Alias Billy the Kid, The Man Behind the Legend*. Santa Fe: Sunstone Press, 1986.

García, Nasario. *Pláticas: Conversations with Hispano Writers of New Mexico*. Lubbock: Texas Tech University Press, 2000.

Franke, Lois Gerber. *J. Frank Torres: Crusader and Judge: An Oral History*. Santa Fe: Sunstone Press, 2007.

Grant, Blanche Chloe, ed. *Kit Carson's Own Story of His Life*. Santa Fe: Sunstone Press, 2007

Fackler, Elizabeth. *Billy the Kid, The Legend of El Chivato*. Santa Fe: Sunstone Press, 2003

Garrett, Pat. *The authentic Life of Billy the Kid*. Santa Fe: Sunstone Press, 2007.

Hunt, Frazier. *The Tragic Days of Billy the Kid*. Santa Fe: Sunstone Press, 2009.

Keleher, William A. *Violence in Lincoln County, 1869 – 1881*. Santa Fe: Sunstone Press, 2007.

La Farge, Oliver. *Santa Fe: The Autobiography of a Southwestern Town*. Norman: University of Oklahoma Press, 1959.

Laughlin, Ruth. *Caballeros, The Romance of Santa Fe and the Southwest*. Santa Fe: Sunstone Press, 2007

Martínez, Valerie, ed. *Lines and Circles, A Celebration of Santa Fe Families*. Santa Fe: Sunstone Press, 2010.

McCord, Richard. *The Other State, New Mexico, USA*. Santa Fe: Sunstone Press: 2003

Melzer, Richard. *Breakdown, How the Secret of the Atomic Bomb was Stolen During World War II*. Santa Fe: Sunstone Press, 2000.

Miller, Jay, *Billy the Kid Rides Again, Digging for the Truth*. Santa Fe: Sunstone Press, 2005.

Nestor, Sarah. *The Native Market of the Spanish New Mexican Craftsman, 1933 – 1940*. Santa Fe, Sunstone Press, 2009.

Nolan, Frederick. *The Life and Death of John Henry Tunstall*. Santa Fe: Sunstone Press, 2009.

Nolan, Frederick. *The Lincoln County War, Revised Edition*. Santa Fe: Sunstone Press, 2009.

Meyer, Doris. *Speaking for Themselves: Neomexicano Cultural Identity and the Spanish-Language Press, 1880-1920*. Albuquerque: The University of New Mexico Press, 1996.

Otero, Miguel Antonio Jr. *The Real Billy the Kid*. Santa Fe: Sunstone Press, 2007.

Pijoan, Teresa. *American Indian Creation Myths*. Santa Fe: Sunstone Press, 2005.

Poe, John William. *The Death of Billy the Kid*. Santa Fe: Sunstone Press, 2006.

Romero, Orlando. *Nambé—Year One*. Albuquerque: The University of New Mexico Press, 2009.

Silverman, Jason. *Untold New Mexico, Stories from a Hidden Past*. Santa Fe: Sunstone Press, 2006.

Simmons, Marc. *New Mexico Mavericks, Stories from a Fabled Past*. Santa Fe: Sunstone Press, 2005

Simmons, Marc. *Stalking Billy the Kid, Brief Sketches of a Short Life*. Santa Fe: Sunstone Press, 2006

Simmons, Marc. *Yesterday in Santa Fe, Episodes in a Turbulent History*. Santa Fe: Sunstone Press, 1989.

Stratton, Porter A. *The Territorial Press of New Mexico 1834-1912*. Albuquerque: The University of New Mexico Press, 1969.

Torrez, Robert J. *New Mexico in 1876-1877: A Newspaperman's View, the Travels and Reports of William D. Dawson*. Los Ranchos de Albuquerque: Rio Grande Books, 2007.

Weigle, Marta, Frances Levine, and Louise Stiver. *Telling New Mexico: A New History*. Santa Fe: Museum of New Mexico Press, 2009.

Weigle, Marta, and Kyle Fiore. *Santa Fe & Taos: The Writer's Era, 1916-1941*. Santa Fe: Sunstone Press, 2008.

Writers' Program of the Work Projects Administration in the State of New Mexico. *The WPA Guide to 1930s New Mexico*. Tucson: University of Arizona Press, 1989.

Suggested Websites
(active at time of publication)

Eagle Books: www.cdc.gov/diabetes/pubs/eagle.htm
Film in New Mexico: www.nmfilmmuseum.org
Pueblo Cultural Center: www.indianpueblo.org
Santa Fe Living Treasures: www.sflivingtreasures.org/
State Historian: www.newmexicohistory.org

4

Faith

Matias Jacobo, as Christ, and Jesus Ruacho, as a soldier, perform in the passion play at Our Lady of Guadalupe Church in April 2010. Photograph by Natalie Guillén.

Faith And Understanding

by
Anne Constable

Lee Moquino's black jacket with his name embroidered on it identifies him as an employee of San Ildefonso Pueblo. But that doesn't tell his whole story. His mother's family has deep roots in the Hispanic community of Truchas. His father's side is from Zia and Santa Clara pueblos. There's also Apache, Kickapoo and Anglo in his blood.

Monsignor Jerome Martínez y Alire, rector of the Cathedral Basilica of St. Francis of Assisi, calls him a "truly multicultural Pueblo Indian." And Moquino, a fluent Spanish speaker who sports spiky hair (red on one side), earrings and a necklace with the image of the Virgin of Guadalupe, calls that "the best description I've ever heard. I love that."

It is impossible to talk about the city today without talking about faith. Not only is faith part of its name, it is a good measure of what makes this venerable community so different from other places in the U.S. For centuries the Catholic church has been a dominant, sometimes contentious, force in Santa Fe, but today, the city and the church are decidedly inclusive.

Moquino, 25, was raised by four generations on his mother's side as a devout Catholic. The family also worshipped at the local morada, a chapter house of the brotherhood of the Penitentes, where Moquino's great-great-grandfather, Carmen Vigil, had been a *hermano*. At the same time, he attended feast days at the pueblos and took part in traditional ceremonies with his paternal grandparents and other relatives.

"I can't distinguish between being pueblo and being Catholic," Moquino said, because "both religions stress taking care of one another and loving each other."

Finding Reconciliation

"After the 'unpleasantries,' we have traditionally gotten along very well," said Martínez y Alire.

But in the 400-plus years of Catholic history in New Mexico, relations were not always so agreeable, and there is still some hurt on the part of the Indians about the way they were conquered and evangelized by the Spanish who came to Nuévo México principally to proclaim the gospel of Jesus Christ and baptize converts.

Those early Spanish brought with them a sense of superiority over the Native people and set about trying to change everything about them, including their religion. According to *Four Hundred Years of Faith*, a book published in 1998 by the Archdiocese of Santa Fe, the friars and the secular leaders vied for the loyalty—and labor—of the Indians. They had some early successes converting Pueblo Indians to Catholicism in villages such as Pecos, but resentment over the abuse grew into rage, exploding in 1680 in the Pueblo Revolt, in which 21 Franciscans were martyred.

The Spanish who returned after the reconquest in 1692 were said to be humbler, "willing to baptize Indian customs and beliefs by giving them Christian meaning and orientation," according to the church history. And out of the reconciliation, "a new more inclusive and adaptive mentality was born, which drew on the strengths of both peoples."

But the Catholic Church was unchallenged. As Martínez y Alire put it, "The church supported the crown, and the crown supported the cross."

After Mexican independence, neither the Spanish nor the Mexican government could afford to fund the church in New Mexico. And because the Franciscans (who were assigned primarily to the pueblos) had never inspired vocations to the priesthood among the local population, there was a lack of clergy to supply the Hispanic churches. Many church buildings fell into disrepair.

The shortage of clergy led to the rise of La Fraternidad Piadosa de Nuestro Padre Jesús Nazareno. Lay Catholics organized themselves into chapters, built moradas or chapels, and provided for spiritual life in remote communities. They held Lenten services, acted out the life of Jesus and Mary in processions and plays, buried the dead, provided for those in need and sought to bring people into the faith.

Their purpose was to inform people about the sacraments so that when they did receive them, they could embrace them, according to Charlie Carrillo, a prominent santero and anthropologist who belongs to a morada in Abiquiú. "The genius of the *hermandad* was that it was grass-roots and it was communal. Faith survives when it's from the people up," he said.

Charlie Carrillo, a prominent santero and anthropologist, belongs to a morada in Abiquiú. Photograph by Luis Sánchez Saturno.

According to the history of the archdiocese, the result was "double-track Catholicism," with the ordained clergy administering the sacraments and the brotherhood ministering to other needs of the people.

The Penitentes, who focused on the passion of Christ, drew national attention for their practice of self-flagellation. According to a 1936 article in *Time* magazine, they began their "bloody emulation of the sufferings of Christ" on Ash Wednesday, when the brothers bowed before a sangrador who gouged crosses on their backs with a jagged piece of glass. "The penitents would keep their wounds open and raw until Easter, often by rubbing rock salt in them," the article said.

During the territorial period, the brotherhood was forced underground. The second in a series of French archbishops, Jean Baptiste Salpointe, considered their practices barbaric—and a threat to the church's power. But the brotherhood survived and kept the faith alive. Today the Penitentes are still private, but not secretive or underground.

Moquino was *hermano mayor segundo* at La Morada de Santa Cruz in 2008 when it opened its Holy Week events to the public. (As of 2010, he is taking a leave of absence from that position.) And hermanos from across New Mexico participated in the celebration of Archbishop Michael J. Sheehan's 25th anniversary in 2008 by singing an *alabado*, or medieval hymn.

The brotherhood nurtures his faith, Moquino said, because it allows the members to "share in the suffering of Christ" by "carrying out penance in the ways taught to them by their ancestors."

Statehood a Threat to the Church

The French archbishops—starting with Jean Baptiste Lamy—who arrived after the conquest of the American Southwest, built up the institutional church and established new schools and hospitals. They persuaded many religious orders (Sisters of Loretto, Christian Brothers, the Sisters of Charity and the Jesuits) to send nuns and brothers to the territory to staff them.

But many of the archbishops and the priests they brought to the territory also had little appreciation for the local culture. They removed native clergy, tried to replace the mission churches with the Gothic and Romanesque edifices more familiar to them and preferred plaster of Paris saints to the beautiful bultos and altar screens made by the descendants of the Spanish colonists to decorate the churches. By 1912, the year New Mexico was finally admitted to the union, there was only one native priest in the archdiocese.

In the years leading up to statehood, the church vigorously fought New Mexico's admission to the union. Sermons opposed a clause in the 1890 constitution that held that schools "shall be under the absolute control of the state, and free from sectarian or church control" and no church schools could receive public funds. A circular was distributed among Catholics warning that "enemies of religion" among the delegates to the constitutional convention would try to "force you to deny your children all kinds of education excepting that of the world."

The constitution was voted down, and New Mexico didn't become a state for another 22 years. The church's primary fears were that the anti-Catholicism among the delegates to the 1890 convention would be institutionalized, said Martínez y Alire, and that New Mexico would ultimately be "swallowed up in a Protestant ocean," if it became part of the union. Statehood was also unpopular in the East with those who thought the territory was "home to too many Mexicans and Catholics. It was too different from the rest of the U.S.," Martínez y Alire said.

The French line of archbishops finally ended in 1919, and the new American-born archbishop began encouraging native vocations. In 1946, a minor seminary was established in Santa Fe.

After statehood, the number of Protestant missionaries increased. The Presbyterians, Baptists and Episcopalians, among others, built churches. Although the first temple wasn't built until the 1950s, Jews gathered together in homes to observe holidays. They also provided financial support to other religious institutions. Rabbi Marvin Schwab of Temple Beth Shalom points to the triangle over the front door of the cathedral and a Jewish star visible from the pulpit at Holy Faith Episcopal Church. "I assume these were thank-yous to the Jewish community," he said.

Meanwhile, nuns and brothers continued to work in many of the state's new public schools. Opposition to their role came to a head in 1951, when the U.S. Supreme Court ruled in favor of Protestants in Dixon who brought suit against the local board of education for allowing Catholic nuns in habits to teach religion as part of the regular curriculum.

A native son, Robert Fortune Sanchez, was ordained the 10th archbishop of Santa Fe before 14,000 people in 1974. Subsequently, the church was rocked by allegations of impropriety by Sanchez (who resigned in 1993) and widespread charges of clergy misconduct, especially by priests assigned to rehabilitation centers like the Servants of the Paraclete in Jemez Springs.

This was a challenging time for the church worldwide, but looking back, Martínez y Alire said, "New Mexico never had any trouble with attendance. Even through the child-abuse scandal, people still came. New Mexico is on the whole a very devout Catholic group."

The churches were buoyed by the influx of immigrants from Mexico and South America. While these native Spanish speakers sometimes met with hostility from native New Mexicans, Martínez y Alire said, their impact on the church has been profound. Today Our Lady of Guadalupe has become "the Mexican national parish" and many of the churches, including the cathedral, offer Masses in Spanish.

A Bittersweet Moment

Despite the increasing diversity of the faith community, Santa Fe is still at its heart a Catholic community.

And Lee Moquino is the face of the new generation. Born in Santa Fe, he was raised in the Pojoaque area, and like every "true New Mexican," he is "related to someone somehow" in many of the villages in the north. His grandparents are Corn Moquino, a potter from Zia Pueblo, and his wife, Christine, from Santa Clara. Moquino graduated from Pojoaque High School and is now an assistant to the governor of San Ildefonso Pueblo. But his passion is pottery. He learned the sgraffito, or scratched, style of decorating pots from his grandfather, Corn, but now makes micaceous cookware in a style he learned from Felipe Ortega.

Now an assistant to the governor of San Ildefonso Pueblo, Moquino is the face of the Catholic Church's new generation.

Despite his youth, Moquino has caught the notice of the archdiocese. As a teenager and a member of Our Lady of Guadalupe parish in Pojoaque, he traveled to Toronto in 2001 to meet the pope with other young Catholics at World Youth Day. Last fall, he was invited to meet Spain's Crown Prince Felipe de Borbón y Grecia and his wife during a 400th anniversary celebration in Santa Fe. Martínez y Alire recalls him saying that the moment was bittersweet. He told the royal couple he was grateful they were there, but not too happy about how it happened.

Although many of the religious ideas the Spanish tried to impose were not so different from Pueblo beliefs, "I think they didn't do it in a compassionate way," he said more recently. "It was more forced on our people. They saw our traditional religious activities as being pagan."

But the people got along, Moquino said, repeating a story told to him by his great-grandmother, who in the 1920s used to make trips with her family from Truchas to what was then called San Juan Pueblo, where they would trade wagon loads of wood for fresh fruits and vegetables. "It was a common bond to survive. They lived in peace. They had a sense of respect, helping each other," he said.

Lee Moquino, then 18, poses with Indian princess Juanita Talache during Fiesta in 2003. Photograph by Jane Phillips.

Today the cathedral holds a Native American Mass during Indian Market, features Aztec dancers during the Feast of Guadalupe, and big pontifical Masses always include a Native dance, chant or readings in Native languages.

For the Feast of St. Joseph at Laguna Pueblo in 2010, Carrillo said he was invited to the homes of four different pueblo members for a meal. But he had to decline because he was expected at the morada in Abiquiú for the Friday Lenten stations of the cross.

"What a wonderful world this is where you can be both [Catholic and Puebloan]," he said. "The Catholic Church has embraced that. It doesn't exist in many places in the world."

Where Diverse Beliefs Are Welcome

by
Anne Constable

When the Reverend Dr. Holly Beaumont came to Santa Fe to interview for a ministerial position at the First Christian Church in 1986, she said she was invited to a meeting of the interfaith alliance, where she was expecting to meet local Catholics, Protestants and Jews.

When Beaumont arrived, she found "there were Buddhists, Hindus, all kinds of new age people, a nice young man from the Unification Church (of Rev. Sun Yung Moon). I thought that for the first time I might find myself in a community where I may not be the most progressive or liberal person. And I might find myself pushed out of my comfort zone."

But four hundred years after the arrival of the Franciscans, Catholicism remains the dominant religion in the City of Holy Faith. There are 350,000 adherents in the archdiocese, many of them new immigrants, and Santa Fe still moves according to the church's liturgical year.

Today the city also boasts three Zen centers (Upaya Zen Center, Maha Bodhi Society of Santa Fe and Mountain Cloud Zen Center), the KSK Buddhist Center, Tibetan shrines, Sufis, Sikhs, at least four Jewish congregations, Muslims (TaHa Mosque), various evangelicals and hundreds of healers attracted by its physical beauty and spiritual history. Among the faithful are descendants of the conversos who fled Spain and Portugal during the Inquisition and practiced Judaism in secret.

City spiritual leaders gathered in January 2010, for the interfaith celebration to mark the 400th anniversary of the founding of the first Catholic parish. Photograph by Jane Phillips.

"Anyone in this town who wants to call himself a minister, calls himself a minister," Beaumont said. In an article in 2010 in *The New York Times*, local author Henry Shukman wrote, "This is a city where the wounded come for healing, and seekers come to find." He described Santa Fe as a "spiritual mini-Mecca for a semi-godless age."

The diversity in the faith community is something that Santa Feans, including Catholics, "treasure," according to Jay Spoonheim, founding pastor of the Lutheran Church of the Servant.

When Spoonheim moved here from California years ago, he said he anticipated a traditional faith community, and "I found, compared to California, this was wilder yet. There was every kind of spirituality here under the sun. It was not at all what I expected." Many of these communities are still poles apart theologically, he added, "but I still don't hear angry voices."

Rabbi Marvin Schwab of Temple Beth Shalom said that in some ways he expected Santa Fe to be "a little more organized" when he got here nine years ago, but "in other ways I expected it to be just as far out as it really is." The city, he noted, "is home to a lot of diverse beliefs" which, in some cases, are "self-proclaimed."

Within blocks of his reform temple on Barcelona Road are a Methodist church, a mosque, a Missouri Synod Lutheran church, an Orthodox church, a Christian Science church, a fundamentalist Presbyterian group and the Unitarians. "Certainly we don't believe all the same things, but we can live as a community of faith in harmony with each other," he said.

After moving to Santa Fe, Schwab helped start the Interfaith Leadership Alliance, which now represents 30 congregations (though none of them is Catholic or evangelical) and meets monthly. Among other things, it is supporting a homeless shelter on Cerrillos Road. "I don't require absolute agreement with all my beliefs or attitudes for someone to be my friend. I require we respect each other," Schwab said. And in Santa Fe, he has found "there are people of good heart and spirit with whom I can disagree vehemently on a given topic," and then walk away with "our arms around each other."

All he wants from an opposing belief system is "intellect and thought," and "this is a place where I can find that." At the heart of all these diverse faiths, he said, is the feeling that "you don't have to accept my theology to believe your religion calls you to save a human life, feed the hungry, clothe the naked and house the homeless."

Santa Fe has always attracted "free thinkers," Beaumont said. Many come here thinking that practicing a faith tradition will not be important to them. But even if they never identify with one faith, "If you settle in this community and you decide to stay, you are just, I think, naturally more accepting of diversity," she said. "To get along in that kind of community means you just learn to enjoy it and to value it. It becomes part of your value system."

Beaumont, legislative advocate for the New Mexico Conference of Churches and former president of Santa Fe Christian and Jewish Dialogue, has lived all over the U.S., but "for me, part of what has kept me here as a person of faith is that I don't want to go off somewhere and fight old battles. I want to see how far we can go as a community like this."

For Charlie Carrillo, a noted santero and author, faith is "the foundation of everything I do in my life, everything I create as an artist." He's a member of both Santa María de la Paz Catholic Community and the Penitente morada in Abiquiú.

Buffalo Dancers from Santa Clara Pueblo begin the January 2010 celebration to mark the 400th anniversary of the founding of the first Catholic parish. The gathering at the Cathedral Basilica of St. Francis of Assisi featured representatives of Native American, Orthodox, Protestant, Jewish, Sikh, Buddhist and Muslim faith groups, who also prayed and collected money for the people of Haiti. Photograph by Jane Phillips.

The new faith communities in Santa Fe siphoned off some Catholics by offering things their church didn't, such as some forms of fellowship, he said. But, he added, "What I've always understood is that people who are secure in their faith never worry about other religions."

He used as an example of religious tolerance the Sikhs in the Española Valley. "They weren't challenged. If you want to build a temple, go for it. A Greek Orthodox shrine, go for it."

And if some people "want to put crystals under their beds, go for it," Carrillo said. "Our faith is strong enough."

Early Confrontation Between Church and State

by
Jason Strykowski

Governor Pedro de Peralta chose the site for Santa Fe to avoid conflict and ease tensions with the natives of the territory. Peralta would have been better served to keep his distance from the Catholic Church.

In 1612, just two years after the founding of Santa Fe, Friar Isidro Ordoñez came to Santa Fe with the strict intentions of assuming control of the church and by extension, the region. Holding the proper paper and charge, Ordoñez would step in as commissary in charge of the New Mexican missions. Ordoñez's ambition and belief in the stern administration of Catholicism coupled with his role as administrator of the Inquisition, made him unpopular with the other friars. And even though the other friars distrusted Ordoñez, he assumed control over the New Mexican mission system.

For Ordoñez, though, control over the missions was not enough. He desired rule over all of the territory. He and Peralta soon butted heads. At first, the two disagreed over the rights of Native laborers employed by the church. But soon the tension between Ordoñez and Peralta escalated over a detachment of soldiers whom Ordoñez met along the trail to Taos. He ordered the men back to Santa Fe to observe Mass, and in so doing, he contradicted Peralta's will and order. Peralta told the soldiers to return.

This willful contradiction perturbed Ordoñez, who sought to punish

Peralta through excommunication. To absolve himself, Peralta would have to appear at Mass barefoot and swear loyalty to the church. The church even insisted that if Peralta did not follow its requests, that no one else should even speak to the governor. The church even went so far as to demand that the royal notary end his service to the governor. As a result of the notary's compliance to the will of the church, Peralta became angry with the notary. Ordoñez sent a representative to plea for the notary's life. Peralta calmed and released the notary, striking a tenuous peace with Ordoñez.

The compromise didn't last. Soon after, Peralta got word that Ordoñez meant to arrest him. Enraged, Peralta marched to Ordoñez's residence and commanded Ordoñez to leave Santa Fe. The two soon exchanged angry words and Peralta brandished a pistol. He actually fired toward Ordoñez, but missed the friar. During the shooting, only one member of the church received a minor wound.

Probably unwilling to do any more damage, Peralta abandoned the effort and soon the capital. He decided to take his grievances to the Spanish authorities in Mexico City. Along the way, Peralta's caravan was intercepted by soldiers and Peralta himself taken prisoner at the Sandia mission.

Unbeknownst to Peralta, Ordoñez had ordered the arrest to keep Peralta from reaching Mexico City. While Peralta endured in prison, Ordoñez exerted his authority over New Mexico. His will became law over both church and state. Peralta managed to escape after eight months of detention only to be recaptured and dragged back to prison in front of numerous natives as an example of punishment for bad behavior.

After a year of imprisonment, Peralta received word that Bernardino de Ceballos would relieve him as governor. But Ceballos soon fell in league with Ordoñez, and Peralta received no reprieve. Ordoñez even went so far as to appear at a court called to review Peralta's role as governor. He intimidated witnesses and made sure there would be no leniency for Peralta. For all intents and purposes, Ordoñez ruled over New Mexico and its small Spanish populations.

Eventually, Peralta exacted some measure of revenge against Ordoñez. After a treacherous journey south during which he was robbed by Ordoñez's men, Peralta reached Mexico City and leveled charges against Ordoñez. After lengthy proceedings, the Spanish authorities punished Ordoñez for his behavior. But the church had already risen to a height of power in the territory.

Personalities: Inspiring Spirit

by
Anne Constable

Fray Angélico Chávez, 1910 – 1996

Fray Angélico Chávez was a priest, historian, author, poet and artist, well-known around Santa Fe for his trademark black beret and an appreciation of cigars and scotch. Before leaving primary school he declared his intention to become a Franciscan friar, and at age 14 went to Cincinnati to train at the Saint Francis Seraphic Seminary, where he made over 40 contributions of lyric poetry and humor, as well as essays on religious themes, to the student-run periodical.

In 1937 he became the first native New Mexican to be ordained a Franciscan priest. His first assignment was in Peña Blanca, where he renovated the church and painted murals of the Stations of the Cross on the church's walls that depicted himself, his family and parishioners. After his assignment to Jémez Pueblo, he began a pilgrimage with La Conquistadora, carrying her to 95 churches and preaching 85 sermons. In 1947, he obtained a copy of a document revealing that Father Alonso de Benavides carried to New Mexico with him in 1625 a crate that Chávez believed contained the bulto now known as Our Lady of Peace.

In 1954, Chávez published an important book called *Origins of New Mexico Families: A Genealogy of the Spanish Colonial Period*. He left the church in 1971 after Vatican II, but three years later Archbishop Robert Sanchez named him official archivist, and in 1989 he moved into the St. Francis Friary.

A passerby stops at the statue of Fray Angélico Chávez in front of the Fray Angélico Chávez History Library on Washington Street. Photograph by Clyde Mueller.

Antonio José Martínez, 1793 – 1867

Ordained in Durango, Mexico, in 1822, Antonio José Martínez returned home to serve in parishes of Tomé, Abiquiú and Taos, where he was known as Padre Martínez. An advocate of religious freedom and active in both religion and politics, Martínez established the first primary schools in New Mexico and purchased a printing press that he used to print the first book printed in New Mexico—*Cuaderno de Ortografía*, 1835. He owned the first newspaper and established an academy in Taos to prepare students for seminary in Mexico. Martínez was often at odds with Archbishop Jean Baptiste Lamy over the archbishop's punishment of denying the sacraments to parishioners who did not pay church fees. He abolished tithing in Taos because of the poverty of the population. Lamy later excommunicated him—on what has been described as shaky legal grounds—but Martínez continued to minister to his flock in his family chapel in Taos.

Leonard Helman, 1926 –

Leonard Helman, a rabbi, tap-dancer, chess champion and guiding light for hundreds of Santa Fe Jews, moved to New Mexico in 1974, where he became the rabbi for about 40 families at Temple Beth Shalom and lawyer for the state's Public Service Commission. He also served as chaplain for the state Legislature. After retiring from the temple in 1991, he moved away, but returned to Santa Fe when local families invited him to lead Congregation Beit Tikva. Helman was known for his inspiring and often funny sermons, including one in which he relates biblical passages to Woody Allen movies. A "Life Master" in bridge (and member of a five-person team that won the Polish national championship), he donated $50,000 toward a new bridge center on Airport Road.

Leonard Helman in 1997. Photograph by Clyde Mueller.

Lobsang Lhalungpa, 1924 – 2008

The Tibetan scholar and Santa Fe Living Treasure became a monk at age five, studied with the Dalai Lama's tutors, and in 1947 became director for Tibetan and Buddhist studies in the Indian Himalayan towns of Darjeeling and Kalimpong. He set up a Buddhist Cultural Center in Kalimpong and a school for local Tibetan children there, but never returned to Tibet. For 15 years he ran a Tibetan radio program to inform people about the conditions in India. He moved to Canada in 1970 and taught at the University of British Columbia. Upon moving to Santa Fe in 1989, he conducted meditation groups and worked on translations of sacred texts. A learned and compassionate man, he influenced many people in his adopted home, teaching them, through his own example, that "compassion is one of the most important things in life" and that "love is kindness," according to Kitty Leaken, a member of one of his meditation groups.

Lobsang Lhalungpa in 1998. Photograph by Steve Northrop.

Katharine Drexel, 1858 – 1955

Canonized in 2000 by Pope John Paul II, St. Katharine was born into a wealthy Pennsylvania family and dedicated her life and fortune to Native Americans and blacks. She established a religious order, the Sisters of the Blessed Sacrament, and financed more than 60 missions and schools. Her first school was St. Catherine Indian School in Santa Fe, where starting in 1887 students learned vocations such as tailoring and baking. The sisters imposed discipline. Students marched to class and to chapel, which was required in the early years. One of the things the Native people appreciated about Drexel, said Patrick

Katharine Drexel. *The Santa Fe New Mexican* **file photograph.**

Toya, the first Pueblo Indian ordained as a deacon in the Catholic Church and a former student at the school, was that "she never said anything about our Indian religion. She said we all pray to one God." The school closed in 1999, and the property was sold to an Albuquerque contractor in 2003.

Jean Baptiste Lamy. Etching from
Illustrated History of New Mexico, 1885, Fifth Edition, **by W. G. Ritch.**

Jean Baptiste Lamy, 1814 – 1888

After New Mexico became a U.S. territory, the American bishops asked the pope for a bishop for the Great Southwest. He created the Vicariate Apostolic of New Mexico and appointed a French priest, Jean Baptiste Lamy. In 1875, Lamy, subject of Willa Cather's novel *Death Comes for the Archbishop*, became the first archbishop of Santa Fe. He built new parishes and established schools, making a number of trips back to France to recruit priests and seminarians for the diocese. He was responsible for building the cathedral, called by the current rector, the Very Reverend Jerome Martínez y Alire, "the cradle of Catholicism for the American Southwest." According to Martínez y Alire, Lamy ran out of money while building the Romanesque cathedral and allowed one of his French priests to gamble with the soldiers at Fort Union. The priest won $2,000 to pay construction costs. Lamy is buried in a crypt under the sanctuary floor of the cathedral.

Robert Fortune Sanchez, 1934 –

Robert Sanchez was the nation's first Hispanic archbishop—and its youngest—when he was appointed archbishop of Santa Fe in 1974 at age 40. Sanchez belonged to the Padres, a group of Mexican-American priests who advocated bringing Hispanics into the church's power structure. He was known for reviving religious traditions in remote areas of the archdiocese and reconciling the Penitentes. Fearing scandal, Sanchez also kept secret growing evidence that priests in the diocese had sexually abused children. His remarkable career ended in 1993 when he resigned in disgrace after several women accused him of sexual misconduct.

Robert Fortune Sanchez. *The Santa Fe New Mexican* **file photograph.**

Mary Lou Cook, 1918 –

Mary Lou Cook, a hat-wearing teacher, minister, volunteer and peace activist who settled in Santa Fe in 1969, is also a founder of the Santa Fe Network for the Common Good, which, twice a year, designates elders from the community as Living Treasures. She herself was named a treasure in 1988. Cook was ordained a minister of the Independent Church of Antioch, which she said in a 1994 story "ordains people in the belief the world needs more ministers." She has performed all kinds of ceremonies ranging from weddings and memorials to land and house blessings to rituals like acknowledging a wonderful dog or getting over an illness.

Mary Lou Cook in 2006. Photograph by Shih Fa Kao.

Yogi Bhajan, 1929 – 2004

In the early 1970s, Yogi Bhajan was given the responsibility to create a Sikh ministry in the West. He founded the ashram Sikh Dharma in 1972 in Española, became a friend to congressional leaders and governors of all parties (many of whom were regulars at his annual birthday party celebration), and traveled the world calling for world peace and religious unity. In 1985 he established International

Yogi Bhajan. *The Santa Fe New Mexican* **file photograph**

Peace Prayer Day. He also helped build a financial empire that came to include 14 corporations such as Yogi Tea and Akal Security (which guards many federal courthouses), opened schools to teach yoga and meditation, and published more than 30 books.

Timeline

1539: Franciscan missionary Fray Marcos de Niza enters New Mexico.

1581: Friars proclaim the Gospel but are martyred.

1598: Oñate expedition, including 10 Franciscans, establishes Spanish colony and Catholic outpost.

1610: Santa Fe founded.

1680: Pueblo Revolt expels Spanish.

1692: Reconquest calls on Indians to return to Christian faith.

1728-1732: First native-born priest, Santiago Roybal, ordained.

1700s: Shortage of ordained clergy leads to founding of Penitente Brotherhood, the Hermanos.

1849: Baptist minister Hiram Walker Reed, en route to California gold fields, sets up place of worship and school.

1851: Bishop Lamy arrives in New Mexico, paving way for schools and a hospital. First Presbyterian missionary arrives.

1863: First official visit by an Episcopal bishop. Holy Faith Episcopal Church founded.

1867: First Presbyterian Church built.

1869: Construction of cathedral begins.

1875: Archdiocese of Santa Fe created.

continued ⇨

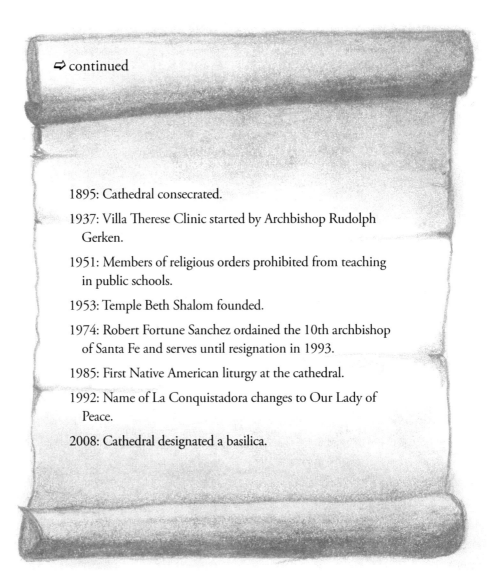

⇨ continued

1895: Cathedral consecrated.

1937: Villa Therese Clinic started by Archbishop Rudolph Gerken.

1951: Members of religious orders prohibited from teaching in public schools.

1953: Temple Beth Shalom founded.

1974: Robert Fortune Sanchez ordained the 10th archbishop of Santa Fe and serves until resignation in 1993.

1985: First Native American liturgy at the cathedral.

1992: Name of La Conquistadora changes to Our Lady of Peace.

2008: Cathedral designated a basilica.

Suggested Books

Aragon, Ray John de. *Padre Martínez and Bishop Lamy*. Santa Fe: Sunstone Press, 2006.

Aragon, Ray John de. *The Penitentes of New Mexico, Brothers of the Light*. Santa Fe: Sunstone Press, 2006.

Aragon, Ray John de, translated from the Spanish. *Recollections of the Life of the Priest Don Antonio José Martínez* by Pedro Sánchez. Santa Fe: Sunstone Press, 2006.

Carrillo, Charles M. *Saints of the Pueblos*. Albuquerque: LPD Press, 2004.

Chávez, Fray Angélico. *But Time and Chance, The Story of Padre Martínez of Taos, 1793-1867*. Santa Fe: Sunstone Press, 1981.

Chávez, Fray Angélico. *La Conquistadora, The Autobiography of an Ancient Statue*. Santa Fe: Sunstone Press, 1975.

Chávez, Fray Angélico. *Our Lady of the Conquest*. Santa Fe: Sunstone Press, 2010.

Chevalier, Jaima. *La Conquistadora, Unveiling the History of Santa Fe's Six Hundred Year Old Religious Icon*. Santa Fe: Sunstone Press, 2010

Fergusson, Erna. *New Mexico: A Pageant of Three Peoples*. New York: Knopf, 1951.

Hackett, Charles Wilson, and Charmion Clair Shelby. *Revolt of the Pueblo Indians of New Mexico and Otermin's Reconquest, 1680-1682; Introduction and Annotations by Charles Wilson Hackett*. Albuquerque: The University of New Mexico Press, 1970.

Herz, Cary. *New Mexico's Crypto-Jews: Image and Memory*. Albuquerque: The University of New Mexico Press, 2007.

Lehmberg, Stanford E. *Holy Faith of Santa Fe, 1863-2000*. Albuquerque: LPD Press, 2004.

McCord, Richard, ed. *Santa Fe Living Treasures, Our Elders, Our Hearts.* Santa Fe: Sunstone Press, 2009.

Ortiz, Alfonso. *The Tewa World; Space, Time, Being, and Becoming in a Pueblo Society.* Chicago: University of Chicago Press, 1969.

Prince, L. Bradord. *New Mexico's Struggle for Statehood.* Santa Fe: Sunstone Press, 2010.

Roberts, David. *The Pueblo Revolt.* New York: Simon & Schuster, 2004.

Rodríguez, Sylvia. *The Matachines Dance: A Ritual Dance of the Indian Pueblos and Mexicano/Hispano Communities.* Santa Fe: Sunstone Press, 2009.

Sanchez, Joseph P. *The Rio Abajo Frontier, 1540-1692: A History of Early Colonial New Mexico.* Albuquerque: Albuquerque Museum, 1987.

Sheehan, Michael J. *Four Hundred Years of Faith: Seeds of Struggle, Harvest of Faith: A History of the Catholic Church in New Mexico.* Santa Fe: Archdiocese of Santa Fe, 1998.

Tobias, Henry J. *A History of the Jews in New Mexico.* Albuquerque: The University of New Mexico Press, 1990.

Weber, David J. *What Caused the Pueblo Revolt of 1680?* Boston: Bedford/St. Martin's, 1999.

Weigle, Marta. *Brothers of Light, Brothers of Blood, The Penitentes of the Southwest.* Santa Fe: Sunstone Press, 2007.

Weigle, Marta. *A Penitente Bibliography.* Santa Fe: Sunstone Press, 2007.

Suggested Websites
(active at time of publication)

History of Cathedral Basilica of St. Francis: www.cbsfa.org/History.asp
Interfaith Leadership Alliance: www.ilasantafe.org/
Rabbi Malka Drucker interview: www.malkadrucker.com/prconver.html
Non-Catholics in late-1800s and early-1900s: www.newmexicohistory.org/filedetails.php?fileID=9948

5

The Land

The hand-dug irrigation ditch has remained a constant in Santa Fe's ever evolving history. Above, burros graze near the acequia, circa 1915. Photograph by T. Harmon Parkhurst, courtesy Palace of the Governors Photo Archives (NMHM/DCA), #11047.

Following the annual cleaning of the Acequia Madre in April 2010, the gate is opened, allowing water to flow into the channel. Photograph by Natalie Guillén.

Nourishing a City: Land, Water and People Intricately Bound

by
Staci Matlock

As a boy, Herman Montoya rode his bicycle east on the dirt road from his family's home in Agua Fría village to St. Francis Cathedral School in downtown Santa Fe. He passed farm fields on his way into town and again after school as he headed the other way, delivering telegrams for Western Union. In spring, summer and fall, he helped on the family farm.

Like others in the village, the Montoyas depended on the Acequia Madre to deliver water to their fields. They grew pinto beans, corn, cucumbers, cantaloupe, hay and fruit trees. Others raised wheat and winter rye. They ran cattle on the Caja del Rio west of Santa Fe.

"We raised all our own food," said Montoya, 99 at the time this book was published.

When he was six, or maybe eight, he began helping clean the ditch each spring. "Or getting in the way," Montoya joked in the Monte Vista Feed Store, the business he started decades ago. His eldest son, George, now runs the store.

Montoya raised his five children to help with the farm and cattle. One son, Michael, remembers going with his grandfather in a horse-drawn buckboard in the 1940s to deliver firewood and coal to customers. "Your hands were frozen, but we didn't complain," Michael Montoya said. "What good would it do?"

Montoya has lived through almost one-fourth of Santa Fe's official history. The city is almost unrecognizable from what he remembers as a boy. The fields are all gone, except a few like his and the nearby Community Farm. The Agua Fría Road is paved. The river he remembers as a year-round flow now carries water only off and on in the spring and summer.

But the acequia, for which he is the longtime mayordomo and a former commissioner, still brings water down to his family's fields and orchard. It has remained a constant in Santa Fe's ever evolving history—400 years of history that was the focus of a citywide celebration in 2010.

For Herman Montoya, Santa Fe is almost unrecognizable from what he remembers as a boy. Photograph by Natalie Guillén.

Nature changed the Santa Fe basin landscape ever so slowly across millions of years. For six millennia, the mountains and plateau around the city provided firewood, edible plants and wild game. The river basin yielded arable land and water for farms. Humans changed the landscape, rapidly and dramatically, especially in the last two centuries.

Without the landscape, and the small river running through it, there would be no Santa Fe. Today people are trying to ensure the landscape and the river can continue sustaining the city and its diverse culture for generations ahead.

Ancient Ones

Some 6,000 years ago, humans roamed the Santa Fe River basin, hunting, gathering food and raising families. The people knew every inch of the land from the mountains to the Rio Grande. Without written language, archaeologists believe, people passed along information about the landscape through storytelling. They kept close watch on the weather, the movement of wildlife, the smallest changes in their environment.

"Archaic people had a very deep knowledge of the land and what the land would produce based on that year's climate," archaeologist Stephen Post said.

Like their pueblo descendants and early Spanish colonists, the Archaic people lived off the land, according to ethnobotanist Mollie Toll, picking weedy perennials and harvesting piñon nuts.

The Archaic people endured unpredictable weather—drought, floods, heat and cold. "It was just as unpredictable then as now," Post said.

In 1000 A.D., the first modern pueblo was built on the terraces above what is now the Scottish Rite Temple on Washington Avenue and Paseo de Peralta. They built their homes of adobe made from the earth and turned nearby trees into vigas, architecture adopted later by Spanish and American settlers. The pueblo people expanded farms and added corn to their staple crops.

In 1400, drought forced many to move. Pueblo people say some of their ancestors were still in the valley when the Spanish arrived. "Why didn't people return full time? That's the million-dollar question," Post said. "Why was it largely depopulated by the time the Spanish arrived?"

Founding a City

When Don Diego de Vargas rode the Camino Real and followed the river into Santa Fe in 1692, he found vegetation "so thick, it obscured the sky," he wrote in his journal.

The Spanish established Santa Fe in 1610 along the river less because of water and arable land than because it was a good location for an outpost from which to govern the nearby pueblos. Water, though, was a big reason to build the Palace of the Governors where it still stands today. Springs, seeps and the Santa Fe River sustained the growing villa. One of the first tasks was creating an irrigation ditch to carry water from the Santa Fe River to homes and fields. This hand-dug ditch—the Acequia Madre—would eventually stretch to the village of Agua Fría, six miles from the Plaza.

When the pueblos revolted against Spanish rule in 1680, they ousted the government from the palace by staging a siege and cutting off the water, according to historians.

The Spanish colonists added local fare to their diet, but also brought new garden vegetables and spices such as beets, carrots, coriander and, of course, chile. The Spanish also introduced new crops such as wheat and domesticated grapes. "They were told by the Spanish government to set up vineyards and olive groves," Mollie Toll said. "But you can't do it up here." Wheat and wine were intensely identified with the Catholic religion, Toll said. In order to be self-sufficient, the missions needed to produce both. Wheat did thrive into the early 1900s in fields all the way to Colorado. Vineyards failed.

Corn, once thought of by the Spanish as poor man's food, had become a staple even by 1846, when Susan Shelby Magoffin arrived on the Santa Fe Trail. "On one square may be a dwelling house, a church," Magoffin wrote in her diary, "and immediately opposite to it occupying the whole square is a cornfield, a fine ornament to a city."

According to historians John Kessell and Rick Hendricks, editors of the Vargas journals, a serious drought in 1695 and 1696 dried up the Santa Fe River. And, according to archaeologist Cordelia Snow, the shortage of water was so severe people were forced to dig wells in the ciénaga (swamp areas) north and east of the plaza to obtain water for drinking. In other years, the river flowed most of the time, and both Stephen Post and Cordelia Snow uncovered trout bones from their excavations in the Palace of the Governors.

People living in Santa Fe as late as the 1940s remember the river flowing almost all year. But by the 1950s, drought, water demands of a growing city and storage reservoirs stopped the flow.

An Acequia Lifeline

Every spring, the Montoyas and others along the Acequia Madre clean the ditch to keep it running, a tradition that dates back to Santa Fe's founding, perhaps earlier. Once they worried only about taking out weeds and trimming back trees. In the last couple of decades they've had to remove mountains of trash—from vending machines to beer bottles—and coax homeless people to move camps before they release the water into the ditch.

Eleanor Ortiz Bové said the Acequia Madre is one of the few unchanged things about Santa Fe in the last 400 years. "The acequia helped nourish Santa Fe from the first settlers until now," said Bové, whose ancestors came to Santa Fe with Vargas.

The state engineer recognized the ditch's water rights as dating to "time immemorial and prior to 1680." "Without irrigation of one kind or another, Santa Fe would never have developed," said Bové's husband, ditch commissioner Phillip Bové.

Kristina Harrigan clears debris from the Acequia Madre during the cleanup of the centuries-old irrigation ditch in April 2010. Photograph by Natalie Guillén.

A 1919 hydrographic survey of the Santa Fe River system listed 40 acequias irrigating 1,300 acres. By 1977, only four ditches were left, irrigating 42 acres of fruit trees, gardens, landscaping and the Montoyas' remaining hay fields.

There was little water for irrigating by then, anyway. Most of the Santa Fe River was impounded in reservoirs east of Santa Fe to serve the city. By 1947 the reservoirs were storing up to 4,131 acre-feet of water a year. "With this large addition to the storage capacity of the water company, the year-round flow of the river essentially stopped," Phillip Bové wrote in a history of the Acequia Madre.

Montoya, Bové and others fought Public Service Company of New Mexico (PNM) for their water rights. PNM and the prior water company claimed the water rights under a permit obtained from the state engineer in the late 1800s. Acequia Cerro Gordo and Acequia Madre users took PNM and the Sangre de Cristo Water Company to court over the water rights in 1990.

State District Judge Art Encinias ruled—in record time for a water case—in favor of the acequias. Encinias noted that, "the urbanized nature of Santa Fe, the virtual disappearance of commercial agriculture in the area and the rise of public utilities as the most common source of water tends to trivialize important water rights. The people, the land and the water are intricately bound together and will be until Santa Fe is entirely paved over."

The acequias and the city now work together under a stipulated agreement to maintain the acequias. But the fight over water remains unfinished. All the water rights along the Santa Fe River still have not been finalized in court.

Full Circle

Santa Fe's growing pains are ongoing, and the landscape around the city continues to change. The hills where Archaic people once roamed, but rarely stayed long, now sprout homes, schools and businesses. New developments are constantly under way, and residents fight to keep some out, like a project planned on the city's northwest side. A multimillion-dollar project to divert water from the Rio Grande, under construction at time of this book's publication, will supplement supplies from the Santa Fe River and city wells.

Locally grown produce for sale on the Plaza around 1890. Photograph by J.R. Riddle, courtesy Palace of the Governors Photo Archives (NMHM/DCA), #76051.

While modern Santa Feans might not want to live the nomadic life of the hunter-gatherer or work as hard as colonial people did to survive, their efforts to restore a relationship with land and water abound. The city, the Santa Fe Watershed Association and other river advocates have worked to restore flows into the Santa Fe River with more regular releases from municipal reservoirs. Youth groups and other volunteers have planted native vegetation and built rock works to reduce erosion and restore the green belt along the river all the way through the city.

The city and county have open space and trails staff collaborating to protect open land and create a network of trails where people can walk or bike.

Farming in Santa Fe faded over the 20th century, but outside the city limits agriculture hung on. And increasingly people in the city wanted to know who raised their food. The result was a burgeoning farmers market in the heart of the city.

The Santa Fe Farmers Market began in the 1960s with people selling produce out of their trucks. By 1999, the market had 170 vendors and more than 160,000 shoppers a year. Now the market has a permanent location at the Santa Fe Railyard.

The Santa Fe Farmers Market in 2005. Photograph by Karl Stolleis.

Miguel Gallegos, the market's manager, said vendors are from the 15 northern counties, including Santa Fe County, but none are from within the city limits. He said the market is averaging 10 to 12 new farmers a year. "The majority are small farms or people who have built a greenhouse," Gallegos said. Inside the city limits, Gallegos has a home garden, as do many residents who are growing their own vegetables and herbs. At least four community gardens have started up in the last year. And in the village of Agua Fría, near Montoya's house, the historic Community Farm is hosting regular plantings and workshops for schoolchildren and families.

And chickens are still legal within city limits, as long as the roosters keep the noise down.

Trailblazers of the Sangre de Cristo Slopes

by
Jason Strykowski

In 1959, an all-day lift ticket at what is now the Santa Fe ski basin cost a grand total of $4. For that sum, skiers could run on 12 miles of trails, although they had to get off the slopes and into their cars before 3 p.m., when the dirt road down to Santa Fe closed. By the mid-1960s, the ski area drew enough outdoor enthusiasts to merit serious discussion of a lodge, but a mere 20 years earlier the resort had been only a dream of Santa Fe skiers.

Discussions of a ski area in the Sangre de Cristos mounted in the 1930s as Santa Feans became jealous of the new resort built in the mountains above Los Alamos. The Rotary Club of Santa Fe and the Chamber of Commerce took action in 1936 and hired a Colorado ski instructor, who suggested lifts at Hyde Memorial State Park. Soon the Santa Fe Winter Sports Club, the U.S. Forest Service and the National Park Service constructed trails and installed a rope tow, the remains of which are still visible.

The trails at Hyde Park drew a small but hearty crowd until World War II, when any plans for expansion and improvement were placed on hold.

The country's postwar transformation led, among other things, to the growing popularity of outdoor recreation. The 10th Mountain Division, which trained to fight in the winter climate and mountainous terrain of northern Italy, also revolutionized the way Americans thought of and equipped themselves for the outdoors. Ernest "Tap" Tapley of Santa Fe helped train the division during the war and redefined wilderness education after it through Outward Bound and the National Outdoor Leadership School.

Members of the 10th Mountain Division, from left, Ted Williams, Ernest 'Tap' Tapley, and Bob Parker at Ski Santa Fe. Photograph by Julie Graber.

Beyond that, the outdoors-oriented men of the 10th Mountain became pioneers of the western ski industry, a group that included Bob Nordhaus of Sandia Peak, who had served in the unit, Buzz Bainbridge of Santa Fe, who had fought alongside the division, and Ernie Blake of Taos, who had volunteered unsuccessfully to join the mountain troops.

Blake and his Swiss-German family brought a love of skiing when they came to the United States in 1938. When Blake moved permanently to New Mexico after his wartime service in the OSS, the predecessor of the CIA, he happened upon a Chamber of Commerce initiative and some local ski enthusiasts who were in the midst of pushing to get the ski area moved up Hyde Park Road to the basin.

The greatest struggle lay in the completion of the road. Controversy arose because the planned road would cross tribal Indian land. The skiers got their wishes when the road pushed through in 1949. Construction of a ski infrastructure began. Skiers traveled to Silverton, Colorado, where they claimed a British-built bi-cable lift used in the mines. They moved the lift to Santa Fe, and the rusty machine, despite the occasional clutch failure, gave skiers a 600-foot lift.

With Blake as manager, the Santa Fe ski basin opened in 1950. He supervised installation of the chairlift, which used seats from B-24 bombers, outdoor writer Daniel Gibson said in a 2005 story in *The Santa Fe New Mexican*. Blake moved to Colorado but continued to scout locations for what became Taos Ski Valley, which he opened in 1955 and ran until his death in 1989.

Bainbridge first came to New Mexico in 1946 as a sales representative for a ski maker, and by the next winter was managing the Hyde Park and Big Tesuque operations. "I'd leave Jean [his wife] at Hyde Park running things and head up to Big Tesuque," he told Gibson in 2005. "I would fire up the torch used to warm that old Cadillac engine we used for the lift, get it warming up and then head back down to check on Jean."

Bainbridge spent a year at present-day Sandia Peak and returned to Santa Fe to run the ski school. After serving in the Korean War, Bainbridge ran the Santa Fe ski basin for five years as general manager. Bainbridge told Gibson: "All I wanted was bodies on the slopes, and so I was always working the lift lines forming ski clubs. I'd ask where a group was from, and say I'd give them each a 50-cent discount if they were a club. They'd elect a president right then and there." A former state tourism director, Bainbridge retired in Santa Fe.

Almost 60 years of stability marked management of the ski area. In 1954, after a propane explosion caused major damage that proved costly, oilman Joe T. Juhan bought Sierras de Santa Fe Corporation and financed improvements that attracted wide attention. Kingsbury Pitcher, whose family now owns Wolf Creek Ski Area, operated the ski basin for the next 30 years, making numerous improvements over the period. In 1984, Ben Abruzzo purchased the ski basin. A famous hot-air balloonist, Abruzzo died a year later in a plane crash, and the family company he formed still manages the ski area.

Work, Words Formed a Sense of Place

by
Rob Dean

To Fabiola Cabeza de Baca, rural life represented the best in people—neighborliness, strong families and healthy habits.

Her long life of 97 plus years at the time this book was published was proof that she knew her stuff and followed her own advice. Born in 1894 on her family's land grant southeast of Las Vegas, New Mexico, Cabeza de Baca appreciated her roots but wanted to know the world, too, living for a time in Spain as a young woman and in Mexico later in her career.

Fabiola Cabeza de Baca, second from left, a prolific writer who chronicled farm and ranch life, celebrates in 1945 with members of La Sociedad Folklórica. Photograph courtesy Palace of the Governors Photo Archives (NMHM/DCA), #9928.

And Cabeza de Baca wrote widely, offering urban dwellers and later generations an authentic view of how material life in Northern New Mexico was so closely tied to the land and a sense of place. She was an educated, independent, well-traveled woman, but always she let others know she drew inspiration from the simple dignity of rural life.

As a teenager on the ranch, she skipped household chores in favor of spending time with the men who worked outside, biographer Maureen Reed said.

Cabeza de Baca taught school for several years after earning a teaching degree. Then her ties to farm and ranch life tugged at her, inspiring her to get a home-economics degree at New Mexico State University and to take a job helping homemakers in the villages of Northern New Mexico. As a Santa Fe County agent, she organized clubs for women and children, taught canning techniques, developed home crafts and found markets for rural products. Eventually, she went as part of a United Nations mission to Mexico to establish a home-economics program and to teach skills in growing and preparing food. Her experiences with cultural change and inequality led her to criticize subtly the static notions of culture and femininity, but in a voice that was "romantic, accommodating, and traditionalist," Reed wrote in *A Woman's Place: Women Writing New Mexico*.

Cabeza de Baca widened her influence through writing. Her popular 1939 cookbook, *Historic Cookery*, included recipes she collected from village cooks and tested in her own kitchen. She published *The Good Life* in 1949 to celebrate the close relationships among village women who overcame the hardships of rural life. In 1953, she published *We Fed Them Cactus*, a compelling blend of folklore, history and memoir that focused on Hispanos who settled the plains.

"Fabiola Cabeza de Baca would probably be surprised and amused at the controversy her life and works created during the Chicano movement of the 1970s and after her death [in 1991]," Kate K. Davis wrote in *American Women Writers, 1900 – 1945*. "Her books received generally good reviews at the time of publication. They have since been criticized as elitist and not representative of the realistic Chicano experience."

Personalities: Forces of Nature

by
Rob Dean

Regular folks work every day to protect the land, use resources wisely and promote a healthy environment. The following profiles offer examples of that commitment over the generations.

Juana Lujan

After the Pueblo Revolt of 1680, the family of Juana Lujan left its farm north of Santa Fe and walked 350 miles to a camp established at present-day Cuidad Juárez. Juana was eight years old. Thirteen years later, she returned with her family to resume farming near San Ildefonso. Lujan's experience was representative of Spanish settlers in the late-17th century, historian Tom Merlan found. As years went by, she acquired enough land to support her three children and their large families. Among her acquisitions was a well-developed ranch property. When she died in 1762, Lujan owned gardens, fields, livestock and implements. Her estate included a 24-room house with a stable and a fruit orchard enclosed by a wall.

Source: New Mexico Farm and Ranch Heritage Museum.

Palemon Martinez

The Santa Fe Farmers Market began as a grass-roots movement, but it took know-how to make it grow. Palemon Martinez had the experience to connect local growers with local consumers. Nudging the farmers market was one way Martinez put his New Mexico State University degree in agricultural education to practical use. Starting in the early 1970s, in the first stages of what would become a 30-year career with the NMSU Cooperative Extension Service, Martinez gave technical and organizational support to help develop what today is a vibrant, colorful symbol of community—the Santa Fe Farmers Market, now in the Railyard. When the League of Women Voters brought the idea from Los Alamos to Santa Fe, the market sprang up spontaneously at the St. Anne's Church parking lot, then moved to Alto Street. "The farmers are usually the ones who organize these markets, but in this case it was the consumers," Martinez said at the time. His work done in Santa Fe more than 20 years later, Martinez continued his work in agriculture as a leader among Taos water users.

Neva Van Peski

A retired economist with the Federal Reserve Board in Washington, DC, Neva Van Peski used her talent for research and numbers-crunching to help figure out Santa Fe's water supply. Because of her enduring curiosity about water and her desire to quantify it, the League of Women Voters activist volunteered in 1990 to compile a list of surface-water rights in Santa Fe County for the state engineer. She also served on the Metropolitan Water Board, the Extraterritorial Zoning Commission, the state's Safe Drinking Water Advisory Group and the Solid Waste Citizens Committee.

Art Sanchez

The city of Santa Fe operates its own water system today because Art Sanchez fought to make it happen. To Sanchez, control of the water utility was essential if the city was to control costs, stabilize supply and manage growth. In the 1990s, Sanchez worked to have the city buy the Sangre de Cristo Water Company from Public Service Company of New Mexico. His talent for accounting and his knowledge of government helped create the financing that made the deal possible. Sanchez served on the City Council until 2000 and died in 2008.

Art Sanchez

John Stephenson in 2005. Photograph by Tina Larkin.

John Stephenson

Sixty years ago, Santa Fe native John Stephenson established the Community Farm, a model for small-scale urban farming. Situated near San Ysidro Park in Agua Fría village, the farm produces fruits and vegetables for charitable organizations that serve the homeless, hungry, disabled and children. The farm, operating as a nonprofit agricultural educational center, is now under the direction of Stephenson's daughter-in-law, Carolyn Stephenson.

Source: Community Farm.

Dale Ball

Just minutes east of downtown Santa Fe is a network of hiking and biking trails through the Sangre de Cristo foothills. The system is named for Dale Ball, the retired banker who had the idea for the trail system and the commitment to put the land managers, funders and construction crews together to make the trail a reality. The foothills trail—winding through city, county, Forest Service and Nature Conservancy land—opened in 2001. Ball's name may live on because of the foothills trail, but he had impact on previous conservation efforts as well. As director of the Santa Fe Conservation Trust, he helped save Atalaya Mountain from development.

Reynaldo "Ray" Romero

Farmers like Ray Romero have had to be ready for anything: 'hoppers that wipe out alfalfa, crop-killing weather, tumbling prices and skyrocketing fuel costs, and, always, the fear of too little water. Romero is keeper of the flame, carrying on the traditions that made La Cienega the breadbasket of Santa Fe. A vibrant livestock and farming region since its settlement in the early 1700s,

Reynaldo "Ray" Romero in 2005. Photograph by Jane Phillips.

La Cienega always has been a valley lush with vegetables, fruit and hay, and a home to families with historical ties to the land—the Moras, Pinos, C' de Bacas, Raels, Mareses, Montoyas. While holding off-farm jobs until his retirement, Romero, in his 70s at the time this book was published, continues to farm and advocate for water irrigators. "This is the way the community was, and the way it should be," he said.

Truman Brigham

Born in rural Arkansas and introduced to ranch life as a teenager in Clovis, New Mexico, Truman Brigham eventually found his life's calling when he started farming north of Santa Fe in 1939. He supplied fresh produce to Santa Fe stores for many years. Meanwhile, he worked as chief gardener at the New Mexico School for the Deaf. As a leading advocate of farm-to-market sustainability, Brigham was the first president of what became the Santa Fe Farmers Market. He died in 1994.

Source: Santa Fe Living Treasures.

Timeline

10,000 – 500 B.C.: Cochise people cultivate crops in earliest evidence of agriculture in the Southwest.

1200 – 1500s: Pueblo Indians establish villages along Rio Grande.

1610: Soon after city's founding, Santa Fe settlers dig Acequia Madre irrigation ditch.

1743: French trappers reach Santa Fe.

1828: Gold is found in Ortiz Mountains.

1848: Mexican-American War ends, paving way for New Mexico to become U.S. territory.

1878: The railroad arrives and opens lands in New Mexico.

1923: Oil is discovered in state.

1947: Santa Fe River reservoirs store city water.

1963 – 1975: Four new dams in Rio Grande basin increase water storage.

1971: Santa Fe Farmers Market organizes after several years of informal gatherings.

1995: City of Santa Fe buys the water utility.

1998: Santa Fe County initiates open space and trails program.

Suggested Books

Bello, A. Kyce, ed. *The Return of the River: Writers, Scholars, and Citizens Speak on Behalf of the Santa Fe River*. Santa Fe: Sunstone Press, 2010.

Crawford, Stanley G. *Mayordomo: Chronicle of an Acequia in Northern New Mexico*. Albuquerque: The University of New Mexico Press, 1993.

DeBuys, William. *Enchantment and Exploitation: The Life and Hard Times of a New Mexico Mountain Range*. Albuquerque: The University of New Mexico Press, 1985.

Dunbar-Ortiz, Roxanne. *Roots of Resistance: A History of Land Tenure in New Mexico*. Norman: The University of Oklahoma Press, 2007.

Freiberger, Harriet. *Lucien Maxwell, Villain or Visionary*. Santa Fe: Sunstone Press, 1999.

Gilbert, Fabiola Cabeza de Baca. *We Fed Them Cactus*. Albuquerque: The University of New Mexico Press, 1954.

Jordan-Bychkov, Terry G. *North American Cattle-Ranching Frontiers: Origins, Diffusion, and Differentiation*. Histories of the American Frontier. Albuquerque: The University of New Mexico Press, 1993.

Keleher, William A. *Maxwell Land Grant*. Santa Fe: Sunstone Press, 2008.

La Farge, Oliver. *The Mother Ditch*. Santa Fe: Sunstone Press, 1983.

Lamar, Howard R. *The Far Southwest, 1846–1912: A Territorial History*. New Haven: Yale University Press, 1966.

Morand, Sheila. *Santa Fe Then and Now*. Santa Fe: Sunstone Press, 1998.

Richards, Rick. *Ski Pioneers: Ernie Blake, His Friends, and the Making of Taos Ski Valley*. Arroyo Seco, New Mexico: Dry Gulch Publishing, 1992.

Rivera, José A. *Acequia Culture: Water, Land, and Community in the Southwest.* Albuquerque: The University of New Mexico Press, 1998.

Rodríguez, Sylvia. Acequia: *Water-Sharing, Sanctity, and Place.* Santa Fe: School for Advanced Research Press, 2006.

Stanley, F. *The Grant That Maxwell Bought.* Santa Fe: Sunstone Press, 2008.

Udall, Stewart L. *The Forgotten Founders: Rethinking the History of the Old West.* Washington, DC: Island Press, 2002.

Vargas, Diego de, John L. Kessell, Rick Hendricks, and Meredith D. Dodge. *Blood on the Boulders: The Journals of Don Diego de Vargas, New Mexico, 1694-97.* Albuquerque: The University of New Mexico Press, 6 volumes, 1998.

Suggested Websites

(active at time of publication)

State acequia association: www.lasacequias.org/
New Mexico Agriculture Department: www.nmdaweb.nmsu.edu/
Santa Fe Farmers Market: www.santafefarmersmarket.com/
Water conservation: www.water2conserve.com/
Wildlife Federation: www.nmwildlife.org/

6

Rogues

Richard C de Baca, who was the deputy state police chief at the time of the 1980 prison riot, walks the halls of the old prison in June 2010. Photograph by Natalie Guillén.

Santa Fe's Sinister Side: Outlaws, Spies and a Shocking Prison Riot

by
Steve Terrell

Santa Fe is a beautiful town, spilling over with art, culture, distinctive architecture, hot chile, turquoise and multicultural quaintness. But scratch the Historic Design Review Board-approved surface of Santa Fe and you'll find that Santa Fe and its surrounding area has a dark side. Songwriter Tom Russell wrote in "The Outcast" that "Your promised land was settled by bastards, drunks and thieves." Santa Fe certainly has had its share of those.

Its history—the city is celebrated 400 years of it throughout 2010—is rich with rogues, scoundrels, religious zealots, killers, con men, lawbrearkers, lawmen and even spies. Writers, filmmakers and museum directors have loved them. Historian William A. Keleher characterized their frontier exploits as "fabulous." In more recent times, author Roger Morris bluntly assessed the inmate-on-inmate violence of the 1980 prison riot as the "devil's butcher shop."

Crime and punishment in all the variations became Richard C de Baca's world during a law-enforcement career that spanned a generation. Still, that 1980 prison riot was a singular horror that disturbed the Santa Fe man the most. "These were barbaric, inhuman acts," he said. C de Baca was the deputy state police chief at the time. C de Baca witnessed a violent eruption on what was likely an unprecedented scale, but bad behavior has marked other episodes in local and regional history. Conquerors were unkind. Men on the frontier could be unforgiving. The harsh territorial prison cast a long-lasting shadow.

Rogues—some more colorful than criminal, some brutally cruel—have disturbed the peace plenty in every corner of Santa Fe, adding a riveting and often unsettling chapter to the story of the city.

In the Beginning

The first Spanish governor of New Mexico, Santa Fe founder Pedro de Peralta, went to prison. But this was because of a power struggle between Peralta and Friar Isidro Ordoñez. The priest declared Peralta a "schismatic heretic" and excommunicated him. History, however has been kinder to Peralta. Santa Fe has named a thoroughfare after him, as well as erecting a heroic statue near the post office downtown.

This struggle for power between the church and secular government proved to be trouble for later governors as well. Historian Marc Simmons, writing last year about Governor Bernardo López de Mendizábal and his successor, the Peruvian-born Governor Diego de Peñalosa, said Mendizábal was arrested for "religious crimes"—the church didn't like his tolerant attitude toward Pueblo religious rites—and eventually died while awaiting the verdict in an Inquisition dungeon.

Peñalosa got into a bitter conflict with church leader Fray Alonso de Posada, at one point even putting Posada under house arrest at the Palace of the Governors. Eventually the governor fled Santa Fe and went to Mexico City. "There he was imprisoned by the Inquisition, charged with 237 crimes, and banished from Spain's colonies in America," Simmons wrote.

And even Don Diego de Vargas, who led the reconquest of Santa Fe, ran into trouble of his own. De Vargas' replacement, Pedro Rodriguez Cubero, came to Santa Fe in 1697 and promptly placed de Vargas under house arrest on charges of graft and misconduct, Simmons wrote. De Vargas was imprisoned for three years, including five months in leg irons, while most of his property was sold at auction. "Later he was exonerated and reappointed governor by the viceroy, too late though to get 'his stuff' back," Simmons continued.

Enter the Anglo

When Anglo settlers began arriving in Santa Fe in the 1800s, many had bad preconceptions about the local Hispanic population. They assumed the locals to be uncivilized. Thus, historian Michael J. Alarid tells us, the newcomers set out to establish a legal code with harsh punishments for these people they thought were in great need of authority.

But Alarid, whose family roots are in Northern New Mexico, said the newcomers were 1.6 times more likely to be indicted for criminal activity than established members of the community. And though the new settlers composed only 18 percent of Santa Fe's population, they were responsible for 12 of the 19 homicides committed between 1847 and 1853.

"There was an influx of soldiers to Santa Fe," Alarid said. "These were single, young men. And of, course, they commit most violent crimes. The new violence was not ethnically based," he continued. "Most of the crimes were committed against drifters and transients."

The new Anglos often sniffed that the locals were being too lenient in punishing criminals—a complaint about Santa Fe and Northern New Mexico juries still echoed today. However, Alarid said that in the cases of those 12 homicides, records can be found for only one guilty verdict being returned by all-Anglo juries. Another guilty verdict was likely, Alarid said, while in a third case, the accused was lynched by an angry mob.

That was Gillion Scallion, a drunken Texan who, along with a friend, loudly bragged about the Lone Star State in the bar at The Exchange Hotel—where La Fonda now stands. The belligerent behavior of the Texans escalated until Scallion pulled out a revolver, vowed to clear the room and began shooting. One of the bullets struck and killed Judge Hugh Smith. Scallion was promptly lynched on the Plaza.

There also was a rise in whiskey-fueled violence. Alarid mentioned fandangos, community parties thrown by rich patrons. But when the Anglos started arriving, local Santa Feans began cashing in on what Alarid calls "commodified fandangos," in which revelers are admitted for a price to a dance filled with gambling and excessive drinking. In 1847, William Bolt, an American soldier, was killed at a Santa Fe fandango commissioned by local German immigrants. Alarid said local Hispanic witnesses refused to cooperate with legal authorities, a typical reaction, he added, when people don't feel they are represented in the political system.

Railroad Days

The West's most famous outlaw, Billy the Kid, lived in Santa Fe briefly when he was a child. His mother, Catherine, married William Antrim at the

First Presbyterian Church downtown in 1873. Shortly after that, the family moved to Silver City, where Billy's life of crime would begin.

The next documented time Billy came to Santa Fe was in 1881. But he wasn't in church. He was in jail on a murder charge. From there he began corresponding with the governor in hopes of gaining freedom in exchange for being an informant against those involved in the Lincoln County War. However, Billy was taken to Mesilla for trial. Found guilty, he escaped only to be shot down in July 1881 at Fort Sumner.

Santa Fe itself, however, was not as wild during this period as nearby Las Vegas, New Mexico. At that time the Santa Fe Railroad had reached Las Vegas and brought with it the requisite gaggle of gamblers, rustlers, gunmen and swindlers that always seemed to fester in railroad towns.

The hanging of Black Jack Ketchum in Clayton, New Mexico, 1901. Photograph by W.A. White, courtesy Palace of the Governors Photo Archives (NMHM/DCA), #128886.

Former territorial Governor Miguel Antonio Otero took note of the violence and corruption in his autobiography. He wrote that "owing to its having developed with the coming of the railroad, [Las Vegas] fell under the control of as vicious and corrupt a set of scoundrels as could be found anywhere in the West."

By 1879, the town was run by a confederation known as the Dodge City Gang, which previously operated out of the infamous Kansas town. The leader was Hyman G. Neill, better known as "Hoodoo Brown," a name given to him by a dance-hall girl. Neill got elected as justice of the peace in "New Town" Las Vegas. In March 1880, Neill and his cronies set up a wealthy Wyoming rancher, Michael Kelliher, who had come to town with a wad of cash to purchase some cattle. In a saloon, a Hoodoo stooge picked a fight with the rancher. Two deputies rushed in to "break up" the fight, but instead shot Kelliher in the head.

Neill, serving as acting coroner, set up an immediate inquest and determined his deputies had fired in self-defense. This, of course, was after he'd lifted Kelliher's wallet, watch and other belongings. Neill split town that night with the widow of one of his deputies who'd been killed a few weeks before. He was picked up in Muskogee, Indian Territory, but somehow managed to be released, even though there had been communication between New Mexico and Muskogee authorities.

In the Ring

Woody Guthrie once sang in his song "Pretty Boy Floyd," "Some will rob you with a six gun, others with a fountain pen." While Santa Fe didn't have civic leaders as outright thuggish as the Dodge City Gang, during the territorial era, this town was infamous for an informal organization called the Santa Fe Ring. This was a group of politicians, lawyers and businessmen who allegedly swindled land-grant owners out of their property. They were involved in government contracts.

Governor Otero wrote, "Nothing was too rotten for the well-known Santa Fe ring to undertake."

Some have denied the existence of a ring, which might have been more of a loose-knit, informal group of cronies than an actual organization. In 2006, Thomas Catron III, a Santa Fe lawyer and grandson of alleged Ring-leader Thomas B. Catron, said, "… the idea that [the Santa Fe Ring] was an early type of Mafia is overblown. [Former state historian] Myra Ellen Jenkins demolished the assertion that [the Santa Fe Ring] was a conspiratorial group that ran the state."

Spies on the Bridge

A world-shaking event occurred June 2, 1945, on the Castillo Street bridge over the Santa Fe River—near present-day Paseo de Peralta. A man named Harry Gold met with a Los Alamos physicist named Klaus Fuchs, a German-born scientist who had fled Nazi Germany. Fuchs handed Gold a packet containing documents concerning a plutonium-implosion device. That was two months before the United States dropped atomic bombs on Japan and revealed the existence of the Manhattan Project in Los Alamos.

The next day, Gold went to the Albuquerque apartment of David Greenglass, the younger brother of Ethel Rosenberg and an Army sergeant who had been assigned to Los Alamos. Greenglass gave Gold another packet of documents. Gold traveled to New York and handed the documents over to a Soviet agent.

In September 1945, Gold and Fuchs met again in Santa Fe to receive more atomic documents. The case didn't unravel until 1949, when the Soviet Union tested its first atomic bomb. Greenglass agreed to testify against his sister and her husband, Julius Rosenberg. The Rosenbergs were executed by the federal government in 1953.

But Gold and Fuchs weren't the only spies to operate out of Santa Fe. In 1985, Ed Howard, a former CIA agent who was working for the Legislative Finance Committee in Santa Fe and living in Eldorado, was under suspicion of spying for the Soviet Union. With the help of his wife Mary, also a CIA operative, Howard gave the FBI the slip and escaped to the Soviet Union. Howard died in Moscow in 2002.

1980 Prison Riot

Richard C de Baca saw a lot of carnage during his 26-year career in the New Mexico State Police. Car wrecks, airplane crashes, murders, suicides. But the worst was in February 1980, following the infamous prison riot south of Santa Fe. Although a few more people died during the Attica prison uprising in New York in 1971, many consider the New Mexico rampage to be the most brutal in the history of American corrections.

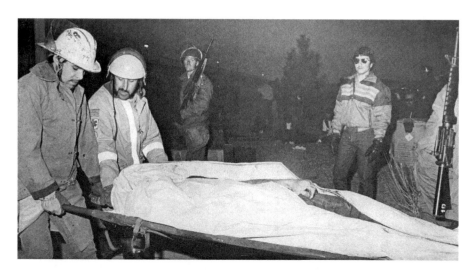

Aftermath of the 1980 prison riot. Photograph by Barbaraellen Koch.

It was a 36-hour bloodbath in which 33 inmates were killed by other inmates and 12 corrections officers were held hostage, some of whom were sodomized, stabbed and beaten.

"We were ankle deep in blood and water," C de Baca said, describing the prison in the immediate aftermath. He was in charge of investigating the specific crimes that took place during the riot.

The riot instigators broke into prison files to find out which of their fellow inmates were "snitches" who cooperated with prison authorities. They broke into the pharmacy and made themselves wild chemical concoctions. Then they went seeking revenge, torturing and killing those deemed snitches.

"One victim was an African-American who had his head hacked off by an ax," C de Baca said, adding that ax marks on the concrete are still visible on the concrete where this inmate lost his life. "Another victim was torched to death," C de Baca added. "The victims were defenseless. What they did was worse than what animals will do."

Only about 100 inmates were responsible for the violence, C de Baca said. Others escaped into the prison, huddling in the cold, while others stayed in their cells and prayed for their lives.

Forty-four inmates were charged with riot-related crimes. C de Baca said it was difficult to prosecute because very few witnesses were willing to cooperate.

Richard C de Baca, shown in the control room of the old state prison in June 2010. Photograph by Natalie Guillén.

The old main facility hasn't housed inmates since 1998. In recent years it's been rented out as a movie set. The state gave permission to shoot the prison comedy *The Longest Yard* there. But in 2007, the state denied permission to filmmaker James Williams to shoot a film version of Roger Morris' book *The Devil's Butcher Shop* at the old prison.

Too many bad memories, prison officials said.

In this June 2010 photo, ax marks, right, remain in the old state prison floor where one inmate was beheaded during the 1980 riot. Photograph by Natalie Guillén.

Billy The Kid: A Legend Is Born

by
Jason Strykowski

On July 14, 1881, William Henry Bonney, aka Patrick Henry McCarty, aka Billy the Kid, met his untimely end. At the time, Bonney had no more than 21 years of life under his gun belt, and his résumé held only a handful of short stints as a ranch hand and occasional monte dealer. Yet, in the years since his death he has become the most famous New Mexican. And, for a time, he visited Santa Fe, but his stay was brief and mostly behind bars.

By the winter of 1880, Bonney was on the run from authorities. He had gunned down at least one lawman, Sheriff William Brady, and was wanted for cattle theft and the murder of a man named Buckshot Roberts. Bonney had even attempted to cut a deal with territorial Governor Lew Wallace, but the deal had unraveled. In exchange for testimony at the murder trial of a lawyer, Bonney would receive a gubernatorial pardon for his crime. Wallace, however, found that he could not abide by those terms. On December 15, 1881, Wallace placed a $500 reward on Bonney's head.

Less than a week later, the recently elected Sheriff Pat Garrett trapped Bonney in a one-room stone hut in Stinking Springs, not too far from Fort Sumner. A prisoner of the territory of New Mexico, Bonney was transported to Santa Fe, where he stayed in a small Water Street jail for several months. From the interior of his cell, Bonney penned a handful of letters to Wallace, pleading for the former Civil War general to make good on his promise and pardon Bonney for his crimes.

William H. Bonney, aka Billy the Kid, circa 1878-80. Photograph courtesy Palace of the Governors Photo Archives (NMHM/DCA), #128785.

On New Year's Day 1881, Bonney pleaded, in his own hand, "I would like to see you for a few moments if you can spare time." Since Wallace and the Palace of the Governors stood only a few minutes' walk away, this made for a meager request, but Wallace never came.

For the next three months, Bonney waited in his Santa Fe cell. On March 27, Bonney made one final appeal to Wallace: "For the last time I ask, will you keep your promise. I start below tomorrow. Send answer by bearer." But, like his previous attempts, Bonney received no answer, and a day later, Bonney was taken in chains to Mesilla to await trial and likely a death sentence. Bonney, however, had no intention of sitting still for the hangman's noose.

A month later, while locked down in the second story of the Lincoln County Courthouse, Bonney made his move. Somehow, he came into the possession of a handgun and shot J.W. Bell, one of the two men holding him. Next, Bonney grabbed a shotgun and walked out to the deck on the second story of the courthouse. From his elevated position, Bonney took aim, yelled, "Hey Bob," and shot Deputy Bob Ollinger. With his manacles still on, Bonney walked down to the dirt road through Lincoln, mounted a horse and galloped out of town.

The escape, coupled with his being shot dead weeks later, propelled Bonney to international celebrity. Soon after his death, a book came out and became the cornerstone of the exaggerated Bonney legend. The book came from the same hand that fired the gun that killed Bonney. Pat Garrett's *The Authentic Life of Billy the Kid* built the young ranch hand into a daring cowboy.

Just over 40 years later, *The Saga of Billy the Kid* by Walter Noble Burns, released in 1926, became an international sensation. Louis B. Mayer purchased the film rights. When finished, Billy the Kid joined a film collection that would grow to more than 60 movies based on the fictional, and sometimes true, adventures of William Bonney.

Around Santa Fe, Bonney remains a presence. In 2004, Governor Bill Richardson attempted to assign Bonney a lawyer to investigate the unfulfilled pardon once promised by Wallace. Always the media darling, Bonney returned to the news that year when two Lincoln County men pushed to exhume his corpse and authenticate it. Rumors persist that Garrett, out of loyalty to Bonney, killed another man and let the young outlaw escape. Bonney's remains may be buried under concrete in Fort Sumner, but his legend is still at large.

Santa Fe Ring: Ruler Of The Territory

by
Jason Strykowski

Returning from the Civil War, veterans searched the United States for opportunities. Some chose to go home, while others hoped to find profit in places they had never before considered.

Famously, some Civil War survivors packed what little they had and headed to the South. Even more intrepid profiteers looked west to make their fortunes. In Santa Fe, a number of these Western "carpetbaggers" discovered power and a nickname for their affiliation. The Santa Fe Ring then dominated New Mexico politics for several decades.

The men loosely tied to this ring were paragons of what Mark Twain coined the "Gilded Age." Members of the Santa Fe Ring had power, money, few scruples and ample opportunity for growth. The Ring encircled lawyers, retailers, military officers, ranchers and politicians. And, if these men of such varied skills had a common interest, it was land speculation and subsequent revenue. The land-grant legacy in New Mexico made the region attractive for the men who would create the Ring. The muddled heritage of these Spanish leftovers translated into thousands of acres of grazing and mining land. New Mexico held unadulterated opportunity.

One of the first to recognize the profitability in land grants, Stephen B. Elkins moved to Mesilla in 1864 to pursue a career as a lawyer. At the time, Elkins possessed only a college degree and an undistinguished record as a Union soldier. But, through a disarming personality and strict resolve, Elkins became a leader in Mesilla. Elkins found success as a lawyer and, boosted by a quick tongue in English and Spanish, he soon found his way to the office of the territorial attorney general. His influence growing, Elkins decided to share the secret of his success with an old friend.

Thomas Benton Catron, circa 1917. Photograph by Wesley Bradfield, courtesy Palace of the Governors Photo Archives (NMHM/DCA), #13309.

Like Elkins, Thomas Benton Catron lived through the war only to struggle through peace time. Elkins' invitation to New Mexico probably came as a minor revelation to Catron, and it didn't take long for Catron to join Elkins on the short list of prominent New Mexicans. The two federally appointed attorneys would need all their influence.

Seated as president of the Maxwell Land Company, Elkins hoped to use his position and connections to increase acreage of the Maxwell Land Grant more than tenfold and therefore boost the company's holdings. Perhaps the most famous of the Spanish land transfers, the Maxwell Land Grant encompassed a parcel that would ultimately cover ground from Southern New Mexico into southern Colorado. At first, though, the grant held less territory, and to get the surveyor to recognize that extra land, Elkins had to cash in on sympathetic links to the Ring. These connections ran throughout Santa Fe and to the Republican Party in Washington.

The Maxwell case opened the gates for investors to stampede into New Mexico. As they rushed in, these investors sought the counsel of Elkins and Catron, whose history of profiteering demanded respect. Elkins and Catron became fixtures in many land exchanges and purchases.

With control of land and government, the Santa Fe Ring became the undisputed power of the territory until some in Colfax County and others in Lincoln County chose to voice their objections with pistols. Fighting erupted in Colfax and, quite famously, later engulfed Lincoln. In both cases, disputes revolved around the Ring's unwillingness to share both resources and controls. And, in both fights, the Ring emerged victorious.

Until 1885, the Ring stayed in control. Only a reformer in territorial Governor Edmund G. Ross and factionalism in the local Republican Party could finally bring an end to the Ring's reign.

Personalities: The Law And The Lawless

by
Rob Dean and Steve Terrell

Silvestre Pacheco

After the Pueblo Revolt of 1680, the Spanish settlers of Santa Fe retreated to present-day El Paso. Tense times followed. One day in 1687, a dispute turned violent between Spanish soldier Silvestre Pacheco and his brother-in-law, Joseph Baca. Pacheco killed Baca and drew a death sentence. On appeal, the governor, who faced a shortage of experienced soldiers, sided with the convicted killer and simply fined Pacheco and ordered him to return to military duty. Pacheco returned to Santa Fe with de Vargas in 1692.
Source: Historian Robert J. Torrez.

Ignacio Sanchez

Not every big case came attached to a major crime. Ignacio Sanchez's offense in 1798 was minor, but his case had wide implications, for in this case the term "rogue" most aptly described the authority figures who lorded over Sanchez. A lasting image of the colonial period portrayed citizens as powerless against the evil alcalde. Sanchez disproved that generalization. Facing arrest for not paying a debt, Sanchez resisted and possibly drew a knife on the authorities. Later, the governor rebuked the local authorities for going too far, and Sanchez was left to cool off, pay the debt and accept jail time. Then Sanchez, who had a record of financial trouble, was lectured about turning his life around. He was told to live within his means and respect his superiors. That was that. Justice served.

Source: Historian Robert J. Torrez.

S.H. Newman

S.H. Newman. Photograph courtesy El Paso Community College.

A teacher turned newsman, Simeon H. Newman, spent time behind bars, although it turned out that he was the victim and his pursuers were the bad guys. Newman used his little Las Vegas, New Mexico, newspaper in the early 1870s to attack political corruption in Santa Fe. His opponents used their political muscle to lock Newman in jail, where he stayed for 63 days while refusing to pay a heavy fine. After a frigid winter, he coughed up a reduced fine and won his release. But the legal fight wiped him out. During his sentence, Newman's opponents had taken control of the newspaper, and the only freedom open to the editor was the freedom to get out of town. Newman resurfaced in Mesilla, once again as a crusading newsman.

Source: El Paso Community College.

Samuel B. Axtell

The Santa Fe Ring had help at the highest level—the governor's office—in its schemes to steal Spanish and Mexican land grants. The Ring-friendly territorial governor from 1875 to 1878 was Samuel Axtell. A Grant appointee, the do-nothing Axtell was swept out of office when a momentary spirit of reform hit Washington, DC. But Axtell's successor in New Mexico, Lew Wallace, failed at reform as others had before him. The talk of corruption around Axtell never resulted in formal charges. He stayed in Santa Fe and thrived, rescuing some of his reputation with a term as chief justice on the Territorial Supreme Court.

Samuel B. Axtell, governor of New Mexico, circa 1881. Photograph by Broadbent & Taylor, courtesy Palace of the Governors Photo Archives (NMHM/DCA), #8787.

Francisco Gonzales y Borrego and His Gang

When a popular, up-and-coming politician was gunned down on the streets of Santa Fe in May 1892, no one could have anticipated the political intrigue and legal twists to follow. But in the end, Francisco Gonzales y Borrego and three accomplices hanged, and a fifth man died while resisting arrest. The crime exposed political gang warfare at its most ruthless. A judge said the motive for assassinating Frank Chavez "was political jealousy, a fear of his popularity and power, and an inordinate desire to remove him from the road of political preferment." Political boss Thomas Catron defended the Borrego gang. During the sensational trial, evidence suggested the motive was revenge for an earlier political murder, and testimony touched on threats against Catron. Borrego and Catron had the benefit of friends in high positions, and the so-called Borrego murder cases stalled in the courts. But a conviction was inevitable. Finally, on April 2, 1897, almost five years after the crime, Borrego and his gang went to the gallows. A scaffold with a huge trap door was specially designed so all four men dropped to their deaths simultaneously—four efficient, orderly death sentences carried out on a single day in Santa Fe.

Sources: Associated Press, William A. Keleher's *The Fabulous Frontier*.

William T. Thornton

The toughest law-and-order governor was William T. Thornton, who served from 1893 to 1897. He talked tough about crime, and his actions matched the rhetoric. Thornton signed off on 13 executions, more than any governor in the period. Criminals must learn that "they violate the law at their peril" and that "justice will surely overtake them," Thornton said. Swift and certain punishment was his way. The last executions under his watch were the four hangings in one day that ended the notorious Borrego murder cases. With those four killings, Thornton had had enough. He left office three days later after he made his final act an unlikely act of mercy. He ordered the release of an 18-year-old who happened to be the brother of the Borregos hanged three days earlier.

Source: Office of the State Historian.

William T. Thornton, second from right, shown on Fort Marcy Hill in 1912. Governors of the period included Herbert James Hagerman, left, Miguel Antonio Otero, behind the wheel, and L. Bradford Prince. Photograph by Aaron B. Craycraft, courtesy Palace of the Governors Photo Archives (NMHM/DCA), #140378.

Secundino Romero

Law enforcement was the Romero family business. Political power was its weapon of choice. While Secundino Romero and his family ran the machine and bankrolled good causes in Las Vegas, New Mexico, he and his brother also spent 16 years in Santa Fe flashing their badges in one job or another. Romero, a one-time San Miguel County sheriff, became the speaker of the House in the early years of statehood. Earlier, politically connected brother Cleofes, also a former sheriff, held the job of warden at the state prison. Speaker Romero's influence in Santa Fe began to fade after 1917. He left the speaker's post, and by then his brother was out as well at the penitentiary. Before becoming speaker, Romero had been U.S. marshal. After leaving the speaker's office, he was ready again to wear a badge. In 1922, a new Republican president overcame considerable anti-Romero opposition to return Romero to the marshal's post, a job he then held for four years.

Secundino Romero

Thomas Johnson and Louis Young

On July 21, 1933, the state first used the electric chair for not one but two men. The first was a Santa Fe man named Thomas Johnson. He was a black man convicted of killing 18-year-old Angelina Jaramillo. But some insist Johnson was framed by authorities and that the real killer was a member of the victim's family. The case was racially charged. Two of the nine people executed by the state have been black. Both were accused of killing Caucasian women. Louis Young was convicted of murdering Eloise Kennedy in 1945. He was a prison inmate who worked as personal handyman at the warden's home in downtown Santa Fe, in Kennedy's neighborhood. As in the Johnson case, serious questions cast doubt on Young's guilt. Young confessed following a late-night interrogation in his cell, though he soon recanted. Like the Johnson case, the racially charged case featured screaming headlines stressing the suspect's race.

Sources: Ralph Melnick's *Justice Betrayed*, defense records and state archives.

Timeline

1610: Pedro de Peralta establishes capital at Santa Fe and begins palace construction.

1680: Spanish Colonial Law gives governor legal as well as civil and military authority.

1680: Pueblo Indians revolt.

1779: Colonial courts carry out first death penalty, a second coming in 1809.

1790: Decade sees growing citizen resistance to despotic local authority.

1812: Reports back to Spain say lack of legal training results in few New Mexico prosecutions.

1846: Kearny Code lays out basis of territorial law.

1848: Treaty of Guadalupe Hidalgo makes New Mexico a U.S. territory.

1876: Lincoln County War gives rise to Billy the Kid, who's killed in 1881.

1885: Federal investigation reveals land fraud by Santa Fe Ring.

1897: Four hang in one day at height of death penalty's acceptance.

1912: New Mexico becomes 47th state.

1933: Thomas Johnson is first to die in electric chair after sensational murder trial.

1945: Spies pass Manhattan Project secrets.

Suggested Books

Airy, Helen. *Whatever Happened to Billy the Kid?* Santa Fe: Sunstone Press, 1993.

Alarid, Michael J. "They Came From the East: Importing Homicide, Violence, and Misconceptions of Soft Justice into Early Santa Fe, New Mexico, 1847-53." *All Trails Lead to Santa Fe*. Santa Fe: Sunstone Press, 2010.

Bullis, Don. *New Mexico's Finest: Peace Officers Killed in the Line of Duty, 1847-2010*. Albuquerque: Rio Grande Books, 2010.

Burton, Jeff. *Dynamite and Six-Shooter*. Santa Fe: Sunstone Press, 2007.

Cline, Donald. *Alias Billy the Kid, The Man Behind the Legend*. Santa Fe: Sunstone Press, 1986.

Crichton, Kyle Samuel. *Law and Order, Ltd., The Rousing Life of Elfego Baca of New Mexico*. Santa Fe: Sunstone Press, 2008.

Cutter, Charles R. *The Legal Culture of Northern New Spain, 1700-1810*. Albuquerque: The University of New Mexico Press, 1995.

Fackler, Elizabeth. *Billy the Kid, The Legend of El Chivato*. Santa Fe: Sunstone Press, 2003.

Freiberger, Harriet. *Lucien Maxwell, Villain or Visionary*. Santa Fe: Sunstone Press, 1999.

Garrett, Pat. *The Authentic Life of Billy the Kid*. Santa Fe: Sunstone Press, 2007.

Hertzog, Peter, ed. *Outlaws of New Mexico*. Santa Fe: Sunstone Press, 1984.

Hunt, Frazier. *The Tragic Days of Billy the Kid*. Santa Fe: Sunstone Press, 2009.

Keleher, William A. *The Fabulous Frontier, 1846-1912*. Santa Fe: Sunstone Press, 2008.

Keleher, William A. *Maxwell Land Grant*. Santa Fe: Sunstone Press, 2008.

Keleher, William A. *Memoirs, Episodes in New Mexico History, 1892-1969*. Santa Fe: Sunstone Press, 2008.

Keleher, William A. *Violence in Lincoln County, 1869-1881*. Santa Fe: Sunstone Press, 2007.

King, Bruce. *Cowboy in the Roundhouse*. Santa Fe: Sunstone Press, 1998.

Lacy, Ann, and Anne Valley-Fox, eds. *Outlaws & Desperados*. Santa Fe: Sunstone Press, 2008.

Melnick, Ralph. *Justice Betrayed: A Double Killing in Old Santa Fe*. Albuquerque: The University of New Mexico Press, 2002.

Melzer, Richard. *Breakdown, How the Secret of the Atomic Bomb was Stolen During World War II*. Santa Fe: Sunstone Press, 2000.

Miller, Jay. *Billy the Kid Rides Again, Digging for the Truth*. Santa Fe: Sunstone Press, 2005.

Mocho, Jill. *Murder and Justice in Frontier New Mexico, 1821-1846*. Albuquerque: The University of New Mexico Press, 1997.

Morris, Roger. *The Devil's Butcher Shop: The New Mexico Prison Uprising*. Albuquerque: The University of New Mexico Press, 1988.

Nolan, Frederick W. *The Billy the Kid Reader*. Norman: University of Oklahoma Press, 2007.

Nolan, Frederick W. *The Lincoln County War, A Documentary History*. Santa Fe: Sunstone Press, 2009.

Nolan, Frederick W. *The West of Billy the Kid*. Norman: University of Oklahoma Press, 1999.

Otero, Miguel Antonio. *My Life on the Frontier, 1864 – 1882*. Santa Fe: Sunstone Press, 2007.

Otero, Miguel Antonio. *My Life on the Frontier, 1882 – 1897*. Santa Fe: Sunstone Press, 2007.

Otero, Miguel Antonio. *My Nine Years As Governor, 1897 – 1906*. Santa Fe: Sunstone Press, 2007.

Otero, Miguel Antonio. *The Real Billy the Kid*. Santa Fe: Sunstone Press, 2007.

Poe, John William. *The Death of Billy the Kid*. Santa Fe: Sunstone Press, 2006.

Sager, Stan. *Viva Elfego, The Case for Elfego Baca, Hispanic Hero*. Santa Fe: Sunstone Press, 2008.

Simmons, Marc. *Murder on the Santa Fe Trail: An International Incident, 1843*. El Paso: Texas Western Press, the University of Texas at El Paso, 1987

Simmons, Marc. *New Mexico Mavericks, Stories from a Fabled Past*. Santa Fe: Sunstone Press, 2005.

Simmons, Marc. *Stalking Billy the Kid, Brief Sketches of a Short Life*. Santa Fe: Sunstone Press, 2006.

Siringo, Charles Angelo. *A Lone Star Cowboy*. Santa Fe: Sunstone Press, 2006.

Siringo, Charles Angelo. *Riata and Spurs, The Story of a Lifetime Spent in the Saddle as Cowboy and Detective*. Santa Fe: Sunstone Press, 2007.

Stanley, F. *No Tears for Black Jack Ketchum*. Santa Fe: Sunstone Press, 2008.

Stanley, F. *The Grant that Maxwell Bought*. Santa Fe: Sunstone Press, 2008.

Tatum, Stephen. *Inventing Billy the Kid: Visions of the Outlaw in America, 1881-1981*. Albuquerque: The University of New Mexico Press, 1982.

Tórrez, Robert J. *Myth of the Hanging Tree: Stories of Crime and Punishment in Territorial New Mexico*. Albuquerque: The University of New Mexico Press, 2008.

Utley, Robert M. *Billy the Kid: A Short and Violent Life*. London: Tauris, 2000.

Westphall, Victor. *Thomas B. Catron and His Era*. Tucson: University of Arizona Press, 1973.

Wilson, John P. *Merchants, Guns, & Money: The Story of Lincoln County and Its Wars*. Santa Fe: Museum of New Mexico Press, 1987.

Suggested Websites

(active at time of publication)

Crime in Colonial period: www.nmbar.org/AboutSBNM/Committees/Historical/ Crime_and_Punishment_In%20Colonial_New_Mexico.pdf
Outlaws and lawmen: www.legendsofamerica.com/LA-OutlawsandLegends.html
Pioneer women in the law: www.nmbar.org/AboutSBNM/Committees/Historical/ Pioneers.pdf
1980 prison riot: www.newmexicohistory.org/filedetails.php?fileID=451

7

Preserving Heritage

From left, City Councilor Miguel Chavez, Aaron Beltran and Christine Ortega, both with YouthWorks!, worked on reapplying mud stucco on the face of the San Miguel Mission in June 2010. Photograph by Luis Sánchez Saturno.

Guardians Of A Vital Heritage: Preservation Essential to Some, Heavy-Handed to Others

by
Tom Sharpe

laims that Santa Fe is the oldest town in the United States, with its oldest house and the oldest church, are exaggerations. But those claims have been used to attract tourists here ever since the railroad arrived.

Of course, Taos Pueblo, the Hopi villages and hundreds of other Native American settlements thrived centuries before Santa Fe was founded by the Spanish—whether in 1610 as celebrated in the 2010 "Cuartocentenario" or 1607, as one document seems to indicate. Historian France V. Scholes found in 1944 a document held by a London antiquities dealer that indirectly supported 1607 as a possible date. Historian Thomas Chavez of the Palace of the Governors rediscovered the document in the 1990s.

Debate around the founding date typified the community's shared passion for history. But by 2010, historians were able to agree that the year 1610 was best for the Santa Fe 400th commemoration.

Long before Europeans found the New World, people were born, lived and died along the banks of the Santa Fe River in what is believed to have been a Tewa village called Ogapoge. Doubts about a pre-Columbian village here were laid to rest early in the 21st century when burials, kivas and other ruins were discovered in archaeological excavations before beginning construction of the Santa Fe Community Convention Center next to City Hall.

But even if Native American towns, houses and places of worship are omitted from the "oldest" contest, St. Augustine, Florida, founded by the Spanish in 1565, beats Santa Fe by more than four decades. St. Augustine's oldest dwelling, the González-Alvarez House, believed to date from the 1600s, easily predates Santa Fe's oldest house at 215 East De Vargas Street, believed to date from the 1700s. But the official history of Santa Fe's oldest house claims it was built on the ruins of an 800-year-old Indian dwelling—switching from European to Native American culture to trump the Florida city.

St. Augustine's oldest church, the Cathedral Basilica of St. Augustine, built in 1797, might predate Santa Fe's Cathedral Basilica of St. Francis of Assisi, begun in 1869 and consecrated, although still unfinished, in 1886. But the Florida church is 87 years younger than even the most recent incarnation of Santa Fe's oldest church.

Debate is an ongoing part of Santa Fe's history, culture and architecture. The discovery of Indian remains downtown meant major changes for the convention center. Even plans for downtown development by the Archdiocese of Santa Fe drew opposition.

Some say we're self-aggrandizing about our culture, heavy-handed with our architecture and downright myth-making about our history. But Santa Fe cares deeply about its heritage—and this was especially evident during its 400th anniversary in 2010.

Oldest Church's Makeover

San Miguel Mission, sometimes called a chapel, at 401 Old Santa Fe Trail, just across East De Vargas Street from the oldest house, was first constructed in 1610, destroyed in 1640, rebuilt in 1645, destroyed again in the Pueblo Revolt of 1680 and rebuilt yet again in 1710.

Its most impressive view is from its wedge-shaped, buttressed backside and its north flank along one-lane East De Vargas Street, where some of the ancient adobe bricks are exposed. The south side of the church, with an entrance to a gift shop under a portal with several large trees on the adjacent state office complex, provides a shady, cool oasis on hot days. The entrance and bell tower, facing Old Santa Fe Trail, currently are obscured with scaffolding for the most ambitious preservation effort in San Miguel Mission's three centuries.

Cornerstones, a Santa Fe-based nonprofit dedicated to the preservation of earthen structures, led the effort—its first major project in town in its decades of preserving some 360 churches and other public buildings in four states and Mexico. Up to 15 volunteers per week worked on the old church, including visitors from around the nation and other countries, and interested locals such as City Councilor Miguel Chavez.

The entrance and bell tower of the San Miguel Mission, facing Old Santa Fe Trail. Photograph by Luis Sánchez Saturno.

"When we conceived this project, the idea was to focus on [volunteers from] the local community but not to restrict anybody," said Cornerstones Executive Director Jake Barrow. "If somebody wants to come help, great, let them in because this is a Santa Fe-type thing. ... People like to make these bricks. It's hard work, but it's fun. It's like one of the girls from Breadloaf (a group of English teachers getting master's degrees) said, 'Wow, you guys have a great job. You get to play in mud every day.'"

The main goal in the ongoing rehabilitation, was to replace the cement-containing stucco on the church's exterior walls with real mud plaster. Cementitious stucco prohibits the evaporation of moisture trapped inside the adobe walls, causing them to deteriorate, while real mud plaster releases moisture via transpiration.

Antonio Martinez, the project foreman for general contractor Paul Taylor of Las Cruces, learned about adobe work in his hometown of Rociada near the San Miguel/Mora County line and began working with Cornerstones on the rehabilitation of the Rociada church.

"People should be concerned about some of these old buildings. Look at all the moisture in that," Martinez said as he studied the water mark on the lower walls of the Lamy Building, built of adobe in 1878 as a dormitory for St. Michael's College and now owned by the state, next door to San Miguel Mission. "This building here is in better condition [than San Miguel Mission] because of the stone foundation. But it's still laid in the lime mortar. When it was covered up with cement, that mortar ... wicks up foundation moisture. ... It can't breathe. So at some point, you end up with what we call 'dead earth.'"

Adobe that has deteriorated to the point of dead earth simply flakes away into loose dirt, incapable of bearing weight and eventually causing the structure to collapse. In the case of San Miguel Mission, some of the internal adobe bricks will have to be replaced. Plans also call for installing a new drainage channel through the campo santo, or graveyard, in front of the mission.

City's Oldest Tourist Attractions

Both Santa Fe's oldest house and its oldest church, as well as several other old buildings along East De Vargas Street including the one housing Upper Crust Pizza (at the time of publication), are owned by St. Michael's High School, originally founded as St. Michael's College in 1859.

For years, the oldest house was rented to a jewelry and curio shop that kept one room as a roadside-attraction museum with a headless dummy—a soldier supposedly beheaded after he complained about a potion sold by a *bruja* (witch). The interior of the shop, at the time this book was published, was being remodeled with plans to lease it out again.

Both the oldest house and the oldest church are in the Barrio Analco—a neighborhood just south of the river that is believed to have been founded by Mexican Indians who sided with the Spanish against the Aztec and accompanied the Spaniards north in their initial colonization of Santa Fe in the early 1600s.

A historical engraving of Santa Fe's oldest house at 215 East De Vargas Street. Photograph courtesy of the Fray Angélico Chávez History Library, Negative #1.91.

The Barrio Analco, the "Yglesia de S. Miguel" and the oldest house—although not labeled that way—appeared on the first known map of Santa Fe by cartographer José de Urrutia in 1766. By the time the railroad line reached Lamy in 1879, both structures, as well as Santa Fe in general, began to get national publicity.

Harper's Weekly of September 13, 1879, devoted a full page to what its unidentified writer called the "oldest town within the whole territory of the United States," with three hand-colored engravings by C. Graham—"from sketches by H. Worrall"—of the cityscape, "the oldest inhabited home in the U.S." and, instead of the Roman Catholic San Miguel Mission, First Presbyterian Church, labeled as "the only Protestant church in Santa Fe."

The article seemed to imply that Santa Fe is older than St. Augustine because it was built on the "old pueblo of Cienyó" discovered by the Coronado expedition into the Southwest, 1540 – 1542. It also sounded an alarm for preservation of Santa Fe's oldest building, the Palace of the Governors, circa 1610: "This interesting old building, on account of repairs repeatedly made upon it nowadays, is fast losing its antique appearance and internal arrangements."

Harper's Weekly returned four years later to promote the city's Tertio-Millennial exposition by devoting several pages of its July 14, 1883, edition to Santa Fe's history. It published five Graham etchings of other scenes of the city, including "the ruins of the ancient pueblo church and college of San Miguel." This time, the magazine predicted that in the near future, Santa Fe "will exchange its ancient and somewhat shabby picturesqueness for the crude glare which characterizes the buildings of our frontier."

"The Oldest House in Santa Fe"—looking not too different than it does today, with exposed river-rock buttresses, a second floor and tiny windows and doors—also was depicted in an unaccredited etching published in the September 8, 1883, edition of *Leslie's Illustrated Newspaper*, another prominent national publication of the late 19th century.

"Until recently Santa Fe has been almost a medieval town in its appearance," Leslie's reported, "but the spirit of enterprise has of late years begun to possess it, and the encroaching Tertio-Millennial promises to give impetus to the progressive movement."

Celebrating, Even When Numbers Don't Add Up

by
Tom Sharpe

Santa Fe's self-promotion of its heritage sometimes defies arithmetic.

In 1883, the city planned a "Tertio-Millennial"—a term contrived to mean one-third of 1,000 or 333. The problem was, that didn't add up. Santa Fe, then thought to have been founded in 1610, would not reach its 333rd year until 1943—60 years later.

But that didn't discourage the party planners.

The Santa Fe New Mexican, which became one of the exposition's most ardent promoters, started off its coverage with an erroneous headline—"One Third of a Century"—indicating how puzzling the term Tertio-Millennial may have been to people of the late 19th century.

But when newspapers in Denver and elsewhere questioned the timing of the anniversary, *The Santa Fe New Mexican* began to defend it, contending that the celebration commemorated "not the founding of the city but [New Mexico's] occupation by the Spanish people and its coming under the influences of European civilization and the christian religion."

An editorial argued that the first Spaniard to explore New Mexico was Alvar Nuñez Cabeza de Vaca in 1538-39, that Francisco Vásquez de Coronado led an armed incursion in 1540-42 and Juan de Oñate established the first colony in 1598. None of those years coincided with a 333rd anniversary, either, and no event was cited from 1550—exactly 333 years before 1883. But the editorial concluded: "In light of these historical facts it will be seen that the Tertio-Millennial is an appropriate name for the celebration which is about to commence under such favorable auspices."

Centennials were the rage in the Victorian Age. The United States had celebrated its first 100 years only seven years earlier. The Tertio-Millennial was Santa Fe's first attempt to promote itself since the transcontinental railroad line reached Lamy in 1879, and the spur was extended to Santa Fe the following year. Mining companies set up booths with examples of their ores, sites and techniques in the exhibition hall erected two blocks north of the Plaza, using the walls of the unfinished "state house," finished later as the U.S. Courthouse. An oval horse-racing track was constructed around the exposition grounds.

Celebrations began July 2, 1883, with a turnout of 10,000 to 12,000 people. "The formal inauguration of a month's festivities was carried out amid much splendor and unbounded enthusiasm," reported *The Santa Fe New Mexican*. "The morning dawned bright and beautiful. At nine o'clock, the first of a salute of thirty-three guns, fired at minute intervals, signaled the crowd into the streets." The evening concluded with "excellent music, graceful dancing and a genuine good time," despite an evening downpour.

The Tertio-Millennial continued for a month, with races of all types, American Indian dances and pageants, including on three successive days, re-enactments of three centuries of history in New Mexico. On July 17, someone tried to burn down the exhibition hall. By early August, as the exposition neared an end, some appeared to grow tired of the controversy surrounding the Tertio-Millennial.

"We now respectfully ask the zealous and hearty support of the whole press of the territory for the exposition," state mining commissioners said in a proclamation. "Now we ask the united press of the territory to sink out of sight for the time being all personal or local feeling with reference to anything unpleasant connected with the exposition heretofore, and join with us unanimously in pushing the high and patriotic objects of the exposition from now until the close."

Reconquering New Mexico

by
Jason Strykowski

Under the leadership of the mysterious Popé and tired of the misery of Spanish dominion, the pueblos successfully removed the yoke of Spanish rule in 1680. The Pueblo Revolt, perhaps the most triumphant of native rebellions, awarded the pueblos freedom after some eight decades of Spanish rule. But, by 1692, pressure from neighboring tribes and continually dry conditions made them vulnerable. Responsibility for the recapture of New Mexico fell to one Spaniard, down on his luck and desperate for redemption.

Using his own money and in danger of losing his status and livelihood permanently, Don Diego de Vargas undertook the reconquest of New Mexico for the Spanish in 1692. Born in Madrid in 1643, Vargas came into a family of considerable standing but meager funds. Vargas' father drove the family into bankruptcy and left young Vargas with few options. To restore the family name and fortune, Vargas opted to try his luck in the New World, where he received a post as justicia mayor of a locale in present-day Oaxaca.

In Mexico, Vargas reversed his fortunes. While he had failed at gentility in Spain, in Mexico he successfully oversaw silver mines near what is now the mountain village of Zacatecas. His superiors took note of the profits turned under Vargas' management. Advancement lay in his future.

In 1688, authorities promised Vargas the governorship of New Mexico, a province they had failed to control for eight years. Although the Spaniards had come to realize that New Mexico promised little material wealth, their claim upon the territory still served to solidify their stature in northern America, not to mention their likely desire to prove their dominance over the Natives.

David Trujillo as Don Diego de Vargas during Fiesta in 2007. Fiesta celebrates the recolonization of Santa Fe by Vargas. Photograph by Jane Phillips

But Vargas would have few resources to display Spanish power. When mustered at El Paso, Vargas presided over a mere 200 soldiers, many of whom were ill-trained or otherwise unprofessional soldiers. The little group was matched against hundreds of miles of unforgiving terrain and thousands of Natives, many of whom would not be glad to see the return of Spanish ordinance.

Some pueblos, however, fared poorly during the dozen years of Spanish absence. A shift in power brought raiding Apaches to pueblo communities. The partial rejection of Spanish crops matched with drought made sustenance difficult for some. Spanish support may have seemed a welcome relief from the pueblo's heavy burdens.

As a result, Vargas met with surprisingly little resistance in the short term. Vargas did find a fight in Santa Fe, where a far larger army of Natives had gathered for a battle, or, at least, a contentious resolution. Wisely, Vargas laid partial siege to the city by cutting off the former capital's water supply. He held the advantage until the Natives relented and negotiated terms for renewed Spanish authority.

Those terms had little meaning until a year later, when Vargas returned with the expression of Spanish rule. He brought with him soldiers and settlers, both of whom had to face renewed Native hostility. A second Pueblo Revolt flared.

Vargas then displayed a gruesome tenacity. His men retook Santa Fe and captured dozens of Native warriors and killed them for their transgressions. Their deaths signaled the beginning of another era of Spanish cruelty. Other Natives were virtually enslaved as laborers for the hundreds of colonists who entered New Mexico and re-established pioneer communities.

As a return on his personal investment and despite numerous challenges, Vargas found himself governor of New Mexico. But his initial contract with Spanish authorities limited his term of leadership to a mere five years beginning in 1688. After all of his work, Vargas had limited time to enjoy his new title. He attempted to stay in office, presumably for the rest of his life and much to the annoyance of his successor.

His persistence earned him a house arrest until 1700, when Vargas traveled to Mexico City to campaign for the restoration of his position. And, despite his general dislike of New Mexico, Vargas regained the governorship, recouped expenses from Spain and took the title to a productive encomienda. At 60, Vargas returned to New Mexico only to fall and die one year later.

Vargas was buried in Santa Fe and an annual celebration commemorates his legacy. But while Vargas proved courageous in his endeavor to retake New Mexico, he also brought about the end of pueblo independence almost singlehandedly.

When the Pueblos Pushed the Spanish Out

by
Jason Strykowski

By the opening of the summer in 1680, a precarious peace lingered in New Mexico. A long drought eradicated crops and livestock. Apaches raided and stole what little food remained on an increasingly frequent basis. Nerves frayed and the pueblo people, who may have sought refuge in their own religious customs, were denied their tradition by Spanish missions.

Among those punished by the church for a dogged devotion to pueblo religion was a war chief from San Juan Pueblo whom the Spanish knew as El Popé. Now regarded as one of the greatest of Pueblo leaders, a scant historical record explains Popé's rise. Most likely, he narrowly escaped execution in 1675 in a purge conducted by missionaries to weaken pueblo religiosity. Five years later, still harboring rightful anger, Popé probably brought his cause to a tribal council.

No written explanation of that meeting exists, but it is likely that Popé used the council to gain the loyalty of other pueblo leaders. They also may have created a strategy to attack and surround the Spanish before the arrival of Spanish goods from Mexico. On August 12, the council reasoned, the Spanish would be most vulnerable. The settlers would have little reason to suspect an attack.

Despite the great distances that separated the pueblos, Popé's leadership brought the tribes together and coordinated an attack. Even with a head start, the Spanish could do little to defend themselves. The pueblo inhabitants vastly outnumbered the Hispanic farmers and missionaries. Most of New Mexico folded in relatively short order.

A 19th century view of San Juan Pueblo, the village of Popé, leader of the Pueblo Revolt of 1680. Photograph by W.H. Rau, Museum of New Mexico/Negative #99997.

The Spanish retreated to Santa Fe to take refuge in the city's thin defenses. What armaments the city did possess could not match the more than 2,000 pueblo soldiers that soon gathered outside the capital. As governor, Antonio de Otermin had few choices and only about 100 men capable of bearing arms. The Spanish fought as long as they could and perhaps inflicted heavy casualties on the Natives. But the siege cut the Spanish off from their water supply, and the Spanish were forced to retreat.

Otermin distributed provisions among those still loyal to him and made ready to march south toward safety. Unbeknownst to those in Santa Fe, other loyalists at Isleta Pueblo had already abandoned New Mexico to seek safety in El Paso. Otermin's party would soon follow.

Popé and his brethren allowed the retreating Spaniards to leave safely, but quickly disposed of Spanish influence. Churches burned, and 21 of the region's 33 missionaries were killed. Pueblo leaders encouraged their brethren to abandon Spanish culture at all costs. They even let loose many of their horses, accidentally providing ponies to the Plains cultures that would soon make the small Spanish workhorses icons of the American West.

The years following the Pueblo Revolt left few historical footprints. Popé somehow lost his life and power, failing in all likelihood to take control of the province. Even without his leadership, pueblos reasserted their unique personalities. Kivas were rebuilt and Native religion restored. The city of Santa Fe itself became a stronghold for Tewas and Tanos.

The Spanish, marooned just south of the Rio Grande near El Paso, did not fare well in the interim. They had trouble with their crops and lived in relative squalor. And, despite the fact they eagerly desired to retake New Mexico, it would take 12 years before a suitable leader would emerge to reclaim in the province. In 1693, Don Diego de Vargas led the Reconquista to take New Mexico back for the Spanish crown.

Despite their continued struggle with drought and raids, the Pueblos were not eager to accept the return of Spanish rule. During the Revolt they had successfully overthrown the Spanish crown and reasserted their cultural traditions. They had no intention of submitting to colonial conquistadors without further resistance. Vargas used careful diplomacy and superior arms to subdue the Pueblos. Even after the successful reconquest, however, the legacy of the Pueblo Revolt ensured some degree of cultural autonomy for the pueblos.

A stable and sedentary Native population has surrounded Santa Fe since its inception, perhaps placing it apart from other North American settlements of Quebec, Jamestown or even St. Augustine. Therefore, the Pueblo Revolt and Spanish reconquest remained at the core of the Santa Fe narrative. Despite uneasy tension that lingers today, the pueblos, with the exception of a handful of violent outbreaks, have tolerated the existence of the capital.

Personalities: Saving Santa Fe

by
Rob Dean

Over the generations, many Santa Fe residents were devoted to saving and protecting the city's heritage. The following individuals illustrate the range of those efforts.

Donaciano Vigil

Born in Santa Fe in 1802, Donaciano Vigil chose when he turned 21 to make the military his career. After U.S. conquest of New Mexico in 1846, Vigil's acceptance of American rule influenced other Hispanos to recognize the reality of the federal presence and calm largely political unrest in the territorial period. During the earlier Spanish colonial period, government and church officials were careful to preserve historical records. After arrival of the Americans, however, it fell to Vigil to champion the cause of saving historical records. As New Mexico's first civil governor, Vigil organized archival records and made it his cause to preserve New Mexico's history.

Source: Office of the State Historian.

Donaciano Vigil, circa 1880. Photograph by Albright Art Parlors, courtesy Palace of the Governors Photo Archives (NMHM/DCA), #11405.

Cleofas Martinez Jaramillo and younger sister May Martinez in 1901. Photograph courtesy Palace of the Governors archives (NMHM/DCA), #9930.

Cleofas Martinez Jaramillo

Her father was a prominent landowner. Her husband was a rising political star. But Cleofas Jaramillo's legacy overtook the men in her life because of her commitment to preserve Hispanic culture. By age 20, when she married in 1898, Jaramillo already knew privilege and influence and proved herself as an excellent student at Loretto Academy. When her husband and three children all died before Jaramillo reached 55, she turned her attention to preserving what she feared was her fading culture. She wrote, "On account of familiarity with the old customs, we had not awakened to the fact that they were worth preserving, until in recent years, and have turned our effort to revive them." In 1935, she co-founded the Sociedad Folklórica, and soon she began a prolific writing career, documenting traditional cooking, storytelling, celebrations and religious customs. She died in 1956.

Source: Tey Diana Rebolledo.

Feliciana Tapia Viarrial

Pojoaque Pueblo grew from near extinction to become the cultural center and economic power it is today. Feliciana Viarrial was a matriarch of the community as it experienced that cultural revitalization. Almost by chance in 1932, her father learned that the federal commissioner of Indian affairs was seeking heirs to Pojoaque tribal lands. Led by Viarrial's father, Jose Antonio Tapia, a caravan of 14 Pojoaque members returned to the pueblo. By 1934, all of the Pojoaque Pueblo land had been fenced. By 1936, the Pojoaque Pueblo became a federally recognized Indian reservation of 11,603 acres. In 1940, just four years after Pojoaque became a recognized reservation, Tapia died. His daughter, Feliciana, who died in 1988, and her son, Jacob Viarrial, carried on the work of developing and strengthening the pueblo.

Feliciana Tapia Viarrial

Carlos Vierra painting murals for Saint Francis Auditorium in 1917. Photograph courtesy Palace of the Governors archives (NMHM/DCA), #30856.

Carlos Vierra

The person arguably most responsible for launching Santa Fe style was Carlos Vierra. A Californian of Portuguese decent, Vierra studied art in New York City before moving to Santa Fe in 1904 to get well. He was a painter who created watercolor images of mission churches and a photographer who used aerial photography to advance the study of prehistoric Native ruins. His association with the Museum of New Mexico fed an interest in traditional architecture. In 1918, he opened eyes in Santa Fe by designing a home that incorporated pueblo influences, particularly a set-back second story. When Vierra died in 1937, his friend Paul Walter, another leading figure in historical preservation, said, "Carlos Vierra left an impression on Santa Fe that will endure for ages. ... That Santa Fe is not only a 'City Different' but also a 'City Beautiful' is more largely owing to him, perhaps, than any other individual."

Source: Maurilio E. Vigil.

William Penhallow Henderson

The Pueblo Spanish Building Company under William Penhallow Henderson was a major contributor to the revival movement in Pueblo-Spanish architecture in the prewar 1900s. Henderson's company designed and built several noteworthy projects, including the present-day School of American Research and Wheelwright Museum. The remodeling of Sena Plaza in downtown Santa Fe in 1927 was a major achievement. Henderson's furniture, influenced by the Spanish colonial period and handmade by craftsmen, was popular locally and nationally.

Source: Corinne P. Sze.

Maria Chabot

If not for Maria Chabot's idea, Indian Market wouldn't be what it is today. Influenced by outdoor markets she saw in Mexico, Chabot brought to Santa Fe the idea of an open-air market on the Plaza. Indian Market began modestly as a fair and exhibition in 1922. With still no permanent home 10 years later, the market stopped for four years. In 1936, Chabot's idea of an outdoor market took hold, and the market was revitalized to run over eight consecutive Saturdays in July and August. Indian Market found its niche. Chabot died in 2001 knowing that the market had gained international fame as Santa Fe's largest event, a celebration of Indian arts and culture that has drawn millions over the years to the city.

Source: Southwestern Association for Indian Arts.

Pedro Ribera Ortega

La Conquistadora needed protection, and The Caballeros de Vargas stepped up to the job. The Caballeros de Vargas needed a leader, and Pedro Ribera Ortega took charge. He is considered the founder of the group organized in 1956 as guardians of the Our Lady of Peace statue, popularly known as La Conquistadora, the oldest image of the Virgin Mary in the United States, first brought to Santa Fe in 1625. The Caballeros de Vargas and the statue have prominent roles in the most visible celebration of heritage, the annual Santa Fe Fiesta. Ortega taught Spanish, Latin and history for 30 years and wrote widely on Santa Fe traditions. He lived simply—a life dominated by books, writing and teaching—and died in 2003.

Source: Center for Southwest Research.

Pedro Ribera Ortega. *The Santa Fe New Mexican* **photo archives.**

José Antonio Esquibel

Hispanos are able to research readily their family histories thanks largely to the work of José Antonio Esquibel. A native of Santa Fe, Esquibel is a historian, lecturer and genealogist. He also is a prolific writer who is equally respected and well known for his willingness to share information on Hispanic heritage with anyone who asks. Esquibel frequently speaks to genealogy groups and presents his meticulous research—both well-known records and newly uncovered information—about Hispanic families.

Source: New Mexican Hispanic Culture Preservation League.

José Antonio Esquibel

Timeline

1200–1500s: Pueblo Indians establish villages in Rio Grande basin.

1680: Spanish Colonial Law gives governor legal as well as civil and military authority.

1598: Juan de Oñate establishes first Spanish settlement.

1609–10: Pedro de Peralta establishes Santa Fe. Book records founding of New Mexico.

1680: Pueblo Revolt forces Spanish to flee.

1692–93: Don Diego de Vargas recolonizes Santa Fe.

1712: Proclamation establishes Fiesta de Santa Fe.

1846: Mexican-American War begins. U.S. Army occupies Santa Fe.

1876: Lincoln County War gives rise to Billy the Kid, who's killed in 1881.

1891: Legislature pays to restore long-neglected archives.

1909: Legislature establishes Museum of New Mexico.

1929: Architect John Gaw Meem remodels La Fonda, blending preservation and design.

1936: Modern Indian Market celebrates Native arts and culture.

1945: Office of the State Historian is created.

1948: Native Americans win the right to vote in state elections.

1958: City enacts historic design ordinance.

Suggested Books

Chávez, Fray Angélico. *La Conquistadora, The Autobiography of an Ancient Statue*. Santa Fe: Sunstone Press, 1983.

Chávez, Fray Angélico. *Our Lady of the Conquest*. Santa Fe: Sunstone Press, 2010.

Chevalier, Jaima. *La Conquistadora, Unveiling the History of Santa Fe's Six Hundred Year Old Religious Icon*. Santa Fe: Sunstone Press, 2010.

Cornerstones Community Partnerships. *Adobe Conservation, A Preservation Handbook*. Santa Fe: Sunstone Press, 2006.

Haozous, Bob, Joseph M. Sanchez, and Lucy R. Lippard. *Bob Haozous: Indigenous Dialogue*. Santa Fe: Institute of American Indian Arts Museum, 2005.

Iowa, Jerome. *Ageless Adobe, History and Preservation in Southwestern Architecture*. Santa Fe: Sunstone Press, 2005.

Montaño, Mary Caroline. *Tradiciones Nuevomexicanas: Hispano Arts and Culture of New Mexico*. Albuquerque: The University of New Mexico Press, 2001.

Montgomery, Charles H. *The Spanish Redemption: Heritage, Power, and Loss on New Mexico's Upper Rio Grande*. Berkeley: University of California Press, 2002.

Nabokov, Peter. *Indian Running: Native American History and Tradition*. 2nd edition Santa Fe: Ancient City Press, 1987

Nieto-Phillips, John M. *The Language of Blood: The Making of Spanish-American Identity in New Mexico, 1880s-1930s*. Albuquerque: The University of New Mexico Press, 2004.

Pacheco, Ana. *Las Comidas De Los Abuelos: La Herencia, a Ten-Year Anniversary Cookbook*. Santa Fe: Gran Via, 2003.

Pérez de Villagrá, Gaspar, Miguel Encinias, Alfred Rodríguez, and Joseph P. Sánchez. *Historia de la Nueva México, 1610*. Pasó por aquí series. Albuquerque: The University of New Mexico Press, 1992.

Preucel, Robert W. *Archaeologies of the Pueblo Revolt: Identity, Meaning, and Renewal in the Pueblo World*. Albuquerque: The University of New Mexico Press, 2007.

Romero, Orlando, ed. *All Trails Lead to Santa Fe*. Santa Fe: Sunstone Press, 2010.

Sando, Joe S., and Herman Agoyo. *Po'pay: Leader of the First American Revolution*. Santa Fe: Clear Light Publishers, 2005.

Sheppard, Carl. *The Saint Francis Murals of Santa Fe, The Commission and the Artists*. Santa Fe: Sunstone Press, 1989.

Trimble, Stephen. *Talking with the Clay: The Art of Pueblo Pottery in the 21st Century*. Santa Fe: School for Advanced Research Press, 2007.

Twitchell, Ralph Emerson. *The Spanish Archives of New Mexico*. Vols. 1 and 2. Santa Fe: Sunstone Press, 2008.

Velarde, Pablita. *Old Father Storyteller*. Santa Fe: Clear Light Publishers, 1989

Weigle, Marta, and Peter White. *The Lore of New Mexico*. Albuquerque: The University of New Mexico Press, 1988.

Wilcox, Michael V. *The Pueblo Revolt and the Mythology of Conquest: An Indigenous Archaeology of Contact*. Berkeley: University of California Press, 2009.

Wilson, Chris. *The Myth of Santa Fe: Creating a Modern Regional Tradition*. Albuquerque: The University of New Mexico Press, 1997.

Suggested Websites
(active at time of publication)

History of Fiesta: www.santafefiesta.org
History of state historian: www.newmexicohistory.org/about_us/history.php
Hispanic Culture: www.nationalhispaniccenter.org
Indian Culture: www.indianartsandculture.org

8

Creativity

Santa Clara Pueblo artist Pablita Velarde (1918 – 2006). Photograph courtesy of the Palace of the Governors Photo Archives (NMHM/DCA), #174190.

Creative to Its Core: Cultures, Colors Inspired an Arts Community

by
Douglas Fairfield

Starting with the rock art of its earliest inhabitants, New Mexico has inspired creative expression for as long as people have lived there. Beginning at least 4,000 years ago, indigenous peoples have communicated through rock art and continue to reveal masterful skills in pottery and textiles. Four hundred years ago, Spanish explorers introduced an art based on religion that depicted both salvation and damnation, not to mention artful metalwork of arms and armor. Other newcomers followed as Santa Fe found itself in the path of America's westward expansion.

The consequent blend of cultures and dramatic landscapes drew hundreds of artists to take up residence in and near Santa Fe until a community congealed and gave birth to an economy based on the creative arts and arts-based tourism.

Santa Fe's 400th birthday in 2010 was an occasion to celebrate the creative impulse that attracts tens of thousands of visitors every year to the state's capital. "New Mexico, and Santa Fe in particular, are places where creativity abounds," said Stuart Ashman, secretary of the Department of Cultural Affairs. "Perhaps as a result of the pioneering spirit of the American West, which required individuals to constantly be resourceful, or as many have said before, the quality of light, the diversity of complex cultures, or perhaps it is the convergence of these over centuries in Santa Fe that has led to the 'City Different' being a place that fosters creative activity and thought."

Imagine Santa Fe without its 200-plus galleries, its museums, the Santa Fe Opera, Indian Market, Spanish Market, film festivals, the Lensic Performing Arts Center, the lowriders, descansos and Zozobra—plus all of the support industries that accommodate them. The city's raison d'être would be utterly diminished, its pulse on life support.

Earliest Artists

Prehistoric rock art—petroglyphs, pictographs and rock carvings—dating back to 2000 B.C. is found throughout New Mexico. Such markings and configurations conceived by the earliest Native peoples referenced the natural world in creative and cryptic ways. In a style known for its delineated simplicity, both figurative and abstract symbols inform contemporary concepts in fine art, jewelry, interior design, furniture, tableware and fashion motifs. Indian dances colorfully convey gratitude, hope and renewal, and Pueblo architecture still inspires Southwest building.

Museums and private collectors worldwide covet ancient pottery and vintage textiles adorned with indigenous designs, including clay vessels once used exclusively for utilitarian purposes. Production of Indian pots, beadwork, jewelry and rugs is integral to the survival of Native artists, as well as Santa Fe's tourist trade. Indian Market—initially called the "Indian Fair" in 1922 as part of Santa Fe Fiesta—is considered the world's pre-eminent sales event for Native art collectors. According to the Santa Fe-based Southwestern Association for Indian Arts, which sponsors the weekend event each August, Indian Market draws nearly 80,000 visitors and about $100 million in revenue to the state.

Indigenous craftwork entered the art market with the coming of the railroad in the late 19th century. Indians toted handmade wares to the train station stops in the frontier towns of Lamy, Las Vegas and Albuquerque. In addition, cross-country excursions to Indian reservations exposed Easterners to Pueblo life and culture. As curator Joseph Traugott wrote in the catalog to a New Mexico Museum of Art exhibition, *The Art of New Mexico: How the West Is One*, "As commercial ventures and cultural change followed the railroads through New Mexico during the 1880s, traders bought obsolete utilitarian items and religious paraphernalia. The early traders transformed them into commodities and energetically responded to requests for souvenirs of Native life. ... [And] Native makers often responded to contact with Victorian America by incorporating new forms, designs and materials." New Mexico's tourism industry was born.

In 1916, painter and teacher William Penhallow Henderson and his wife, Alice Corbin Henderson, a poet and associate editor of *Poetry* magazine, left Chicago for Santa Fe, where Alice was treated at Sunmount Sanitorium for advanced tuberculosis. A practicing architect, Henderson in 1926 established The Pueblo Spanish Building Company, devoted to creating Spanish-Pueblo Revival, or 'Santa Fe Style,' architecture and furniture. Photograph courtesy of the Palace of the Governors Photo Archives (NMHM/DCA), #013325.

By the 1920s, tourists were visiting Native enclaves. "In 1926, Fred Harvey and R. Hunter Clarkson developed auto side trips called the Indian Detours [which linked Las Vegas and Santa Fe hotels with] sightseeing trips to living pueblos, archaeological sites and geographical wonders, then [dropped] the 'Detourists' at their next train connection," historian Deborah Slaney wrote in *Jewel of the Railroad Era: Albuquerque's Alvarado Hotel*. Native artists continue to sell their wares under the portal at the Palace of the Governors, as well as on the plaza in Albuquerque's Old Town district.

The Spanish influence, both in religion and sacred art, is likewise essential to Santa Fe. Cathedrals and Catholic-based missions are graced with devotional iconography, and handcrafted santos (painted icons on wood panels), bultos (saints carved from wood) and altarpieces are found in museum shops and galleries.

El Día de los Muertos—the Day of the Dead—is a solemn and joyous Mexican tradition also celebrated in New Mexico. From October 31 to November 2, families honor deceased relatives by decorating their grave sites and creating elaborate memorials in their homes. Of particular note are the myriad ways in which artisans depict skeletal figures in various media in festive, communal postures, from singing and dancing to eating and drinking.

Such tradition and artistry by Hispanic artisans is found during Spanish Market the last full weekend in July. The colorful event—originally sponsored by the Spanish Colonial Arts Society in 1926 through the mid-1930s, then reintroduced in 1965—is now produced by the Museum of Spanish Colonial Art. Contemporary Hispanic Market runs concurrent with Spanish Market and showcases the best in nontraditional Hispanic art in various media.

Clusters of Creativity

To the north of Santa Fe, Taos is an oasis of respite and rejuvenation for artists who find it far removed—down-to-earth, exotic and less stressful—from their workaday lives elsewhere. In 1915, *The Santa Fe New Mexican* described Taos as a "mecca for tourists and artists [with] spectacular red men ... right at our door."

The serendipitous event that led to the founding of the Taos Society of Artists occurred in 1898, when New York artists Bert Geer Phillips and Ernest L. Blumenschein found their way into Taos while traveling to Mexico through New Mexico. When their wagon wheel broke, the men found Taos the closest settlement where the wheel could be fixed.

Phillips decided to stay in Taos, and Blumenschein moved there permanently in 1920. In 1915, the pair established the Taos Society of Artists, an exclusive group of painters visually taken by the vernacular subjects of Indians, adobe structures, provincial living conditions and spectacular landscapes, all under crystal-clear skies. The original group included Phillips, Blumenschein, E. Irving Couse, W. Herbert "Buck" Dunton, Oscar Berninghaus and Joseph

Henry Sharp (the man who recommended that Phillips and Blumenschein visit New Mexico following his first trip to Santa Fe in 1883).

Other noteworthy individuals who upheld Taos as a place for artistic endeavors were artist Emil Bisttram and socialite Mabel Dodge Luhan. According to art historian David Witt, Bisttram "founded the first contemporary art gallery in Taos, created its first art school, co-founded (with Raymond Jonson) the Transcendental Painting Group in the 1930s, and pushed into existence the Taos Artists Association and its artist cooperative Stables Gallery in the 1950s."

The transformation of Mabel Dodge from New York luminary to Taos guru is legendary. Her bohemian lifestyle and embrace of all that was Indian drew a stream of East Coast visionaries to her Southwest salon beginning in 1918. On 12 acres adjacent to Taos Pueblo, she built a three-story house with 22 rooms, five guest houses and a separate gatehouse to accommodate like-minded aesthetes.

During her lifetime, Dodge Luhan (she married Taos Pueblo member Antonio Luhan) was host to writers, painters, photographers and performing artists. Nearly a decade after Dodge Luhan's death, actor/director/artist Dennis Hopper purchased the Mabel Dodge Luhan House, where a new generation of counterculture types did their thing. Today, members of the arts intelligentsia still seek creative inspiration and renewal in Northern New Mexico.

The Santa Fe Art Colony was less structured, less organized and not chartered like its brethren to the north. "I try not to refer to the early artist community [in Santa Fe] as the Santa Fe Art Colony," local gallerist and arts writer Stacia Lewandowski said. "Even Gustave Baumann said as much in discussing Santa Fe—that what appealed to him about the situation here was precisely that there was not a tightly knit group of artists here, all working in common spirit—as is reflected by other art-colony type places."

For 50 years, painter/printmaker/marionette maker Baumann called Santa Fe home. According to Lewandowski, the art-colony moniker came via newspaper writers and the publication *El Palacio*, which lumped together artists of differing mind-sets as part of the local "art colony." Traugott put it succinctly in the *How the West Is One* catalog: "The artists moving to New Mexico after World War I brought along their artistic biases and aesthetic baggage."

Those who contributed to Santa Fe's artistic milieu during the first decades of the 20th century are a who's who of Southwest American art and modernism.

The most closely knit group of artists associated with Santa Fe at that time was *Los Cinco Pintores* (The Five Painters). Active from 1921 to 1926, its members were Jozef Bakos, Fremont F. Ellis, Walter Mruk, Willard Nash and William Schuster. "All five were under the age of thirty, full of high spirits and professing a popular view of art," writes art historian Sharyn Udall in *Modernist Painting in New Mexico*. "A shortage of funds seldom stood in the way of their optimism; the *Cincos* soon began to share raucous parties and built neighboring adobes on Camino del Monte Sol, for which they were affectionately labeled 'the five nuts in the adobe huts.'"

In 1923, another coalition of artists—most part of art circles in Taos and Santa Fe—organized themselves as the New Mexico Painters. "The group was a nebulous organization and attracted established painters who were modernists or were incorporating aspects of modernist style into their academic paintings," Traugott wrote.

Also during that decade, landscape painter Warren Rollins—the "dean of the Santa Fe Art Colony"—became the first president of the Santa Fe Arts Club. Although never successful financially, it was a clearinghouse for diverse cultural events in Santa Fe and sponsored guest speakers and artists' receptions.

In 1938, the most experimental art group in New Mexico—the Transcendental Group of Painters—came together through the efforts of Bisttram and Jonson. A partial reading of their artistic philosophy—taken from their first group exhibition in Santa Fe—is telling:

> The Transcendental Painting Group is … concerned with the development and presentation of various types of non-representational painting; painting that finds its source in the creative imagination and does not depend upon the objective approach. The word Transcendental … best expresses its aim, which is to carry painting beyond the appearance of the physical world, through new concepts of space, color, light and design, to imaginative realms that are idealistic and spiritual. The work does not concern itself with political, economic or other social problems.

Passing on cultural treasures

Until the city's galleries took root starting in the 1960s, the Palace of the Governors, as well as the Museum of Fine Arts (built in 1917 as the

Museum of New Mexico Art Gallery and now called the New Mexico Museum of Art) were exhibition venues for New Mexico artists. The museum's collection database now contains the names of 2,900 artists who lived in New Mexico at one time or another.

But as art historian Julie Schimmel noted in her introductory essay to *Santa Fe Art Colony*, as early as 1886, W.P. Blair's pharmacy hosted an exhibit of paintings by art teachers Harold Elderkin and his wife, along with student work from their classes at the Plaza Art Studio. In the late 1890s, the Seligman Brothers general store installed work by landscape painter George Stanley.

The Hal West Gallery on Canyon Road. Photograph by Roy Rosen

The current gallery scene in Santa Fe began modestly in the 1960s. According to Lewandowski, Jean Seth was a key player in promoting its growth. "[Jean] operated the Seth Gallery on Canyon Road in the mid-1960s," she said. "She handled contemporary artists, both Anglo and Native American, along with works by established Santa Fe/New Mexico artists. Willard Clark [with his daughter] also had a gallery, the DAS Gallery, on Canyon Road that started in the '60s. These were important establishments that helped spur the real growth that followed in the 1970s."

Today, every possible genre, medium and style of art can be seen in Santa Fe, including historic, modernist and contemporary. In three distinct locales—Canyon Road, the Plaza and the Railyard—galleries outnumber grocery stores and car dealerships combined. In fact, for the past few years, Santa Fe has been one of the top three art markets in the country, keeping in lock step with New York and Los Angeles.

Educational institutions in New Mexico have stoked creative fires for decades, boasting some of the nation's most forward-looking art students and faculty. Among them have been painter Richard Diebenkorn, who studied at The University of New Mexico during the 1950s, and Elaine de Kooning, a visiting professor there from 1958 to 1959. Photographer and photo historian Beaumont Newhall, who founded New York's Museum of Modern Art photography department in 1940, was a faculty member at The University of New Mexico from 1971 to 1984. In 1970, as part of their School of Art and Art History and under the guidance of Clinton Adams and Garo Antreasian, Tamarind Institute moved to Albuquerque from Los Angeles and has since hosted a distinguished roster of the world's top printmakers.

An act of Congress in 1962 established the Institute of American Indian Arts (IAIA). Overseen by George Boyce and artist Lloyd Kiva New, original faculty members included Allan Houser, Fritz Scholder and Charles Loloma. More recently, Melanie Yazzie, Charlene Teters and Linda Lomahaftewa, among others, have provided formal art instruction to Native students from throughout North America.

But formal art education for Indians predated the founding of IAIA by decades. In 1932, Dorothy Dunn, a recent graduate of the School of the Art Institute of Chicago, established the Studio School at the Santa Fe Indian School. Rigid in her teaching methods and demanding a style geared more to illustration than fine art, Dunn nevertheless nurtured a sense of creativity and confidence in her students that allowed some to make a living as artists.

Further opportunities for art education in Santa Fe include the New Mexico School for the Arts, St. John's College, Santa Fe Art Institute, Santa Fe Community College, Santa Fe Photography Workshops and Santa Fe University of Art and Design (formerly the College of Santa Fe).

Those who simply love to admire creativity can travel throughout the state and take part in 43 studio tours that occur annually between April and December. From Farmington to Santa Fe to Silver City, artistic currents in

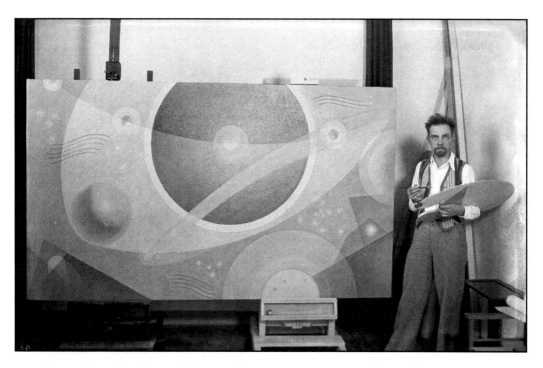

After moving to Santa Fe in 1924 to pursue his painting career, Raymond Jonson (1891 – 1982) began his work with abstract landscapes and quickly moved toward nonobjective painting. Photograph by T. Harmon Parkhurst, courtesy Palace of the Governors Photo Archives (NMHM/DCA), # 073938.

Artists Linked With Associations or Organizations

Santa Fe Indian School:

T.C. Cannon, Earl Biss, Marcus Amerman, Dan Namingha, Kevin Red Star, Roxanne Swentzel, Harrison Begay and Pablita Velarde.

Los Cinco Pintores **(The Five Painters) of Santa Fe:**

Jozef Bakos, Fremont F. Ellis, Walter Mruk, Willard Nash and William Schuster.

Santa Fe Art Colony:

In her book *Santa Fe Art Colony*, art historian Sharyn Udall listed Frank Applegate, Cyrus Baldridge, Henry Balink, Gustave Baumann, E. Boyd, Paul Burlin, Gerald Cassidy, Andrew Dasburg, Randall Davey, Stuart Davis, Marsden Hartley, William Henderson, Robert Henri, Russell Vernon Hunter, Raymond Jonson, Gina Knee, Alfred Morang, B.J.O. Nordfeldt, Sheldon Parsons, Julius Rolshoven, John Sloan, Theodore Van Soelen, and Carlos Vierra, who, in 1904, became Santa Fe's first resident artist.

Transcendental Group of Painters:

Co-founders Emil Bisttram and Raymond Jonson brought together artists Robert Gribboek, Lawren Harris, William Lumpkins, Florence Miller, Pelton, H. Towner Pierce and Stuart Walker.

Taos Society of Artists:

Walter Ufer, Victor Higgins, Randall Davey, Robert Henri, and John Sloan, all of whom spent time in Santa Fe as well, according to David Witt's book *Modernists in Taos*.

The Taos Colony:

Led by Mabel Dodge Luhan, it included writers Mary Austin, Willa Cather, Aldous Huxley, Spud Johnson, D.H. Lawrence and Jean Toomer; painters Andrew Dasburg, Dorothy Brett, Maynard Dixon, Nicolai Fechin, Ernest Knee, Marsden Hartley, John Marin, Georgia O'Keeffe, Cady Wells and Agnes Pelton; photographers Laura Gilpin, Ansel Adams, Edward Weston and Paul Strand; composer and conductor Leopold Stokowski; theater designer Robert Edmond Jones; choreographer Martha Graham; and social theorist Carl Jung. This list is from author Lois Rudnick's *Utopian Vistas*.

Native Artists Still Exploring 'The Edge'

by
Paul Weideman

What's trendy in Native American art? Well, just about everything if the categories for Santa Fe Indian Market are any indicator. Ceramic pots, turquoise-and-silver jewelry, beadwork, quillwork, concho belts, wooden carvings and rugs are all in demand at this annual event, which features quality, Native-made art pieces from all over the continent.

Many of the styles are traditional, but the market is also a barometer of what's new and unusual. At the first market in 1922, the black-on-black pots by Maria Martinez (San Ildefonso) were all the rage. In 1995, she and Apache artist Allan Houser won lifetime achievement awards from the Southwestern Association for Indian Arts (SWAIA), presenter of Indian Market. The Museum of New Mexico launched Indian Market to "provide the opportunity to simultaneously educate the potter and the buyer to appreciate Indian art as it had been before its transformation by non-Native cultures into curios and souvenirs," according to SWAIA.

The annual market takes place in an atmosphere of camaraderie among artists and collectors. In 1969, when the market was still small enough to fit under the portal of the Palace of the Governors, *The Santa Fe New Mexican* said, "The event gives one the opportunity of buying a fine piece of traditional Southwestern Indian art directly from the Indian who made it."

The palette of Native artworks in the 21st century includes distinctly contemporary items, like wall sculptures by Hopi artist Arlo Namingha that are abstract landscapes in woods, limestone and aluminum, and handblown glass figures with silver dust by Tony Jojola of Isleta Pueblo.

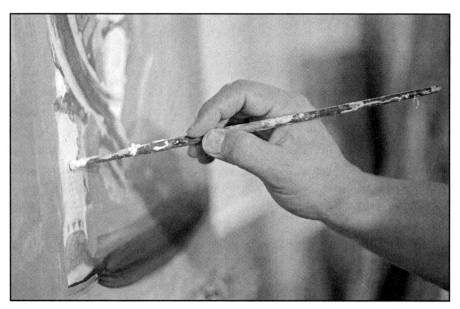

Works by Mateo Romero include realistic paintings of ceremonial dances, as well as more abstract works like lithographs and mixed-media paintings. Photographs by Luis Sánchez Saturno.

Mateo Romero makes realistic paintings of ceremonial dances, as well as more abstract works like lithographs and mixed-media paintings. The son of Cochití Pueblo watercolorist Santiago Romero was born and raised in the San Francisco Bay Area. After undergraduate work at Dartmouth College, he earned a master's degree in printmaking from The University of New Mexico.

In a conversation about today's Native artists, he said influences vary wildly. "Dan Lomahaftewa was influenced by Hopi petroglyph and pictograph art, so you can look at his work and say, 'This is an example of an artist with kind of a thesis element in his work,'" Romero said. "Then you look at the Fort Marion artists, Plains Indians who were basically imprisoned [at Fort Marion in St. Augustine, Florida, starting in 1875 as part of the Indian Wars] and began making ledger art to sell as a means to support themselves and their families. In a sense, it's kind of the beginning of one evolution of Native artists who are producing work for an external audience for money."

The paintings of Fritz Scholder encapsulate a history of painting, Romero said. "His work maybe starts with Cezanne and the modernism of the multiple perspectives, then from there I'd look at Matisse with the kind of flat color fields and fauvism, and then I'd look at the Bay Area abstract figurative stuff like Nathan Oliveira, who was a heavy influence in Scholder's early work. Scholder also borrowed heavily from T.C. Cannon and Bill Soza Warsoldier when he was a student…. In his history is all that stuff that comes before him."

The "Indian art" world in 2010 embraced video, digital photography and diverse works by installation and performance artists. "And there's actually a street-art movement, where people are doing graffiti art, like Native guerrilla art," Romero said. "The edge is where things occur. It's never the center where the art changes."

Romero doesn't claim to be on that edge. "People who come too close to making a living with art like me get known for a certain kind of work," he said. "But I also think the kind of weird, interesting, quirky stuff that is on the edge becomes the center eventually. Will Wilson is an edgy guy, and right now he might be considered the videograph, digital installation guy who's not that well understood, but in five or 10 years that may totally change. It's just the process of people consuming art and artists."

Santeros Nurture Tradition, Innovation

by
Michael Abatemarco

An image of San Rafael, painted in 1780 by Spanish soldier, cartographer and engineer Bernardo Miera y Pacheco, is among the oldest examples of the santero tradition in New Mexico in existence. Miera y Pacheco came to Santa Fe in 1754 in service to Spain, and his creation was originally commissioned by Doña Apolonia de Sandoval, a prominent Santa Fean; it's now in the Museum of Spanish Colonial Art. Miera y Pacheco is considered the first santero in New Mexico.

Commissioned to create *rerados* (altarpieces), bultos (figures carved in the round) and retablos (icons of saints painted on wood panels) by private citizens and by the Catholic church, saint makers of today continue the tradition of early santeros like Miera y Pacheco.

By the late 18th and early 19th centuries, saint makers had developed a distinct visual vocabulary that included a lexicon of popular saints. As devout Catholics, santeros lived and worked close to the church. According to art historian Charlie Carrillo, a barrio that was home to a collective of artisans and other woodworkers stood across from St. Francis Cathedral in downtown Santa Fe. "The entire district was where all the woodworkers of Santa Fe lived," said Carrillo, whose work is the subject of a book, *Charlie Carrillo: Tradition & Soul/Tradición y Alma* by Barbe Awalt and Paul Rhetts. "It was one extended family and they controlled the entire woodworking

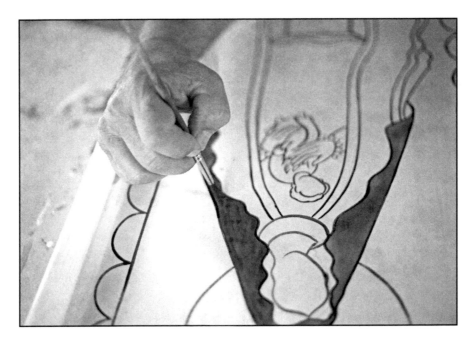

Art historian and santero Charlie Carrillo works on a retablo of La Conquistadora in July 2010. Photograph by Luis Sánchez Saturno

During Spanish colonial times, artisans who painted or sculpted images of saints were called *pintores* or *escultores*. "Colonial documents have lots of references to some of the great santeros being referred to as *pintores*," Carrillo said. "The word 'santero' was never used during the colonial period. That word was introduced by Anglo patrons in the 1920s and '30s."

The railroad in the 19th century brought manufactured paints and dyes and pre-cut lumber, and these commodities changed the lives of some santeros. Traditional saint makers had used natural pigments to color their work, and these had to be gathered and ground by hand. They included egg temperas, oil colors and vegetal dyes, and their preferred panels were made of soft woods such as cottonwood and pine. "That [original] tradition continues from the 1750s uninterrupted until the present," said Carrillo, "even though people say it died in the 1900s."

Not all practicing santeros, including Carrillo, depict saints within a strict iconographic lexicon. He sees room for innovation in techniques and imagery. Contemporary artist Luis Tapia, for instance, depicts ordinary people in artwork intended as social commentary. Early in his career, Tapia was criticized by other santeros for introducing bright colors and acrylic paints into his work. Tapia no longer exhibits with the traditional Spanish Market because of the market's strict guidelines for materials and techniques.

"I started dealing more with social issues and issues relating to the Catholic church," Tapia said. "My work was getting more intense with regard to those issues." In 2008, Tapia exhibited *Man Without a Heart*, a sculpture ridiculing the hypocrisy of pedophile priests who continue to administer religious rites, as part of an exhibition called ¡Orale! at the former Owings Dewey Gallery.

But the santero tradition has always seen trends. Figures such as San Isidro and the Virgin of Guadalupe have always been popular, while santos like San Pasqual are more popular today than in Spanish colonial times. "I've never seen a San Pasqual from colonial New Mexico," said Carrillo. "They don't exist."

Today, the traditional market allows more innovation than it did in the 1970s, when Tapia exhibited there. "They're allowing the artists to be more creative, which is what they should have done since Day One," he said.

Images of the santero are an enduring tradition, Carrillo said. "There will always be a place for these devotional paintings. But then there's going to be the clients and the galleries who enjoy seeing things that step out of boundaries. So I think there's room for everybody."

Contemporary artist Luis Tapia and his grandson, Andres Garcia, work on a chair in July 2010.
Photograph by Katharine Egli.

Personalities: Inspiring Santa Fe

by
Rob DeWalt, Michael Abatemarco and Paul Weideman

María Benítez

New Mexico native, flamenco legend and Institute of Spanish Arts founder María Benítez may have "retired" a few years ago, but her participation and influence in the local arts community dances on. After moving to Santa Fe in the early 1970s, Benítez established her dance company, María Benítez Teatro Flamenco, and presented 12-week summer performance seasons until 2008. She also developed Flamenco's Next Generation, the local youth company (ages 10-18), in 2001 and has been a dancer and choreographer for the Santa Fe Opera. Her first collaboration with SFO was a 1975 production of Manuel de Falla's *La Vida*

María Benítez in 2007. Photograph by Ramsay de Give.

Breve, and she choreographed 2006's production of *Carmen*. Also in 2006, Benítez was honored with Spain's most prestigious award for artistic achievement, La Cruz de la Orden de Isabel la Católica. Among regional accolades, she has been awarded the New Mexico Governor's Award for Excellence in the Arts and the city of Santa Fe Mayor's Arts Award.

John Crosby

Musician/composer John Crosby (1926–2002) founded the Santa Fe Opera in 1957 with $20,000 in seed money borrowed from his father. He served as the opera's general director for 44 seasons. During the opera's first season, Crosby impressed audiences with the staging of Igor Stravinsky's *The Rake's Progress*. Stravinsky oversaw the production personally, solidifying Santa Fe Opera's place as a young but ambitious player on the international operatic stage. (Crosby went on to mount all of Stravinsky's stage works, although Strauss became a more indelible Santa Fe Opera trademark.) During Crosby's tenure, he introduced and fostered the singer and technician apprentice programs, commissioned or presented U.S. debuts of works by Britten, Henze, Menotti, Penderecki and many others, and established Santa Fe as one of the world's top destinations for enjoying opera.

John Crosby. Photograph courtesy of the Santa Fe Opera.

The Rubber Lady on the Plaza in 1988. Photograph by Leslie Tallant.

The Rubber Lady

After arriving in Santa Fe in the late 1970s, the Rubber Lady appeared at local galleries, museums and public spaces for more than a decade. The performance artist's identity was once a closely guarded secret (no, we're not telling you who she is), and today she continues to passionately participate in Santa Fe's arts community, as do a few people who stood in for her on occasion. Her presence often stirred up as much controversy as it did lively conversation: Her rubber suit was stolen in 1981 but was eventually recovered in a bus-station locker, and in 1983 *The Santa Fe New Mexican* printed a letter from a reader complaining that she was "downright weird." Still, the Rubber Lady typified the open-mindedness, creativity and optimism—and provided the requisite absurdism during absurd times—that allowed Santa Fe's arts community to weather the era's Wall Street excesses and an economic recession. What's old is new again.

Paula Castillo

Paula Castillo creates some of the heaviest art around: Her rather visceral sculptures are made from recycled steel, and she thinks about complexity science while she's making them. The Belen native, now a longtime resident of the village of Cordova, earned her bachelor's degree at The University of New Mexico and her master's at the College of Santa Fe. The wonderful shapes and surfaces she has coaxed from industrial refuse range up to the monumental. Two of these, *Dos Arboles, Dos Hermanas* and *Rio Grande Colcha*, frame the entrance of the New Mexico History Museum.

Paula Castillo. Photograph courtesy Palace of the Governors Photo Archives (NMHM/DCA) Neg. #013325.

T.C. Cannon

Kiowa painter T.C. Cannon was born in Oklahoma and attended the Institute of American Indian Arts as a teenager in the mid-1960s. Also a poet and musician, he went on to develop a distinctive style that sometimes incorporated social commentary. "His large, bold paintings often stirred controversy for their humorous or bitter portrayal of their Indian subjects," said a story in *The Santa Fe New*

T.C. Cannon. Photograph by Herbert Lotz, courtesy Palace of the Governors Photo Archives (NMHM/DCA) Neg. #HP.2010.15.7.

Mexican the day after Cannon was killed in a car crash in the spring of 1978. Two years earlier, he appeared in the book *Song From the Earth: American Indian Painting.* "I have something to say about the experience that comes out of being an Indian, but it is also a lot bigger than just my race," he told author Jamake Highwater. "It's got to do with my own mythology, the one I make up myself. That's what I want to express in my paintings."

Laura Gilpin

Photographer Laura Gilpin began taking pictures of New Mexico's landscape and Pueblo Indians in the 1920s and went on to document Navajo people beginning in 1930. The Colorado native moved to Santa Fe in 1946 and died here 33 years later. Her books include *The Rio Grande: River of Destiny* (1949) and *The Enduring Navajo* (1968). Our state has been home to many inspired photographers. Among the most famous photographic images of New Mexico are Ansel Adams' *Moonrise, Hernandez, New Mexico* (1941) and *Saint Francis Church, Ranchos de Taos, New Mexico* (c. 1929). Other noteworthy resident or visiting photographers or teachers of photography included William Henry Jackson, Edward S. Curtis, Dorothea Lange, Beaumont Newhall, Edward Weston, Eliot Porter, Henri Cartier-Bresson, Van Deren Coke and Paul Caponigro.

Laura Gilpin. Photograph courtesy Palace of the Governors Photo Archives (NMHM/DCA), # 013325.

Rose B. Simpson

Rose B. Simpson, daughter of Santa Clara ceramic sculptor Roxanne Swentzell and Anglo contemporary artist Patrick Simpson, has practiced sculpture, printmaking, creative writing, dance and music. Simpson was the lead singer in the local bands Chocolate Helicopter and The Wake Singers. Her art portfolio includes autobiographical, figure-based pieces such as *Punk Rock Doll, 2007* and a joint project with her aunt, Nora Naranjo-Morse, and cousin, Eliza Naranjo-Morse, for SITE Santa Fe's 2008 biennial. Other works are difficult to describe. She is working toward her master of fine arts degree in ceramics at the Rhode Island School of Design.

Rose B. Simpson. Courtesy photograph from *The Santa Fe New Mexican* archives.

Arthur Lopez

Arthur Lopez has been doing solo exhibitions at Parks Gallery in Taos since 2003, not long after he began carving santos full time. The Santa Fe native began his career as a santero in his late 20s, making bultos and retablos, after a career working as a graphic artist. Although Lopez is comfortable working with traditional images of saints in the New Mexico santero tradition, his innovations and his social commentaries on contemporary issues are his claim to fame in the contemporary art world. Lopez steps away from traditional imagery, while maintaining the santero's traditions of gathering wood to carve and paint by hand with natural pigments. His sculptures often present scathing commentary on themes of social justice, politics and religion. What emerges is a highly stylized and expressive art form that resembles the statuesque carvings of earlier forms but speaks to the world of today, rendered with extraordinary attention to detail.

Arthur Lopez in 2005. Photograph by Jane Phillips.

Timeline

Before 1500s: Natives elevate weaving to a high art, creating baskets, clothing, sandals and utensils.

1598: Spanish colonial life raises to art form activities associated with everyday life and religious practice—carving, tin work and weaving.

1821: Santa Fe Trail opens.

1878: Railroad opens migration from the east.

1898: First movie filmed in New Mexico.

1915: Taos Society of Artists organizes.

1917: New Mexico builds the Museum of Art.

1921 – 1926: Los Cinco Pintores, the five painters, active in Santa Fe.

1922: Indian Market begins.

1926: Spanish Colonial Arts Society forms.

1932: Studio School opens at Santa Fe Indian School.

1995: SITE Santa Fe opens to celebrate contemporary art.

Suggested Books

Carrillo, Charles. *Saints of the Pueblos*. Los Ranchos de Albuquerque: LPD Press, 2004.

Chauvenet, Beatrice. *Hewett and Friends: A Biography of Santa Fe's Vibrant Era*. Santa Fe: Museum of New Mexico Press, 1983.

Cirillo, Dexter, Michel Monteaux, and Stephen Northup. *Southwestern Indian Jewelry*. New York: Abbeville Press, 1992.

D'Emilio, Sandra, and Suzan Campbell. *Visions & Visionaries: The Art and Artists of the Santa Fe Railway*. Salt Lake City: Peregrine Smith Books, 1991.

Feder, Norman. *American Indian Art*. New York: Harrison House/H.N. Abrams, 1982.

Flynn, Kathryn A. *Treasures on New Mexico Trails, Discover New Deal Art and Architecture*. Santa Fe: Sunstone Press, 1995.

Foster, Barbara Spencer. *Fremont F. Ellis, Last of Los Cinco Pintores of Santa Fe*. Santa Fe: Sunstone Press, 2010.

Garman, Ed. *The Art of Raymond Jonson, Painter*. Albuquerque: The University of New Mexico Press, 1976.

Garmhausen, Winona. *History of Indian Arts Education in Santa Fe: The Institute of American Indian Arts with Historical Background, 1890 – 1962*. Santa Fe: Sunstone Press, 1988.

Hammett, Jerilou, Kingsley Hammett and Peter Scholz. *The Essence of Santa Fe: From a Way of Life to a Style*. Santa Fe: Ancient City Press, 2006.

Hassrick, Peter H., Elizabeth J. Cunningham, and Ernest Leonard Blumenschein. *In Contemporary Rhythm: The Art of Ernest L. Blumenschein*. Norman: University of Oklahoma Press, 2008.

Hoefer, Jacqueline. *A More Abundant Life, New Deal Artists and Public Art in New Mexico*. Santa Fe: Sunstone Press, 2003.

Levin, Eli. *Santa Fe Bohemia*. Santa Fe: Sunstone Press, 2006.

Lisle, Laurie. *Portrait of an Artist: A Biography of Georgia O'Keeffe*. New York: Washington Square Press, 1980.

Luhan, Mabel Dodge. *Lorenzo in Taos*. Santa Fe: Sunstone Press, 2007.

Luhan, Mabel Dodge. *Winter in Taos*. Santa Fe: Sunstone Press, 2007/

Mather, Christine, and Sharon Woods. *Santa Fe Style*. New York: Rizzoli, 1986.

Nestor, Sarah. *The Native Market of the Spanish New Mexican Craftsmen, Santa Fe, 1933 – 1940*. Santa Fe: Sunstone Press, 2009.

Reily, Nancy Hopkins. *Georgia O'Keeffe, A Private Friendship: Part I, Walking the Sun Prairie Land*. Santa Fe: Sunstone Press, 2007.

Reily, Nancy Hopkins. *Georgia O'Keeffe, A Private Friendship: Part II, Walking the Abiquiu and Ghost Ranch Land*. Santa Fe: Sunstone Press, 2009.

Robertson, Edna, and Sarah Nestor. *Artists of the Canyons and Caminos: Santa Fe, Early Twentieth Century*. Layton: Ancient City Press, 2006.

Rudnick, Lois, ed. *Intimate Memories, The Autobiography of Mabel Dodge Luhan*. Santa Fe: Sunstone Press, 2008.

Rudnick, Lois. *Utopian Vistas: The Mabel Dodge Luhan House and the American Counterculture*. Albuquerque: The University of New Mexico Press, 1998.

Schaafsma, Polly. *Indian Rock Art of the Southwest*. Santa Fe: School of American Research, 1980.

Slaney, Deborah Christine, and David Nufer. *Jewel of the Railroad Era: Albuquerque's Alvarado Hotel*. Albuquerque: Albuquerque Museum, 2009.

Udall, Sharyn Rohlfsen. *Modernist Painting in New Mexico. 1913 – 1935*. Albuquerque: The University of New Mexico Press, 1984.

Udall, Sharyn Rohlfsen. *Santa Fe Art Colony, 1900-1942*. Santa Fe: Gerald Peters Gallery, 1987.

Verzuh, Valerie K, and Addison Doty. *A River Apart: The Pottery of Cochiti & Santo Domingo Pueblos*. Santa Fe: Museum of New Mexico Press, 2008.

Weigle, Marta, and Kyle Fiore. *Santa Fe and Taos, The Writer's Era, 1916 – 1941.* Santa Fe: Sunstone Press, 2008.

Wells, Cady, Lois Palken Rudnick, Robin Farwell Gavin, and Sharyn Rohlfsen Udall. *Cady Wells and Southwestern Modernism.* Santa Fe: Museum of New Mexico Press, 2009.

White, Robert R. *The Taos Society of Artists.* Albuquerque: The University of New Mexico Press, 1983.

Wilson, Chris. *The Myth of Santa Fe, Creating a Modern Regional Tradition.* Albuquerque: The University of New Mexico Press, 1997.

Witt, David. *Modernists in Taos: From Dasburg to Martin.* Santa Fe: Red Crane Books, 2002.

Wurzburger, Rebecca, and Tom Aageson, Alex Pattakos and Sabrina Pratt, eds. *Creative Tourism, A Global Conversation: How to Provide Unique Creative Experiences for Travelers Worldwide.* Santa Fe: Sunstone Press, 2010.

Suggested websites
(active at time of publication)

Art Santa Fe: www.artsantafe.com
Institute of American Indian Arts: www.iaia.edu/index.php
Pablita Velarde: www.newmexicohistory.org/filedetails_docs.php?fileID=417
Spanish Colonial Arts: www.spanishcolonial.org

9

Learning

Anita Nugent (Gerlach) teaches science at Santa Fe High in September 2010.

César Chávez Elementary School fourth-grade teacher Fernando Morales gets a hug goodbye from Lalyla Garcia, 9, in September 2010. Photographs by Jane Phillips.

Enduring Love of Learning: Teaching is a Gift that Runs in the Family

by
Robert Nott

For close to three centuries—before New Mexico achieved statehood in 1912—the state's school system developed and transformed under the governance of three different flags. Education in the state was heavily influenced by the various cultures, the impact of the Catholic church, and political upheaval and corruption.

Missionaries and their wives often served as teachers from the 1600s through the 1800s, imparting their version of the "3 Rs"—reading, writing and religion—on students, often with the purpose of Christianizing Native Americans of all ages. "Little is known about their qualifications as teachers except that they were religious and knew the English language," authors John B. Mondragón and Ernest S. Stapleton note in their 2005 history, *Public Education in New Mexico*. The state's School Code of 1860, for instance, simply specified that people who wanted to teach had to prove they could read and write. Fortunately, the state requires a bachelor's degree and teaching license these days.

Over 400 years, curriculum has changed as technological advances continue to make computers, SMART boards and document cameras as necessary as pencil and paper in the classroom.

But one element that has remained consistent over the years is the passion and dedication of teachers. Just 40 teachers were listed in the 1840 state census. For the 2010-2011 school year, New Mexico had budgeted about 21,000 teachers. Santa Fe Public Schools employed roughly 900 teachers.

This is the story of three of them, at the start of the school year in September, 2010.

"This is the most exciting profession in the world," Fernando Morales said.

Around 1:40 p.m. every day the fourth-graders in Fernando Morales' portable classroom at César Chávez Elementary School look at the clock on the wall. They're anticipating story time at 2 p.m., which Morales uses to "promote the love of reading."

"I'm trying to share my love of learning with them," he said.

It's paying off. He got a beautiful note from one of his kids two Mondays ago, which read, "Thank you for the best first day of school I ever had." Just this week, another student said to him, "This year I like coming to school every day!"

Morales likes coming to school, too. This is his fifth year. He started out in college studying pre-law, until the enthusiastic teaching style of a professor at New Mexico Highlands University—Daniel Holguin—inspired him to change course. Morales had already applied to The University of New Mexico's law school in 2005. He still has the university's response letter, although he said, "I have not opened it to see if I was accepted or not."

Instead he got his teaching degree at the College of Santa Fe and started at César Chávez as a second-grade teacher. His family isn't surprised: His late grandma, Ruth L. Dominguez, taught in a three-room schoolhouse in Chamisal back in the 1950s, and both his mother, Yolanda Morales, and his father, Gene Morales, still work as educators in Albuquerque Public Schools. Plus he has "cousins, aunts, siblings" who teach—all but one in New Mexico. His wife, Amy, teaches fifth grade at César Chávez.

His grandmother told him stories of teaching in the old days. Some things have changed; others have not. "I've thought about the past," he said. "It would have been interesting to be teaching in not necessarily a slower paced time, but a time when you relied on the old pencil and paper. I think there was a lot more creativity in the school room 50 or 100 years ago."

His classroom is filled with books, colorful objects, maps, animal figurines and an energetic lizard in a glass cage. (One student said it is a gecko; another claims it is a gila monster. Either way, nobody tries to pet it.)

César Chávez Elementary School fourth-grade teacher Fernando Morales in his classroom. Photograph by Jane Phillips

He encourages parental involvement but doesn't blame parents for kids' academic failure: "A lot of parents are working two jobs just to survive." But he still recalls his own worst day at school: "A kid showed up with evidence that she was being beaten by her stepmother. She couldn't concentrate that day. She spent 80 percent of the day crying. But she was much safer at school than at home, so she stayed here."

He's in his early 30s, and wants to teach until he retires. "To me, it's a very noble profession, to be able to make a difference in the lives of these children," he said. He runs into former students who remember him, who run up to him and hug him and tell him about their most recent academic achievements.

"They tell me how proud they are that they got an 'A' on a test," he said. "They still want you to be proud of them. And I always want to be proud of them."

"I want them to follow in my footsteps," Christina Lujan said.

It's 1 p.m. or so in the gym at Nava Elementary School, and the Cookie Monster is loose. He's hungry, and he'll happily gobble up the other first-graders in physical education teacher Christina Lujan's gym class.

Lujan knows that a lot of people think she's got it made. After all, she doesn't have to grade homework or keep the kids quiet during a math test. But it's not always easy to corral 30-some students and engage them in a coordinated athletic exercise—although the first-graders do like playing the catch-and-evade game of Cookie Monster. When that class leaves, she shifts gears, working with sixth-graders to teach them the proper technique behind football.

Lujan, 46, stays on her feet for seven or eight class periods in a row (minus a 30-minute lunch break). She taught at Ortiz Middle School for five years before transferring to Nava. One day an English teacher at Ortiz said to her, "You have it so easy."

"And then he had to take over my class one day," Lujan recalled. "He came back exhausted and said, 'I was wrong. I couldn't even take roll.' "

PE teacher Christina Lujan, a fourth-generation teacher, gets an exercise ready for her first-graders at Nava Elementary School in September 2010. Photograph by Jane Phillips.

A graduate of Santa Fe High and a long-distance runner, Lujan received a cross country scholarship at Navajo Community College (now Diné College) in Tsaile, Arizona. She earned her bachelor's and master's at New Mexico Highlands University. She started teaching physical education at Capshaw Middle School in 1990. Lujan's great-grandfather was superintendent of Union County, New Mexico, up Clayton way, back about 90 years ago. Her great-aunt, Amalia Castillo Bernal, raised Lujan's mother, Alice—both women became teachers.

Bernal ran the typical one-room school house in Colfax County, in northeastern New Mexico, in the 1920s and 1930s. "She was everything: the principal, the teacher, even the janitor," Lujan said. "My mother would go with her to school early to build a fire to keep the school house warm."

These women taught Lujan a valuable lesson about her trade: "You won't make much money. It's hard. You have to love what you do."

In this day and age, Lujan said, a teacher must double as counselor, disciplinarian, parent, friend and even confidante.

"You have to be everything to them," she said. "I try to be a positive role model."

Parents don't usually come by to talk to her during parent/teacher conferences; they're not that concerned if their child is failing gym class. But Lujan said she's rarely wrong when it comes to correlating how children are doing in her class with their academic standing in other areas.

"I can tell which kids do well in the classroom and which do not," she said. "I'll see the other teachers in the lounge and say, 'He can't read, can he?' They'll say, 'How did you know?'

"Because he can't skip. You can tell by how they pay attention, how they follow the rules, how they move."

She stresses cooperation, not competition, in sports. "For me, it's not about winning or losing, it's about exercise," she said. "I want them all to feel comfortable when they are exercising and not feel like they're bad at P.E." She bemoans the lack of physical activity that children get outside of school today. Too much TV, not enough play time, she thinks. Technology keeps kids glued to video and computer screens way too much, in her view.

She understands why people think the school system is failing their children, but she also believes it's not an entirely accurate picture. "Nobody gives us credit for what their kids are learning," she said. "And I don't think tests are a good measure of success. I know kids who are doing well in school but perform badly on tests."

"I'm proud of what I do. My passion is being active, and I want my kids to share that passion. The best thing about this is having contact with the kids, being there for them. I want them to follow in my footsteps."

"You'll learn life … in physics class," Anita Nugent (Gerlach) said.

She's 66 years old and stands just over five feet tall, and she's wearing a crazy contraption on her head that's made out of an old wire hanger and a pair of small weights. It looks like the outline of a court jester's crown, and as she turns in a circle under it, and it remains stationary, it demonstrates the theory of inertia to her class.

She tells her students that knowledge of science can come in handy as she teaches them about displacement—the difference between the initial and final destination of an object or person.

"See, if Mom and Dad ground you for the weekend, but you sneak out when they're not looking and take the car to the mall and then come back and park the car exactly where it was when you started, and they ask if you went anywhere while they were gone, you can truthfully tell them that your displacement was zero," she once told her students.

Anita Nugent (Gerlach) has been teaching in New Mexico for 25 years. Photograph by Jane Phillips.

"All that hoopla about kids and how awful they are—nonsense," Anita explained. "If you respect them and gain their respect, you can make it work."

She's Texas-born. Her uncle and aunt were educators around Eastland, Texas, in the 1940s; he worked into the 1990s. Her cousins are educators in Texas to this day. She's going on 50 years of teaching—or about an eighth of Santa Fe's 400 years. She's been teaching in New Mexico for 25 years.

And things changed since her early days: "When I started, the emphasis was on the three Rs. Students got one elective a year—maybe. Everyone had to take P.E. The female teachers had to wear skirts, the men had to wear shirts and slacks—and no facial hair allowed. And those horrible Ditto [copy] machines!" Back then, a teacher's starting salary was about $3,000 a year, she said. Still, she could afford a down payment on a $21,000 custom-built house in a private subdivision. Now a starting teacher earns $30,000 in his or her first year. "But you're not going to buy a house like that today—not for $21,000," she said.

She knows that today's students have short attention spans thanks to the fast-paced world of media. So she looks for ways to engage them, adding a theatrical flair (she's a former dancer) to her methods.

Yet she's not sure she would have wanted to be a teacher here 100 years or so ago. "They watched your private life in a way that we watch the private lives of our politicians today, and that was probably even more true in a small town," she noted.

"Even when I started teaching in the high school, I had to sign a moral turpitude contract, saying that if anything in my private life led to questions about my morality, I could lose my licensure for teaching." Then, too, female teachers generally could not marry in the 1800s and even early 1900s, she said.

But she suspects students had a better chance of acquiring a good background education then because teachers, "didn't have to cover so much ground, and students today have to learn a lot more than what we had to learn in school." Teachers work harder than most people realize, she said: "You take your job home with you, and you also take home the hearts of your students." Facebook keeps her in touch with a lot of former students. At 47 years of teaching, with an average of 120 students a year (a low figure, she maintains), she figures she's seen 6,000 students pass through her classroom.

"Not only do we touch the kids' lives, they touch ours," she said. "I still love the kids. I can't imagine teaching if you don't love your students. They keep you young."

Students line up for registration at Santa Fe High School in 1963. Photograph courtesy Palace of the Governors Photo Archives (NMHM/DCA), #29344.

Squabbles over School Funding, Reform Timeless

by
Rob Dean

Consider two statements separated by nearly 200 years but bound by an enduring plea for money to run Santa Fe schools.

In 1812, Pedro Bautista Pino, New Mexico's representative to the Spanish parliament, appealed to the king for financial help, saying:

> "Even in [Santa Fe] it has been impossible to engage a teacher and to furnish education for everyone. ... This condition gives rise to expressions of discouragement by many people who notice the latent scientific ability of the children in this province."

In 2009, Santa Fe teacher Lisa Randall issued this warning about budget cuts: "I'm bracing for too many kids in the classroom, too few materials, overworked administrators, and an already very-tired group of colleagues who have been dealt another blow. ... And achievement scores are not going to go up."

Long before and long after the formation of Santa Fe Public Schools in 1896, the community has argued over school funding and reform. Did most of those squabbles happen in days gone by? Yes. Are they relevant today? You decide. But given that Santa Fe schools absorbed nearly $7 million in budget cuts this year, it is worth considering what happened at several key moments between the Spanish colonial period and statehood.

One of the earliest and strongest arguments for better schools came in that report to the king in 1812. Pino arrived in Spain to take his seat in a new session of the parliament and soon delivered his written report on conditions in New Mexico.

One topic Pino addressed was education. He argued that education would give opportunities to individuals and promote prosperity for the community. At the time, only families wealthy enough to help pay the teacher could afford to send children to school. Further, Pino called for higher education so New Mexico could train its own as priests, doctors and judges. "I am leaving this matter to the consideration of your majesty," Pino concluded. The plea went unanswered.

After almost 10 years of waiting, new hope for pro-education Santa Feans followed Mexican independence. But hope quickly turned to disappointment when in 1822, a year after independence, the provincial assembly established public schools in New Mexico but failed to supply funding. The school system existed on paper but continued for years to underserve the community. In 1844, free schools opened again in Santa Fe only because Governor Mariano Martinez de Lejanza was willing to pay out of his pocket for the schools and two teachers brought in from Europe.

The next opportunity to take stock of education came during the U.S. military occupation of Santa Fe. Governor Donaciano Vigil's report to the Legislature in 1847 said the whole territory of New Mexico had only one school, in Santa Fe, and that school had but one teacher. Vigil called for a public school in every village in New Mexico. Lawmakers gave the idea a thumbs down.

After decades of division, what happened next made all previous school debates seem like nap time in kindergarten. In March 1884, in the midst of a legislative debate on school-funding reform, a citizens committee appointed by the county commission delivered a report that shook Santa Fe and ignited a very public quarrel.

When the committee appeared before a grand jury and offered the report alleging misuse of funds, the grand jury refused to hear the report. Not to be denied, the committee instead took the report straight to the public and detailed the allegations in a hearing open to the whole community. The report made two serious charges about the handling of local school taxes. The first charge said county school officials were illegally funneling one-sixth of public-school money to religious schools. The second made the case that two Catholic institutions received all of the money, while schools run by Protestants and the Christian Brothers were shut out of the funding.

The citizens committee called on the Legislature to abolish the local tax and to stop public funding of church schools. Without reform, the committee said, "this school tax in the place of advancing popular and general education will be a fund for the propagation of the religious dogmas of the majority."

Loretto Academy, circa 1900. Photograph courtesy Palace of the Governors Photo Archives (NMHM/DCA), #158295.

The mother superior of Loretto Academy, a recipient of taxpayer money, fought back through the newspaper, deflecting the specific charges by making the sympathetic case that her school served poor students. The mother superior did not directly challenge the charges, instead choosing to attack her accusers for exaggerating the facts.

The citizens committee, particularly spokesman José Manuel Martin, showed considerable courage by standing up to pressure from a community inclined to support the Sisters of Loretto and Sisters of Charity. In a published response to the mother superior, Martin demanded that the state "give us an efficient public school entirely free from sectarian control, and the sooner the better."

That spring, the territorial Legislature enacted a package of school reforms, just as Martin and his committee had wanted. The legislation shifted responsibility for public schools from the county school superintendent to the newly created local school districts and governing boards. That basic structure has stayed in place since.

Archaeological Institute Helped Define City

by
Jason Strykowski

Adolph Bandelier was broke. Although he had received a $1,200 grant to explore the indigenous peoples and wondrous ruins of New Mexico, that money went quickly to travel and supplies. Exasperated, curious and probably a little bitter, Bandelier investigated the disbursements of funds dedicated to archaeology by American institutions. The vast majority of gifts and funds, he found, went to classics, the study of ancient civilizations in Europe. Very little money and very little attention went to scholarship of American antiquities. The United States needed a center for its own archaeology.

In Chicago, the Archaeological Institute of America, almost 20 years old by 1893, was caught in the midst of an economic "panic." They had to broaden their support base to say vital. The institute had funded Bandelier but had done little else to study the Americas. In 1901, to remedy that issue, they created a Committee on American Archaeology and soon enrolled such luminaries as Frederic Putnam, Charles P. Bowditch, Franz Boas, Charles Lummis, Jesse Walter Fewkes, Alice Cunningham Fletcher and Edgar Lee Hewett to oversee this new wing. The committee was appointed with the task of further studying the cultures of the Americas, and, of course, attracting more American donors from regions in the West.

Their interest in American antiquities dovetailed perfectly with a greater fascination in natural and cultural resources gripping the United States. Soon, the Antiquities Act would be in place to protect the great cliff cities of the Southwest and, a decade later, the National Park Service would be formed to administer and steward such treasures into the future. Following a horseback trip from Santa Fe to Chiapas, Mexico, Hewett reasoned that the time was right to found a school of American archaeology and that Santa Fe was the place to do it.

School of American Research board meeting at Puyé in 1909. Photograph courtesy Palace of the Governors Photo Archives (NMHM/DCA), #13328.

Under the guidance of Alice Fletcher, the Archaeological Institute met in 1907 to discuss such a school. And, despite vehement opposition from some members, a decision was made. A School of American Archaeology would open in Santa Fe.

Hewett, a former president at New Mexico Normal University (now New Mexico Highlands) and well-regarded archaeologist, took over leadership of the new school. Fortunately, Hewett had supporters in Santa Fe and his plans to assume control of the Palace of the Governors were confirmed by the territorial government. Better yet, territorial Governor Nathan Jaffa also created a Museum for the Territory of New Mexico and tied that organization to Hewett's school, making Hewett president. Within a year, Hewett was planning and guiding field schools from Santa Fe to what is now Bandelier National Monument and other sites in the region.

Hewett, however, was not yet satisfied. He expanded the field schools to other parts of the Southwest. He established a museum at the old Palace. Hewett also planned and presented lectures across the country. In 1915, he took his showmanship to another level as he helped organize displays on Southwestern and Latin American archaeology for the Panama-California Exposition in San Diego. Now, Hewett had an international audience.

Back in Santa Fe, the School of American Archaeology, which Hewett had now dubbed the School of American Research, took an active role in the arts community. Hewett himself encouraged the work of a potter from San Ildefonso Pueblo and her husband. Maria and Julian Martinez had previously joined him on a dig by the Puyé Cliff Dwellings, and, recognizing their talents, Hewett had pushed the couple to try to re-create the types of pots they found on their digs. Combined with input from local shops, Martinez's distinctive black-on-black was born.

In his interest in Pueblo art, Hewett had company. In 1922, the school organized a Southwest Indian Fair. Others in Santa Fe organized the Indian Arts Fund, and even John D. Rockefeller Jr. visited Santa Fe in the hopes of donating money to the preservation of such art. The Arts Fund collection and Rockefeller's support soon became the basis for the Laboratory of Anthropology.

Yet another educational institution showed interest in archaeology, and in 1927 Hewett chaired the new Departments of Anthropology and Archaeology at The University of New Mexico. Hewett delighted in the partnership, throwing himself fully into the new departments and arranging ambitious field schools for his students.

Until his death in 1946, Hewett remained ambitious in his leadership and work. His projects extended well beyond the Southwest into Central and Latin America.

Always in search of more involvement and exposure, Hewett would have been pleased to see that just a year after his passing, the Laboratory of Anthropology and the Museum of New Mexico merged. And, while the director of the school had since 1909 assumed the unpaid role of museum director, the Laboratory of Anthropology did not directly join the school. All the same, the most important archaeological institutions in New Mexico were nearly consolidated, for a time.

Just over a decade later, the New Mexico attorney general struck down this archaeological powerhouse as unconstitutional, breaking it up into the school and museum. The school found further independence in 1970 as it severed its ties to the Archaeological Institute of America and shortly thereafter relocated to its current location at an estate formerly owned by the White sisters, arts patrons and activists.

Now known as the School for Advanced Research, the educational facility celebrated its centennial in 2007 and presently hosts a wide array of think-tank activities far surpassing even the broad programs implemented by Hewett. Among its offerings, the school counts residencies for visiting scholars, member field trips and a scholarly press.

Personalities: Teachers, Scores and Money

by
Rob Dean

Over time, any list of Santa Fe's leading citizens has included people who stood up for teachers, pushed for student achievement and did so by spending tax money wisely.

Marcelino Abreu

If you think the idea of measuring yearly school progress started with No Child Left Behind Act of 2001, think again. One of the first public school teachers in Santa Fe was Marcelino Abreu, probably the first educator to give the public a report card on the schools. He did that in 1830 with a report that listed 12 students who made the grade. In particular, Abreu named three students who began the year with no math skills but ended the year having mastered addition and multiplication. Since 1808, city leaders clearly had seen education as a means to strengthen the community but struggled to pay for open-admission schools. Finally in 1827, under Mexican rule, regulations outlined a school system and a curriculum based primarily on Christian doctrine. Not long afterward, the school run by Abreu opened.

Source: *UFOs Over Galisteo* by Robert J. Tórrez.

Geronima Cruz Montoya

From 1937 to 1962, Geronima Cruz Montoya directed the Studio School of painting at Santa Fe Indian School. The Studio School, founded in 1932 by Dorothy Dunn, was controversial because it advanced the notion that Indian School students could learn academic concepts by creating visual arts. A native of Ohkay Owingeh, Montoya became Dunn's first student and then her successor as school director. Meantime, Montoya continued to create her own art, earned a college degree, created an adult program for the northern pueblos and founded a Native American crafts cooperative. By 1962, feeling tied up in federal red tape, she stopped teaching. Earlier this year, at 95, Montoya was honored as the 2010 Indian Market poster artist.

Source: *The Worlds of P'otsúnú* by Jeanne Shutes and Jill Mellick.

Geronima Cruz Montoya in 2004. Photograph by Jane Phillips.

St. Michael's High School, circa 1925. The Miguel Chavez building was torn down after the Christian Brothers sold the land to the state. Photograph by T. Harmon Parkhurst, courtesy Palace of the Governors Photo Archives (NMHM/DCA), #50927.

Brother Botulph

The Christian Brothers opened present-day St. Michael's High School in 1859. When the first burst of energy began to fade, a new generation of Brothers considered closing the school in 1870. Peter J. Schneider, known as Brother Botulph, saved the school, recruited Brothers to teach in Santa Fe and established a training program for local students wanting to teach. St. Michael's, chartered as the College of the Christian Brothers, graduated its first class in 1876. Botulph raised money in 1878 for a new classroom building that still stands today as the Lamy Building on Old Santa Fe Trail. Brother Botulph died in 1906.

Source: St. Michael's High School.

Estafanita 'Esther' Martinez

Estafanita 'Esther' Martinez in 1996. Photograph by Steve Northup.

In her mid-50s, Estafanita Martinez quite unexpectedly became a teacher. Then in 20 years as Tewa instructor and director of bilingual education at San Juan Day School, she did as much as anyone to preserve her native Tewa language. She attended Santa Fe and Albuquerque Indian schools, where students were taught to shed Native language and culture. When she became a classroom volunteer in the late 1960s, Martinez proved to be a gifted storyteller and found the inspiration to save and record the old stories in Tewa. She wrote a Tewa dictionary and two collections of stories. After Martinez's death in 2004, Congress passed the Native Languages Preservation Act in her name.

Source: Matthew J. Martinez.

John V. Conway

A New Mexico native, son of an Irish father and Spanish mother, and graduate of St. Michael's High School and The University of New Mexico, John V. Conway got his start in Santa Fe in the hotel and restaurant business. His lasting mark, however, was his long career of expanding access to education. Conway became county superintendent of schools in 1900 and worked for more than 20 years as an innovator and reformer. He led a building boom that brought comfortable classrooms and modern equipment to local schools, many in rural areas. To serve adults who had little formal education, Conway opened the schools at night and offered classes in reading, spelling and composition.

Source: *Leading Facts in New Mexico History* by Ralph Emerson Twitchell.

Manuel 'Bob' Chávez

From 1887 to 1998, St. Catherine Indian School inspired intense loyalty among the students and families it served. Bob Chávez of Cochiti Pueblo exemplified that lifelong commitment to the boarding school situated near Rosario Cemetery. A successful artist who worked in a basement studio at the school, Chávez neither forgot

Manuel 'Bob' Chávez in 2001. Photograph by Katherine Kimball.

that a St. Kate's teacher had encouraged him to pursue art nor that the school equipped him mentally and spiritually to survive the Bataan Death March and a World War II prison camp. For 52 years, Chávez volunteered at the school as a teacher, coach and fundraiser. He died in 2003, five years after the school closed.

Source: Office of the New Mexico State Historian.

Edward Ortiz

In the 1980s, a nationally recognized reformer led Santa Fe Public Schools. Edward Ortiz, Santa Fe's first Hispanic superintendent, gave teachers an expanded role in the management of their schools. In 1989, he became known as the first superintendent in the country to give teachers and parents the power to choose their new principal. Ortiz's death during surgery shocked the community. He was only 53. "He was the heart and soul of Santa Fe education," a school board member said.

Edward Ortiz

Lorraine Goldman

As budgets got tighter and burdens on teachers grew heavier, Lorraine Goldman saw that businesses, service clubs and volunteers needed to step up. She was director of Partners in Education from 1990 to 2001 and perfected the art of squeezing thousands of dollars and service hours out of businesses in support of education. From those allies she recruited, Goldman collected money for classroom supplies, field trips, internships and awards. When a teacher needs money or resources, Goldman once said, "All they do is call." Since retiring from Partners, Goldman has stayed active in community service. Partners is still going strong, too, making sure education is everyone's job.

Lorraine Goldman at the 2010 Santa Fe school board meeting. Photograph by Luis Sánchez Saturno.

Timeline

1812: New Mexico representative to Spain asks crown to fund schools.

1826: Vicar of New Mexico uses own money to start Santa Fe school.

1832: Mexican officials report one public school in Santa Fe with private funds paying for teacher.

1844: Governor Martinez de Lejanza establishes public school.

1851: Archbishop Lamy starts first English school, a year before Army wife Anne Howe opens nonsectarian English school.

1853: Sisters of Loretto open school to youth from across New Mexico.

1859: Christian Brothers establish St. Michael's College.

1860: Legislation places schools under jurisdiction of probate judges.

1863: New law creates Board of Education with members including governor, Supreme Court justices and archbishop.

1884: Legislature modernizes school system, defining local districts and establishing funding system.

1887: St. Catherine Indian School opens; it would operate for 111 years.

1890: Santa Fe Indian School opens.

1896: Santa Fe Public Schools comes into being.

1964: St. John's College opens.

1983: Legislature establishes Santa Fe Community College.

Suggested Books

Gallegos, Bernardo P. *Literacy, Education, and Society in New Mexico, 1693-1821.* Albuquerque: The University of New Mexico Press, 1992.

Garmhausen, Winona. *History of Indian Arts Education in Santa Fe: The Institute of American Indian Arts with Historical Background, 1890 to 1962.* Santa Fe: Sunstone Press, 1988

Hyer, Sally. *One House, One Voice, One Heart: Native American Education at the Santa Fe Indian School.* Santa Fe: Museum of New Mexico Press, 1990.

Mondragón, John B., and Ernest S. Stapleton. *Public Education in New Mexico.* Albuquerque: The University of New Mexico Press, 2005.

Nathan, Fred. *Making New Mexico's Public Schools World Class through Decentralization, Competition and Choice.* Santa Fe: Think New Mexico, 2000.

Reed, Benjamin M. *A History of Education in New Mexico.* Santa Fe: New Mexican Printing Company, 1911.

Simmons, Marc. *Charles F. Lummis, Author and Adventurer.* Santa Fe: Sunstone Press, 2008.

Telgen, Diane. "Nina Otero-Warren." *Notable Hispanic American women.* Detroit: Gale Research, 1993.

Tórrez, Robert J. "An Early Report Card." *UFOs Over Galisteo and Other Stories of New Mexico's History.* Albuquerque: The University of New Mexico Press, 2004.

West, Beverly. "Mother Magdalen and the Sisters of Loretto: Pioneers of Education." *More Than Petticoats. Remarkable New Mexico Women.* Guilford, Connecticut: TwoDot, 2001.

Whaley, Charlotte. *Nina Otero-Warren of Santa Fe.* Santa Fe: Sunstone Press, 2007.

Wiley, Tom. *Politics and Purse Strings in New Mexico's Public Schools.* Albuquerque: The University of New Mexico Press, 1965.

Suggested websites
(active at time of publication)

Santa Fe schools: www.sfps.info/
History of St. Michael's High School: www.stmichaelssf.org/about/mission_&_history/
History of St. Kate's: www.newmexicohistory.org/filedetails.php?fileID=21300

10

Power

State Democratic Party Chairman Javier Gonzales, left, and his father, former Santa Fe Mayor George Gonzales, at their radio station, AM 810 Que Suave, in September 2010. Photograph by Luis Sánchez Saturno.

Alva Simpson of Abiquiú, who ran for New Mexico governor in 1954, speaks with former governor Dave Cargo, right. Photograph by Barbaraellen Koch.

Where Power and Idealism Collide
Backroom Deals and Public Politicking

by
Julie Ann Grimm

t's easy to put Santa Fe on an island," Javier Gonzales said. "It's easy to say, 'That's where those guys can make those crazy policies.'" In 2010, as state Democratic Party chairman, Gonzales could see that the rest of New Mexico cannot disassociate Santa Fe from the exercise of political influence and power. But to Gonzales, Santa Fe is more than the state capital. It's his hometown.

"Those of us here in Santa Fe, we are very proud of it," he said. "This community has been defined by so much more than politics. And sadly, what the rest of the state sometimes does is to define us as a community that is just purely politically driven rather than a community built on family and culture and diversity."

It is undeniable, he said, that Santa Fe is the political center of New Mexico. Any survey of history or the many government buildings would show that. Throughout 2010, Santa Fe remembered and honored its 400 years of history, including the fundamental fact that the city has been a seat of government since its founding.

"Government—that is your dominant industry out there," economist Larry Waldman said matter-of-factly.

Political insiders like Gonzales know what it means for Santa Fe to be the capital city. The city always has been a place of conventions, rallies and protests—reasons for activist Santa Feans to act on the impulse to question authority. From its early days, Santa Fe has been at the intersection of money and influence, serving as a magnet for bankers, lawyers and developers. The struggle for power has turned deadly serious at times, to the point that assassinations were part of the political history.

Government is known largely as the economic engine for Santa Fe, said Waldman, an analyst with the Bureau of Business and Economic Research at The University of New Mexico in Albuquerque. "It's a major, well-paying employer," he said, noting city data that show government workers in Santa Fe earned an average of 21 percent more than all other workers in the county and 27 percent more than workers in all other industries statewide.

But beyond jobs, there also is a long tradition of activism on a personal level, said Gonzales, who is both a member of a public-spirited family and a political-party pragmatist. There are families, he said, "who have, within their own structure, placed public service of high value, and that has been consistent over generations."

As a party chair, Gonzales enjoys a political process that accommodates progress while respecting tradition. In 2010, New Mexico had a key moment in its political history. For the first time, New Mexicans elected a female governor, choosing Republican Susana Martinez over Democrat Diane Denish, the former lieutenant governor.

Whole Family Involved

Gonzales' own family tree is full of people who left lasting impressions on Santa Fe politics. His father, George, was mayor and a candidate for Congress; his godfather, Johnny Vigil, was the county Democratic chairman for six years in the 1960s; and a more distant ancestor on his mother's side was the state auditor.

It seemed natural, almost expected, that Javier Gonzales would make his mark. At 26, he challenged and defeated an incumbent Santa Fe county commissioner, won re-election four years later and in 2002 left office because of term limits after eight years. During that time, he considered running for Congress, and he served during his final term as board president of the National Association of Counties.

State Democratic Party Chairman Javier Gonzales, left, talks with his father, former Mayor George Gonzales. Photograph by Luis Sánchez Saturno.

"We worked really hard," he said of his entrance to elected office. "But there is no doubt that my family name, my dad's name, and certainly the [family's] radio station helped. There were a lot of contributing factors that allowed me to win outside of just me.

"I think that's part of the whole four hundred years of Santa Fe, through the generations. Family plays a role, not just for those in government, but also in business or in the nonprofit world. With the northern New Mexico family, when an individual gets involved, the whole family gets involved."

Still, Gonzales was reluctant to attribute power to any particular family or families. He said that even though voter participation is low, the government structure gives people a loud voice if they use it. "I don't know that I would call them powerful families," he said, referring instead to families that value service—people like Bruce King, a county commissioner who went on to serve three terms as governor, whose son Gary has served as attorney general and whose niece Rhonda, in 2010, is a state senator.

"I think it's more of a testament to the values that families have about public service and the obligation that we have to it more than an accumulation of power," Gonzales said. "I don't think that we live in a day where just one family by its existence can single-handedly influence."

Personal Campaign Style

One successful politician who grasped the nature of personal politics was former Governor David Cargo. In the 1960s, his four years as an Albuquerque legislator followed by two terms as governor allowed him to witness what he said was a drastic change in the way things were done in New Mexico. As of 2010, Cargo, an attorney, still works on labor issues. He is proud of his role as governor in filing a successful lawsuit that resulted in redrawn legislative districts in which Hispanics, Native Americans and women could compete as candidates.

As a Republican in a Democratic stronghold, Cargo benefited from the help of "potent northern New Mexico politicians." Before the New Deal, Republicans held many statewide offices and a majority in the Legislature, but urban population surges during and after the Depression favored the Democrats.

Former Governor David Cargo and family. Photograph from *The Santa Fe New Mexican* **archives.**

So how did Cargo win the hearts of Democrats in 1966 to become, at 37, New Mexico's youngest governor? Part of his success, he said, came because as a young attorney, he shared an office with a brother-in-law to Dennis Chavez, the Democrat who held a U.S. Senate seat from 1935 to 1962. Although Chavez died four years before Cargo ran for governor, his influence persisted.

"He was an old-style politician," Cargo recalled. "He would name off the list of people, and he would say, 'You go campaign for Dave Cargo,' and they would."

Cargo said he carried northern New Mexico by campaigning the old way.

"I would go out into personal campaigning," he said. "I didn't have any money. I spent about sixteen thousand dollars getting elected governor. Bill Richardson spent sixteen million and Susana Martinez is spending money till it doesn't quit. ... During the whole campaign for governor, I don't think I ever stayed in a hotel or motel. I stayed in the homes of people supporting me and usually they were people who Dennis Chavez recommended."

Backroom Politics

Chavez also was the reason Cargo won support in Santa Fe County, where during a series of meetings in smoke-filled rooms at La Fonda, leading Democrats threw their support to Cargo. He recalled witnessing stacks of cash, and wine and whiskey donated by liquor mogul George Maloof being delivered to political leaders who needed encouragement.

The intimacy of New Mexico's politics and the red-carpet treatment Santa Fe gives politicians make New Mexico unique," Cargo said. "You have a state government that is really much more influential here than in other places."

Even as he chuckled at "the way things were" during his campaign, Cargo said he tried to change the way state officials handed out jobs. His predecessor, Jack Campbell, had set up the state's first personnel act, but Cargo said hiring as he took office still wasn't based on merit.

"It was all political," he said. "I wanted to reform it because it was a horrible system."

Cargo's record reflected the times. He served at the height of the civil-rights movement, and some schools in New Mexico were still segregated.

Former Governor David Cargo attends the 40th anniversary of the return of Blue Lake at Taos Pueblo in September 2010. Photograph by Megan Bowers Avina.

He helped pass the state's first human-rights legislation and set an example for crossing long-established lines by appointing Hispanos to his Cabinet and funneling public-works projects to an all-black community south of Las Cruces. Cargo's late ex-wife, Ida Jo Robeson, was the state's first Hispanic first lady since 1918. When Taos Pueblo fought the federal government over its sacred lands at Blue Lake, Cargo recruited President Richard Nixon to help.

Cargo found minority groups at a disadvantage. "There was not a single Indian in the Legislature, and the Anglos really did control things," he said.

400 Years of Power

How particular racial, ethnic or demographic groups have used power has been an issue in Santa Fe for four centuries. Today, representation of women and Native Americans in positions of leadership seems disproportionately small. Founded as a colonial capital, Santa Fe sprung up in a region that had been home to Indian people long before the Spanish arrived to put the territory on Europe's map. The first two capitals of the colony of New Spain were to the north, at present-day Okhay Owingeh and San Gabriel, both settled and abandoned by members of Oñate's exploratory party in the last years of the 16th century.

When Pedro de Peralta arrived in New Mexico as the first colonial governor, he established the capital in a strategic location. In 1610, construction began over the ruins of Tanoan Indian village, and Peralta formally named it Villa Real de la Santa Fe, or Royal City of Holy Faith.

After decades of oppression, Native Americans exerted their own power by overthrowing the colonial government in what's known as the Pueblo Revolt of 1680. The Spanish returned 12 years later.

New Mexico was part of Mexico after independence from Spain in 1821. U.S. troops entered Santa Fe in 1846, and New Mexico was governed as a U.S. territory from 1848 to 1912. Washington appointed territorial officials in Santa Fe, but voters chose local office holders through elections. After a 64-year quest for statehood, New Mexico in 1912 joined the union and won, among other things, the right to elect its leaders and representatives.

Females in Politics

Debbie Jaramillo was the first female mayor of Santa Fe, serving from 1994 to 1998. But another rare female candidate, former City Manager Asenath Kepler, lost to incumbent Mayor David Coss in 2010.

Debbie Jaramillo

Women haven't appeared in Santa Fe political offices or statewide elected roles as often as their male counterparts. The reasons aren't that different from what happens across the nation. Women are burdened by the inability to raise money and by family responsibilities, explained Rebecca Frenkel, a member of the League of Women Voters. Nonetheless, women have been influential, she said, and League members used the organization's 60th anniversary in 2010 to publicize the role of women.

"We've found out about women in New Mexico who participated in the women's suffrage movement and who were instrumental in establishing the League of Women Voters nationally," she said. "There have always been women in Santa Fe who have been involved in some aspect of political action. ... They have been very active, but not always in the role of elected officials."

Statistics from Emerge New Mexico, a group that recruits and trains women to run for office, put New Mexico 12th in the nation for its number of women serving in the Legislature. Still, in 2010, the state House and Senate remain 70 percent male.

Reena Szczepanski, Emerge director, said women don't run as often as men, research shows, because they are less likely to feel qualified. "It's not that voters don't want to see women in office or that there are more barriers for women who decide to run," she said. "What we have seen in the research is that women are less likely to decide they want to run.

"Patterns might change," Szczepanski continued. "Having at least four years of a woman governor should serve to inspire women that they can get to elected office, that they can serve their community."

Tax Hike Leaves Santa Fe Under Siege

by
Jason Strykowski

Members of the small colony were not accustomed to paying taxes. They had yet to see any tangible result of what they had contributed and they were hesitant, even angered, at the prospect of paying more. So when the time came for an appreciable hike, the people of northern New Mexico rebelled. Often referred to as the Chimayó Rebellion, the 1837 insurrection in New Mexico was a violent, but short, outpouring of resistance to changes in leadership and management of the northern territories of Mexico.

A fundamentally diverse community of Pueblos, Hispanos and other Native peoples who had been adopted into Spanish society, Chimayó and other communities nearby were a true product of Spanish colonization. But the Spanish left in 1821, forced out by the Mexicans, and a fragile society would have to be restructured. In 1835, the Mexican government chose a rising political star named Albino Pérez to take control of New Mexico.

Pérez arrived to New Mexico just as major changes were taking hold throughout Mexico. General Antonio López de Santa Anna instituted a new centralist government in 1836, ending more than a dozen years of relative independence in New Mexico. Among other federally mandated changes, was a tax to be collected in the provinces and sent to the federal capital.

Talking among themselves, the people of Northern New Mexico shared their concerns over this new tax and managed to inflate the tax burden. In short order, the rumor mill transformed into the war machine. People in the area were by then accustomed to using arms and forming militias as defense against raiders. As a consequence, the Mexican authorities had little choice but to take seriously an August 1 proclamation drafted in Rio Arriba. The document made it clear that the people of Rio Arriba would not stand for the federal changes. Pérez had little choice but to respond.

At La Mesilla, more than a thousand disgruntled Natives, Hispanos and others ambushed the governor and his small entourage. Much of the governor's contingent immediately defected and joined the rebels. A number of the governor's men were taken prisoner, but Pérez himself was able to escape to Santa Fe. Word reached Santo Domingo and a party was sent north to finish the job. Pérez fought with fist and dagger, but a bullet got the best of him and soon the governor was beheaded, his head placed on a pike. Nearly 20 Pérez supporters were killed in the fight, one of whom was castrated while still alive.

The rebels took power and installed their own governor only to see him greeted with additional violent opposition. Tempers flared and the people of Santa Fe soon had good cause to worry once again. Hundreds of men from the north and south were mobilizing to take Santa Fe.

On September 21, 1837, Manuel Armijo, former governor and entrepreneur, led some thousand men to Santa Fe where 3,000 men under the recently installed rebel government stood ready to defend their newly won power. Faced with Armijo's superior arms, the rebels surrendered to Armijo's terms. They signed a treaty, surrendered some of the key leaders of the rebellion and the fighting ended. Out of the new terms, Armijo rose as governor of New Mexico.

Even with an army under his control and an official appointment as governor, Armijo still faced a continuing threat of rebellion. Another outbreak in Truchas provoked Armijo into seeking troops from Chihuahua, Mexico. This display of power coupled with Armijo's decision to execute prisoners taken earlier, helped stir New Mexicans to peace.

Armijo also had the wisdom to lower taxes and reduce strain on militias by taking better care of New Mexican troops. The new peace also rebuilt confidence in the safety of the Santa Fe Trail, bringing much needed trade back to the region. Although Americans distrusted Armijo, the lucrative Santa Fe Trail could not be ignored.

Within a decade, New Mexico would become property of the United States and what few gains were won by these revolts would have little to do with the new territorial government set up by the Americans. Perhaps, worse yet, New Mexicans would be from the end of the rebellion onward under the control of a centralized government.

Famous American Explorer Jailed in Santa Fe

by
Jason Strykowski

The expedition unraveled rapidly. Despite an impressive force of some 600 soldiers and a nearly equal number of horses, the group's progress slowed, and the distance between Santa Fe and the American border seemed to lengthen. A mutiny, significant loss of livestock and Indian raids nearly doomed Lieutenant Don Facundo Malgares' trip. But despite being depleted by the strenuous journey, Malgares reached his objective—a small ragtag group of Americans led by an explorer named Zebulon Montgomery Pike.

Perhaps best known today for the peak in Colorado that bears his name, Lieutenant Pike explored and recorded much of the Spanish-owned Southwest for the United States in 1805 and 1807. A gifted soldier, Pike died at the young age of 34 during the War of 1812. He had spent his entire adulthood in the American Army.

Pike also had the misfortune of exploring large sections of North America just as other American navigators were taking an even more impressive jaunt through the Louisiana Territory and all the way to the Pacific. Like Pike, Meriwether Lewis and William Clark set out to explore the West under the directives of President Thomas Jefferson and for the explicit purpose of charting the resources that would fuel the new "Empire of Liberty."

The Spanish authorities had heard of Pike's plans long before he reached Santa Fe, and in 1807, Pike was taken prisoner by Malgares' forces. Fortunately for Pike, his guards were more akin to guides who took him as a willing guest throughout New Mexico. Lewis and Clark may have had a splendid lead in Sacagawea, but Pike received a full tour.

Lieutenant Zebulon Montgomery Pike. Photograph courtesy Palace of the Governors Photo Archives (NMHM/DCA), #7757.

He was escorted all the way to Santa Fe, where both the governor of New Mexico and a small crowd awaited him. The reception embarrassed the weary Pike. After months on trail over mountain and plains, Pike must have appeared exhausted. Worse yet for the career soldier, his uniform had long ago been replaced with moccasins, blankets and fox fur. Pike did not make a reputable appearance for formal court.

After marching through Tesuque and south into the capital, Pike found Santa Fe to be a strange sight. Of the city, he wrote in his journal:

"Its appears [sic] from a distance, struck my mind with the same effect as a fleet of the flat bottomed boats, which are seen in the spring and fall seasons, descending the Ohio River. There are two churches, the magnificence of whose steeples form a striking contrast to the miserable appearances of the houses. ... The public square is in the centre of the town; on the north side of which is situated the palace [as they term it] or government house."

As Pike was walked through some of the buildings, he probably found less cause to be embarrassed by his own dress as he spotted buffalo, bear and other animal skins filling some of the chambers. Pike's appearance then caused him little problem, but his reputation as a spy did.

Ironically enough, Pike earned his traitorous label through his affiliation with General James Wilkinson, a Spanish mole. Wilkinson was being paid by the Spanish for information at the same time he was one of the highest-ranking American soldiers. Wilkinson also had a much-discussed relationship with the fallen politician Aaron Burr. It was widely claimed that the two had hatched a plot to take a large chunk of Spanish land and found their own nation. The governor of New Mexico was likely concerned that Pike was conducting reconnaissance for the Burr-Wilkinson plot.

Pike was not entirely forthcoming with Governor Joaquín de Real Alencaster and underreported the number in his party by one Dr. J.H. Robinson. Unfortunately for Pike, Robinson had already spoken with the Spanish and given them a different head count. Even more damning in the governor's opinion were the papers he confiscated from Pike's trunk.

Alencaster wanted the Americans investigated further so he ordered them to Chihuahua, Mexico, where they would meet with other Spanish officials for questioning. Pike protested, but ultimately joined a number of locals as they headed south through New Spain toward Chihuahua. Despite guards and the denial of his prized journal, Pike still had opportunity to see much of the country, including Albuquerque, El Paso and the many native communities along the way.

At Chihuahua, Pike relinquished many of his notes but faced no formal prosecution from the government of New Spain. His notes would stay in Mexico for a century before being rediscovered and returned to the United States. Pike immediately went back to the United States, dropped off by the Spanish at the American border in Louisiana.

Despite being insulted by the Spanish, Pike still managed to enjoy his time in New Spain. He interacted with people who entertained him and saw unique places. Once back in the United States, in fact, Pike devoted much of his time to sharing these memories with other Americans as he edited his journals for publication. His efforts paid off, and the journals were published in 1810, making Pike into an even greater celebrity. He stayed in the Army until his death during the War of 1812 just a few years later. Along the way, he received numerous postings at a handful of forts, one of America's most visible soldiers.

Although he never reached the level of fame attained by Lewis and Clark, Pike had enjoyed his time in the spotlight. His journal, in fact, made it to print before that of Lewis and Clark. Had he lived, Pike might even have joined William Henry Harrison and Andrew Jackson as extremely successful veterans of the War of 1812. As it happened, Pike was buried in upstate New York, where he remains despite a campaign in Colorado to have his remains sent to be reinterred near Pike's Peak.

Personalities: Mastering the Art of the Possible

by
Rob Dean

These people from Santa Fe history represent the many colorful political figures who balanced high hopes and pragmatism, often with mixed results.

Pedro Bautista Pino

By 1812, after more than 200 years of Spanish colonial rule, New Mexicans wanted more financial help from Spain but felt neglected by their faraway European masters. New Mexico sent representative Pedro Bautista Pino to Spain to ask the parliament for aid. Pino, later described as the most able statesman born in New Mexico, delivered a written report lobbying the Spanish crown for money to stimulate agriculture, industry and commerce, and to develop teachers, writers, lawyers and doctors. Its national power in decline by that time, Spain was not willing or able to come through.

Source: *Foreigners in Their Native Land* by David J. Weber.

Concha Ortiz y Pino de Kleven

Energetic yet generous with her time, Concha Ortiz y Pino de Kleven made friends easily but never stopped pushing them to do the right thing. She had a full life that stretched from 1910 to 2006, summarized by her biographer this way: "Concha became a college student in Washington, DC, a state legislator in New Mexico, a faculty wife at The University of New Mexico, the boss-lady of a 100,000-acre ranch, a widow, a board member of 60 or more organizations working to make the world a better place, a champion for women and the handicapped and Hispanic culture and the arts and the poor." Winning an election in 1937, she represented the sixth generation of her family to serve in the Legislature. She came to Santa Fe as the youngest member of that body and later was the first woman in America to be a legislative majority whip. She built a strong pro-education legislative record, and today her name graces a state office building.

Source: *Concha!* by Kathryn M. Córdova.

Concha Ortiz y Pino de Kleven and sheepherder with Caracul lambs at Jose Ortiz y Pino Ranch, Galisteo, 1939. New Mexico State Tourist Bureau, courtesy Palace of the Governors Photo Archives (NMHM/DCA), #59021.

Mariano Martínez de Lejanza

Quality of life has been part of the Santa Fe agenda for a long time. The frontier was very much a matter of day-to-day survival, but in 1844 Governor Mariano Martínez de Lejanza had the foresight to look beyond the routine affairs of the day to imagine a community of the future. He created a large park south of Rosario Chapel, established a public school, helped young men pursue advanced military training and planted cottonwoods on the Plaza. His tree-lined avenue leading to the Rosario park was a space that even in 1844 had quite a modern feel. Santa Feans gathered there to enjoy entertainment provided by musicians, acrobats and rope walkers.

Miguel Trujillo

Native Americans won the right to vote in 1924 through federal legislation, but New Mexico and four other states continued to deny voting rights in state elections. That changed in August 1948. Sitting in Santa Fe, a panel of federal judges ruled that the voting ban constituted discrimination based on race. The man who won the right to vote was Miguel Trujillo of Isleta, a World War II veteran, university graduate student and head teacher at Laguna Pueblo. He died in 1987. Trujillo succeeded in 1948 where a similar legal challenge had failed just a month earlier. In that case, a class action originating at Tesuque Pueblo unsuccessfully sought to force the Santa Fe county clerk to list the plaintiffs as qualified voters.

Source: *Native Vote* by Daniel McCool and others.

Miguel Trujillo, with daughter Josephine in the late 1940s. Photograph courtesy Josephine Waconda.

George Julian

The loose association of bankers, lawyers and politicians known as the Santa Fe Ring operated in the shadows. George Julian showed that bringing backroom deals into the open was the best safeguard against corruption. President Grover Cleveland sent Julian, an ex-Indiana congressman, to New Mexico to investigate land fraud. He found that indeed a ring representing business and political interests had been stealing property from the heirs to Spanish and Mexican land grants. Not only did he report his findings to Washington, but he also in 1887 published the story in a national magazine, naming the ringleaders

George Julian

and detailing their misdeeds so that the whole country might learn of the scandal. The Santa Fe Ring soon faded from the scene.

Frank Chavez

Politics escalated from dirty to deadly in 1892 when a rising politician was gunned down on a dark street outside his home. The victim was Frank Chavez, a popular Democrat and tough former sheriff who had enemies. "The brutes have murdered me," he cried as he fell, adding to the mounting evidence that thugs operated in Santa Fe to do politicians' dirty work. The murder had political overtones. In that election year, the issue was statehood, and New Mexicans were to decide which approach best served them in making their case in Washington: the aggressive, abrasive style of Republican Thomas B. Catron or the gentle persuasion of Democrat Antonio Joseph. The Chavez assassination raised doubts whether political debate could ever be civil or the rule of law ever prevail. The case also proved that justice could win in the end, when three years later a jury convicted a gang of five of the killing.

Source: *The Far Southwest* by Howard R. Lamar.

Pedro Perea

The struggle for statehood lasted 60 years and survived half a dozen major setbacks. Several of the strongest champions of statehood died before New Mexico finally became the 47th state in 1912. Pedro Perea was one of those fathers of statehood who didn't live to see his dream fulfilled. He died in 1906. College educated and successful as a rancher and Santa Fe banker, Perea won election as delegate to the U.S. Congress in 1898, a critical time in the statehood debate. At the time, prejudice in Congress and the Eastern press blocked statehood for a territory that was heavily Hispanic, Spanish-speaking and Catholic. The able Perea was credited with breaking down the prejudice and ignorance about New Mexico.

Pedro Perea, circa 1890. Photograph courtesy Palace of the Governors Photo Archives (NMHM/DCA), #7755.

Source: *New Mexico's Fight for Statehood* by Marion Dargan.

Soledad Chacón

Although the state was slow to ratify the amendment giving women the right to vote in 1920, New Mexico voters two years later anointed Soledad Chacón as the nation's first Hispanic woman to win a statewide election. After winning the office of secretary of state at the young age of 32, Chacón arrived in Santa Fe with the added distinction of being the first woman in the country to hold that office. Within a decade, two other Hispanic women followed in her footsteps to become secretaries of state. Chacón died prematurely at 46 in 1936.

Source: *Soledad Chávez Chacón* by Dan D. Chávez.

Timeline

1610: Pedro de Peralta establishes Santa Fe as seat of government.

1680: Pueblo Revolt forces Spanish to flee.

1693: Don Diego de Vargas recolonizes Santa Fe.

1807: Zebulon Pike leads first Anglo-American expedition into New Mexico.

1821: Mexico declares independence from Spain; Santa Fe Trail opens.

1837: Chimayó Revolt against Mexican taxation leads to assassination of Governor Albino Pérez.

1846: U.S. Army enters Santa Fe and annexes New Mexico to the United States.

1848: Treaty of Guadalupe Hidalgo makes New Mexico a U.S. territory, not a state.

1863: New Mexico is partitioned in half; Territory of Arizona is created.

1910: New Mexico Constitution drafted in preparation for statehood.

1912: New Mexico admitted as 47th state.

1920: Nineteenth Amendment gives women right to vote.

1942 – 1945: New Mexicans make major contributions to U.S. victory in World War II.

1948: Native Americans win federal case to gain state voting rights.

1966: New state Capitol opens.

Suggested Books

Cargo, David Francis. *Lonesome Dave, The Story of New Mexico Governor David Francis Cargo*. Santa Fe: Sunstone Press, 2010.

Chavez, Thomas E. *New Mexico Past and Future*. Albuquerque: The University of New Mexico Press, 2006.

Córdova, Kathryn M. *Concha!: Concha Ortiz Y Pino, Matriarch of a 300-Year-Old New Mexico Legacy*. Santa Fe: Gran Via, 2004.

Garnder, Richard. *Grito!: Reies Tijerina and the New Mexico Land Grant War of 1967*. New York: Harper & Row, 1971.

Griswold, del C. R. *The Treaty of Guadalupe Hidalgo: A Legacy of Conflict*. Norman: University of Oklahoma Press, 1990.

DeBuys, William. *Enchantment and Exploitation The Life and Hard Times of a New Mexico Mountain Range*. Albuquerque: The University of New Mexico Press, 1985.

Holmes, Jack Ellsworth. *Politics in New Mexico*. Albuquerque: The University of New Mexico Press, 1967.

Garcia, F. Chris, and Paul L. Hain. *Governing New Mexico*. Albuquerque: The University of New Mexico Press, 2006.

Gordon-McCutchan, R. C., and Frank Waters. *The Taos Indians and the Battle for Blue Lake*. Santa Fe: Red Crane Books, 1991.

King, Bruce, and Charles Poling. *Cowboy in the Roundhouse: A Political Life*. Santa Fe: Sunstone Press, 1998.

Larson, Robert W. *New Mexico's Quest for Statehood, 1846-1912*. Albuquerque: The University of New Mexico Press, 1968.

Lowitt, Richard. *Bronson M. Cutting: Progressive Politician*. Albuquerque: The University of New Mexico Press, 1992.

Mason, W. Dale. *Indian Gaming: Tribal Sovereignty and American Politics*. Norman: University of Oklahoma Press, 2000.

McCulloch, Frank. *Revolution and Rebellion, How Taxes Cost a Governor His Life In 1830s New Mexico*. Santa Fe: Sunstone Press, 2001.

Nolan, Frederick W. *The Lincoln County War: A Documentary History*. Santa Fe: Sunstone Press, 2009.

Perrigo, Lynn I. *Hispanos, Historic Leaders in New Mexico*. Santa Fe: Sunstone Press, 1985.

Prince, L. Bradford. *New Mexico's Struggle for Statehood*. Santa Fe: Sunstone Press, 2010.

Roybal, David. *Taking on Giants: Fabián Chávez, Jr. and New Mexico Politics*. Albuquerque: The University of New Mexico Press, 2008.

Tobias, Henry Jack, and Charles E. Woodhouse. *Santa Fe: A Modern History, 1890 – 1990*. Albuquerque: The University of New Mexico Press, 2001.

Vigil, Maurilio E. *Los Patrones: Profiles of Hispanic Political Leaders in New Mexico History*. Washington, DC: University Press of America, 1980.

Whaley, Charlotte. *Nina Otero-Warren of Santa Fe*. Santa Fe: Sunstone Press, 2007.

Wilkins, David E. *American Indian Politics and the American Political System*. Lanham: Rowman & Littlefield, 2007.

Suggested Websites
(active at time of publication)

Institute for Public Law: www.ipl.unm.edu
League of Women Voters: www.lwvsfc.org
Sen. Dennis Chavez: www.dennischavez.org/archives/view/56/index.html
Statehood fight: www.newmexicohistory.org/filedetails.php?fileID=24195
Think New Mexico: www.thinknewmexico.org

11

Warriors

Three generations of the Chavez family, including Alexine Chavez, her father, Ray, and grandfather Refugio, have served in the U.S. military. Photograph by Natalie Guillén

Answering the Call: Three Generations of Military Service

by
Kate Nash

Alexine Chavez was a senior in high school when she passed by a military recruiting center on St. Michael's Drive in Santa Fe. With a spur of the moment feeling egging her on, she did a U-turn and headed into the center. Inside, the Air Force recruiter persuaded her to join, and she was hooked, joining not once but twice since then.

More than nine years later in 2010, Chavez has seen two tours of Iraq, plus deployments to Saudi Arabia, Japan and countless weekends of training. While her decision to join seemed spontaneous, with a grandfather who served in World War II, a father who put in 20 years at the New Mexico National Guard, and an uncle who served in Vietnam, the service might just be in her blood. Her contribution to the country, and that of her father, Ray, and grandfather, Refugio, who joined her in a recent interview, represent the city's military history dating back more than 60 years. In a broader sense, it also embodies the men and women of the City Different who have served since Santa Fe was founded 400 years ago.

The military history of Santa Fe—capital of a state with more than 200,000 veterans—includes tales of a pueblo revolt, a role in the Civil War, sons lost in Korea. It is flush with stories of those who survived a death march in the Philippines, of Buffalo Soldiers and Rough Riders, of those who went to Afghanistan and of a strong anti-war movement. It includes the yarn of Pancho Villa, and the creation of the atomic bomb.

And it includes the Chavezes. Each signed up for the military in a different era and for distinct reasons. Each had unique experiences. And each puts a face on Santa Fe's sacrifice.

Refugio: POW in WWII

Refugio Chavez was 20 and living in Santa Fe in 1940, without a stable job in sight. With an eighth-grade education, he had been working construction when he could. The Army seemed like his best option, paying $30 a month. He enlisted and shipped off to World War II with the 8th Cavalry Division, against his father's better judgment. To sign up for the training, he needed parental permission.

"My dad signed for me," said Chavez, who recently turned 90 in 2010. "He didn't want to do it, but finally he signed."

In France, Chavez was captured and taken to Germany where he was held for 18 months. For meals, he got two bowls of cabbage soup a day. He did all right, he said, even without meat or bread, but worried about his family in New Mexico.

"My mom didn't know where I was. At first they got a telegram that I was missing in action, then that I was a POW."

When he was liberated in 1945, he said he had never been so happy to see American soldiers. He was able to call his parents back home to give them the news. It would be several more months before he would see them in person, given the logistics of returning to Santa Fe after being discharged. So much has changed since that war, Chavez said, including the number of troops who come back alive. Some 2,263 New Mexicans died in World War II.

"Thanks to God I came back," he said. "I didn't think I was going to make it. They didn't kill me. I was lucky."

Lucky to be alive, Chavez said, and grateful to be back home. The first thing he did was eat a steak, he recalled, then rest, then look for work. One of more than 50,000 New Mexicans who served in World War II, he ended up as a mechanic working the bowling machines at the now-closed Coronado Lanes. Later, when his son Pete went to fight in Vietnam, Refugio Chavez would watch television news every night for word of the U.S. troops.

By coincidence, Refugio one night saw Pete in the background of a scene a reporter had filed from Cambodia. Although Pete had been sending letters to his family with some information on his time in the service, there was such a lag time and Refugio often wondered whether his son was okay. He was, and "By ten o'clock, the whole neighborhood knew about it," Ray Chavez said, gesturing up and down the Third Street neighborhood where Refugio still lives.

These days, Pete doesn't like to talk about Vietnam. And Refugio Chavez doesn't watch the news as much.

Ray: Better Off in the Guard

Ray Chavez thought about the Army after his brother Pete joined. But Pete made him change his mind on a trip back home six months before he was discharged. "He said, 'You don't want to join the Army. If you can join the National Guard you'd be better off.'" So in March of 1971, Ray joined the guard, where his brother also ended up when he came back from Vietnam. Ray put in six years, finished his advanced individual training with the supply section for a heavy equipment maintenance company, then got out in 1977 with no intention of going back. Again, Pete made him change his mind. "He said, 'Go back and finish your twenty years,'" Ray Chavez said.

Chavez was 40 at the time. The physical training was the hardest part. In 2010, Chavez, then 57, was glad to see some of the old friends he'd had in the Guard, something he had missed. At work, he played a key role in keeping the military equipment going, ordering all the mechanical parts needed. He trained with Army members and traveled to Germany, Italy, and Panama for annual training.

One of the highlights for him was running a whole supply unit during a drill weekend in Camp Dodge, Iowa. "I was kind of thrown in there," he recalled. "Usually, when you go for drill weekend, you kind of help them out," he said. Then deployments to Iraq started coming for his unit, something in which Chavez wasn't interested.

He switched to the 93rd troop command, a nondeployable unit that supports those who are sent overseas. "Deployments for me are good for a single person," said Chavez, who has two daughters and a son. He retired in 2002 and as of 2010 works in the human resources department at the National Guard.

Military life has changed for him, too, now that his daughter, Alexine, is in the Air Force—something he said he at first discouraged. "I told her to join the Guard and get a taste before you decide to join," he said. "I didn't feel comfortable with her doing it ... being all the deployments, I figured she doesn't belong being exposed to that kind of danger. She surprises me though."

To get through Alexine's deployments, Chavez looked forward to hearing from her, just as he once had waited for news from his brother, and just as his grandparents waited for news of his father. "I just prayed and thought, 'Let God take care of her.'"

Along with e-mail instead of telegrams, with cross-oceanic flights instead of boat rides, attitudes toward military members have also changed, Chavez said—even in a town that's known for its active peace movement and dotted typically with anti-war signs. "I think people in general have made an extra effort to recognize our work. When my brother came back from Vietnam, they didn't have anything ... anybody waiting. I think the recognition has changed."

Alexine: 9/11 Marked Start

Alexine knew she didn't want to go to college, so as her time at Capital High was ending in 2001, she was searching for her path. The stop at the recruiting center set her on her way. At first, her parents didn't know anything about her plans. "Finally I told them I am going to join, and they said, 'What?' My mom was really ... she didn't want me to go."

But go she did. And became a member of the security forces, no less. Basic training was supposed to start September 11 of that year. Because of the terrorist attacks of that day, the training started a week late. Still, Chavez went. During her nine years in the Air Force, including six on active duty, she went twice to Iraq, and to Japan and Saudi Arabia.

If her father and grandfather hadn't been in the service, she might not have known so much about being deployed, about serving a country from thousands of miles away. "It actually did help. I don't think I would have known anything about the military," she said.

Alexine Chavez served nine years in the Air Force before joining the reserves. Photograph courtesy of Alexine Chavez.

She got out of active duty in early 2007, after her first tour of Iraq, but that didn't last. Within a few months, she joined the reserves. "I wasn't going to go back into the military, I decided to be a civilian, but I missed it a lot and I felt like I need to be in the military," Chavez said. "I didn't know what I wanted to do. I was kind of lost, I guess. I needed to get into the reserves to transition to civilian life again."

By 2008 she was back in Iraq for six months. She kept in touch with Santa Fe through the Internet. Her family kept her linked to life back home. "I missed the food bad," she said.

At training in Missouri, Chavez's mom, Santanita, sent her green chile. It wasn't the same. "It was in baggies and on dry ice."

To Alexine, one of a growing number of women in the Air Force, life in the military is nothing new. To her grandfather, it's a bit of a novelty. The women of his generation played a different role in the military. "They were nurses," he said.

At the Ready for 400 Years

The story of the Chavez family was similar to that of many in the Guard, said the New Mexico National Guard adjutant general, Major General Kenny Montoya. "Almost all of us have a father and grandfather who served," he said. "Traditionally in New Mexico, I think it's part of our culture that we have to serve."

Working for the Guard has become increasingly popular, Montoya said. Recruiting numbers have increased for the past few years, helping the Guard meet its recruiting goals. It had a membership of 4,050 in 2010, and the New Mexico Guard planned to add several new units of about 180 people, including a military police company, a special operations unit and an intelligence unit, Montoya said. Many of the new recruits signed up straight out of high school, Montoya said, a shift in recent years from men and women on active duty or other walks of life who joined the guard in their older years.

"Younger people are seeing the Guard is doing everything the active duty [soldiers] do and more at home. If people in Chama are snowed in and elderly people need their medicine, the Guard is going to get it." The seeming ease with which Montoya was signing up new members in New Mexico tracked with national recruiting numbers.

According to information published by the Department of Defense for the 2010 fiscal year, both the air and army Guard had successful recruiting missions. The Air National Guard signed up 6,983 people, 109 percent of its goal of 6,430, and 57,204 people joined the Army National Guard, 95 percent of its goal of 60,000, the Department of Defense reported. The Army Guard had 362,015 members while the Air Guard had 107,676. Both branches had retention rates above 90 percent.

Montoya said the National Guard system traces its roots back to New Mexico and to Don Juan de Oñate, who when he came through the state in 1598 left some of his troops behind, telling them they were no longer on active duty.

It was also the Guard that played a key role when Pancho Villa crossed into New Mexico. "He raided the regular Army, but it was the Guard who was called out to track him down," Montoya said.

While more might be signing up with the Guard, and while the work is rewarding for many, it comes with a somber task. The men and women of the guard this year alone have buried 600 veterans, many who served in World War II. "Our World War II vets are passing away in large numbers, and that's really hard seeing great New Mexicans that you looked up to your whole life," he said. "That generation is going away."

Bataan: Death March for
World War II Soldiers

by
Bob Quick

The Bataan Death March, one of many Japanese war crimes in World War II, took place in April 1942 in the Philippine Islands. Thousands of American and Allied soldiers died in the march, which was an important event in New Mexico because hundreds of New Mexico soldiers, including those from Santa Fe, were stationed in the Philippines and captured by the Japanese.

Of the 1,800 New Mexicans who took part in the Bataan Death March, only half survived the war to return home. The rest died of disease and starvation and maltreatment in captivity.

The survivors who returned to Santa Fe after the war have faithfully gathered at the Santa Fe Bataan Memorial Building every April 9, the day of surrender to the Japanese.

"That's the day we cried," said the late Jimmy Lopez, a member of the 200th Coast Artillery, as were many of the New Mexico Bataan Death March veterans who lived in Santa Fe. Lopez and other death march survivors discussed their experiences for an article published in *The Santa Fe New Mexican* in 1992, the 50th anniversary of the Bataan Death March.

It all started in Manila with a Japanese attack 10 hours after the air raid on Pearl Harbor. As they did in Hawaii, the Japanese caught the Americans unprepared. The 200th later covered the retreat of U.S. and Filipino soldiers from Manila to prepared positions in Bataan, a 40-mile long jungle-covered peninsula that juts into Manila Bay. It was the plan of General Douglas MacArthur, U.S. commander in the Philippines, for American and Filipino troops to hold out for six months, long enough for reinforcements to arrive from the United States.

But no help arrived, and on Bataan, food supplies dwindled and morale sagged. Soldiers started eating cavalry horses and foraged in the jungle for food. Back home in the newspapers, the beleaguered soldiers became known as "the battling bastards of Bataan."

MacArthur left by torpedo boat on March 11, putting morale even lower. It finally became clear that further resistance was futile, and 12,000 American and 64,000 Filipino troops surrendered on April 9, 1942. The Japanese didn't expect to capture as many soldiers as they did, and their

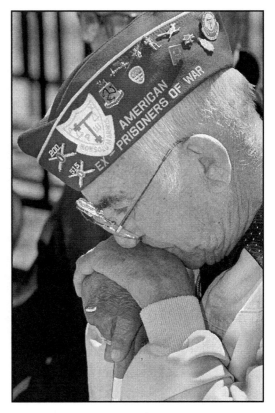

Bataan Death March survivor Arthur Smith in 1998. Photograph by Clyde Mueller.

plans to deal with them fell apart. There weren't enough trucks to take captives to prisoner-of-war camps, and the prisoners' weakness from sickness and hunger made it difficult for them to walk.

But the Japanese forced the prisoners to keep moving, sick or not, and thus began the infamous "death march" of Bataan. It started in Mariveles, a small port at the tip of the peninsula, and ended about 60 miles north in the village of San Fernando.

By the time it was over, more than 10,000 American and Filipino soldiers were dead. The late Manuel Armijo, a Bataan veteran from Santa Fe, remembered bodies lying lifeless along the path of the march. "They wouldn't mess around with sick people," Lopez recalled. "Once you fell down, the guards just stuck a bayonet through you or shot you. We had the best and worst of the Japanese Army," Lopez said. "We knew we were at their mercy."

Bataan Death March survivor Manuel Armijo at age 92 in 2004. Photograph by Steve Babuljak.

In his documentary film about the Bataan Death March, *Colors of Courage: Sons of New Mexico*, Anthony Martinez said it was his impression that the Japanese "never intended for any of these men to live. If they lost the war, the Japanese intended to murder all of them." Martinez includes in his film an interview of a Japanese guard, Yukio Yamabe, who took part in the march. The interview was arranged with the help of a Japanese film crew in Yamabe's hometown of Osaka. "He felt no remorse whatsoever," Martinez said in a 2002 story in *The Santa Fe New Mexican*. "He felt very strongly what happened there (on the march) was simply war."

Yamabe did express regret about one incident during them march, and that was when a Japanese officer decapitated an American prisoner after another officer's sword had only partially severed his head." "I didn't understand why he had to be that cruel," was Yamabe's reaction to the beheading, Martinez said.

Glorieta Battle: Civil War Comes to New Mexico

by
Jason Strykowski

The Battle of Glorieta Pass marked the most momentous battle in the Southwestern theater of the Civil War, and it was fought just miles from Santa Fe. Just a year into the Civil War, the lack of resources that would ultimately be a partial cause of the Confederacy's defeat had not yet become crippling. Optimistic that they could exact some wealth from areas with fewer Union forces, the Confederates hatched a plan. Under President Jefferson Davis, the Confederacy had set its sights on the left coast. If they could take control of the Santa Fe Trail, the Confederates could move west and north toward gold in California and Colorado. But first the Confederates had to capture Fort Union to clear the path.

The Confederates began their march at the opening of 1862. A group of Texas volunteers led by General Henry Sibley progressed up the Rio Grande, beating Edward Canby's Union soldiers at the Battle of Valverde before taking Albuquerque. Sibley's men rolled through Santa Fe that March and prepared to advance into the Sangre de Cristo Mountains toward Fort Union. Leading some 300 men, Major Charles Pyron camped at Apache Canyon. From there they could push though Glorieta Pass and on to Colorado.

John Chivington's Union forces, however, beat Pyron to the punch. On March 26, Chivington attacked with some 400 Union soldiers. At first,

Chivington's troops were repulsed, but flanking the Confederates, Chivington's men managed to push back the Confederate line.

Revisiting the battlefield at Glorieta Pass, June 1880. Photograph by Ben Wittick, courtesy Palace of the Governors Photo Archives (NMHM/DCA), #42922.

Fighting resumed on March 28 after each side took time to be reinforced. The Confederates swelled their ranks to more than 1,000 men while the Union now had a force of more than 1,300. The Union command opted to split its party, sending some into the Pass and others to flank the Confederates.

In Glorieta Pass, the Confederates under Colonel William P. Scurry held strong, forcing the Union back and securing control over the pass. After forcing the Union into several retreats, Scurry's men took a major tactical advantage by gaining control of a ridge overlooking Union forces. Sharpshooters forced the Union back and a Confederate offensive soon broke the Union line. Scurry's men had taken Glorieta Pass.

Unfortunately for Scurry, the flanking Union soldiers had managed to take the Confederate supply train, effectively isolating Scurry's men and making their advance impossible. No longer able to sustain their progress, the Confederates were forced to retreat. Deprived of their supplies, Scurry reported that his men were so destitute that they slept the night after the battle without blankets.

Sibley's men returned along the Rio Grande to Texas. The Union gave chase, forcing the Confederates to return control of Albuquerque to the Union. Never again would the Confederacy or Texas volunteers present a serious threat to New Mexico or the heart of the Southwest.

The defeat doomed the Confederate's campaign in the Southwest, making an overland route to the Pacific highly unlikely. Perhaps gold from the Western mines might have changed the course of the war for the Confederacy, but it was unable to access the great wealth of California and Colorado.

In New Mexico, the aftermath of Glorieta Pass restructured the Union Army and much of the Territory as consequence. After leading 2,000 volunteers from California to New Mexico, Gen. James H. Carleton relieved Canby and assumed command of the Military Department of New Mexico. An experienced desert fighter, Carleton changed the face of war against Native Americans and ultimately instituted the disastrous "Long Walk of the Navajos."

Unknown War Story: Italians Relocated to Santa Fe in 1942

by
James McGrath Morris

When it opened, the exhibit that ran from June 2010 to September of that year at the Los Alamos Historical Museum on the internment of thousands of German civilians during World War II illuminated what a writer called "one of the least known chapters in American history." True enough, but few Americans know that Santa Fe played a role in another equally unknown relocation.

In 2008, I received an e-mail from overseas. "I learned that you are writing a new Joseph Pulitzer biography and that you live in Tesuque," wrote John Pulitzer, an Italian biology professor whose grandfather may have been a distant cousin of the famous Pulitzer. "In nineteen forty-two, we (I was six years old), and some of our Italian and Russian-Italian friends were forced to leave California and, artists all, drawn by the Santa Fe myth, emigrated, of course, to New Mexico."

The emigration was part of the hysteria when the United States was drawn into World War II that led to the imprisonment of Japanese Americans. Italians, and even Italian Americans, were branded "enemy aliens" and ordered to move from certain areas of the country. Nearly 600,000 Italian Americans were subjected to arrest, searches, curfews, forced relocation and in some cases internment.

John's Italian father was a successful architect in Los Angeles who had done work for such famous Americans as Edward G. Robinson. But that was not on the mind of the FBI agents who showed up at their house one day, confiscated his father's personal papers, and told them they would have to move. They selected Santa Fe for their wartime home.

"We rented a house in Tesuque from Hunter Clarkson, I believe a leading player in creating the Santa Fe myth," John explained. "Clarkson was also our neighbor and helped my father plough a field where we grew giant cabbages. My sister was born in June of nineteen forty-two and baptized in Tesuque at the nearby small church of Saint Ysidro. I was going through my father's diary of that year and thought it would be fun to recapture with my family the half-remembered places and events of that time."

Posters like "Enemy Ears Are Listening" were common in World War II. They reflected the fear of espionage. In 1942, the United States detained and moved Americans with ancestral ties to enemies Japan, Germany and Italy. Present-day Casa Solana in Santa Fe was the site of an internment camp for some 4,500 men of Japanese ancestry designated as enemy aliens by virtue of their standing as leaders in their communities. Some Italian Nationals also were moved to Santa Fe but not interned. *Uncivil Liberties* by California historian Stephen Fox is about the Italian-American relocation program. National Archives Identifier 514209.

So it came that on a Sunday morning, armed with topographical maps and a small red-leather diary, John, his wife, Adriana, their 12-year-old son and I headed out to explore the back roads of Tesuque. We found San Ysidro church up a narrow dirt road off Bishop's Lodge Road. We were fortunate because we arrived as Sunday Mass was ending. The church is closed the remainder of the time. This gave John a chance to see the church's interior where he had last been in 1942. As he stood outside, John recognized the orchards leading down the hill slope and the irrigation ditches. One could tell that the place, the sights, and the smells were bringing back memories.

Becky Martinez, a gregarious and charming parishioner whose family has lived in the Tesuque valley for generations, quickly agreed to help us in our quest to find the house John's family rented. All we had was an aging black-and-white photo and his memories. We followed her to a house that seemed like it could have been a remodeled version of the one John lived in, but it was not quite right. Content that we had at least seen the church and been close to his old childhood haunts, we began to drive back to the Tesuque Village Market. Suddenly I spotted a small blue sign hanging on a pole in a driveway. It read, "Rancho Piano, V. Babin." I slammed on the brakes. I remembered John talking about eating borsht at the house of a neighboring Russian pianist and composer named Victor Babin.

Slowly we walked up the overgrown path leading to the house. "Hello, anyone here," I called out. A man appeared. I introduced myself and explained our mission. The man said he was only a guest in the house. Meanwhile, John excitedly recognized the place and picked out a spot where his family joined Babin for meals.

We again showed the 1942 photograph of John's house. "You know, Charlie Miner might know where the house is," said the man. "He has been here thirty-five years and knows just about everything."

Miner operates the Tesuque Glass Works that he created in an old chicken coop in the 1970s on land that had been part of an artist's commune during the 1960s.

So we headed down to the glass studio and asked for Miner. When we found him he was in state of concern. He was heading up to Rancho Piano because he had heard that some strangers were wandering around his property taking photographs. Recently the place had been broken into and, as it is also where Babin is buried, fans of his work have been known to wander in uninvited. His worry was understandable but after we explained that we had asked politely if we could come onto the property and no harm had been intended, his fears were allayed.

Relieved, Miner immediately took an interest in John's story. He looked at the photo and said, "That's Karen Schmidt's house." Schmidt inherited the house from her grandmother almost 20 years ago. Santa Fe and Taos artists had once frequented it. In fact, as she worked to restore the house, Schmidt discovered more than 600 oil, pastel and watercolor paintings done by her grandfather Albert Schmidt.

Miner produced a phone number. She wasn't in, so John had to show the house to his wife and children from the road. But, after a journey of thousands of miles and many years, he had come home.

Personalities: Soldiers, Service, Sacrifice

by
Rob Dean

From the Spanish *cuadrilla* that founded Santa Fe to the Native bands that led the Pueblo Revolt, from the Presidio cavalry to the Great War foot soldiers, Santa Fe residents have responded when called to armed service. The following are among those who made their marks as front-line fighters or unsung heroes.

Colonel Kit Carson in 1864. Photograph courtesy Palace of the Governors Photo Archives (NMHM/ DCA), #7151

Colonel Kit Carson

At 16, Kit Carson followed the Santa Fe Trail to escape the humdrum life as an apprentice saddle maker in Franklin, Missouri. Carson became famous as a trapper, trader, military guide and army officer. He rode with U.S. Army commanders John C. Fremont, Stephen Watts Kearny and James Carleton. Under orders, Carson waged a military campaign against the Navajos, executing the brutal scorched-earth policy of 1863. He later served in Colorado, where he died at 58. He was buried in Taos alongside his wife, Maria Josefa Jaramillo Carson.

Source: *Blood and Thunder* by Hampton Sides.

Major Albert Myer

Major Albert Myer. Photograph courtesy Library of Congress

Modern battlefield communications started in Santa Fe. Trained as a doctor and inspired to develop a communication system for the deaf, Albert Myer joined the U.S. Army and worked out a system of flag signals that allowed one unit to talk with another at a distance. Myer perfected his system while assigned to Santa Fe in 1860. The Union army used the signaling system to help win the Civil War. Myer, who was reassigned from Santa Fe to Washington, D.C., became the father of the Signal Corps for his system known as aerial telegraphy. After the war, Santa Fe became the southwestern headquarters for the Signal Corps, operator of the latest advance in communications, the telegraph system.

Source: *Getting the Message Through* by Rebecca Robbins Raines.

Major Jose Sena

During the battle of Valverde, while other U.S. companies refused to cross the Rio Grande, Jose D. Sena led the men of his Union company across the river through a shower of bullets. The charge didn't prevent a Confederate victory that day in 1862, but it did earn him respect as a U.S. Army officer. After the war, he was in charge of the rebuilding of Fort Marcy. Later he served as Santa Fe County sheriff, became a trusted court interpreter and practiced law. He was an inspiring speaker and pro-statehood spokesman until his 1892 death. In 1865, he brought his patriotism and skills as an orator together to deliver on the Plaza a stirring eulogy for the fallen President Lincoln.

Louisa Canby

U.S. troops under Henry Canby were the heroes of Glorieta, while down the trail it was the colonel's wife, Louisa, who became the "angel of Santa Fe." In a series of battles ending at Glorieta Pass in 1862, U.S. troops stopped Confederate expansion from Texas into the Southwest. On March 29, fighting a late-season snow as well as the enemy, the Texans retreated to Santa Fe in need of blankets for the sick and wounded. Louisa Canby organized army wives on the Union side to give the Confederates badly needed medical attention, earning her a place in history for her humanitarian efforts.

Source: *Women of the New Mexico Frontier* by Cheryl J. Foote.

Louisa Canby. Photograph courtesy National Archives

Rough Riders, Troop E, in San Antonio, Texas, 1898. Photograph courtesy Palace of the Governors Photo Archives (NMHM/DCA), #55017

Sergeant Thomas Ledgwidge

When the Spanish-American War broke out and Teddy Roosevelt mustered his famous Rough Riders, New Mexicans were eager to prove their loyalty to the United States. Santa Fe names filled the roster of 150 men who made up Troop E. One of the sergeants was Thomas Ledgwidge. Of the decisive charge up San Juan Hill in 1898, he recounted, "We went up with a whoop and a yell, and sent the Spaniards running for their second line of entrenchments." The misery of war, however, took much of the bravado out of men such as Ledgwidge, who afterward observed humbly, "We had brave men and we had cowards."

Source: *The New York Times.*

Theodore Rouault

Although he never wore a military uniform and never went to Europe, Theodore Rouault was part of the Great War. He fought the battle of Santa Fe, the battle for respect. Rouault was the state game warden during World

War I, when a Kansas City writer published a letter in a national magazine questioning whether New Mexicans possessed the will to guard America's border. Rouault declared open season on the writer of the "scurrilous letter." Rouault, a descendant of Hispanic settlers, saw the letter as a racist attack. His response to the letter offered a virtual report on New Mexico's eager patriotism in time of war. He said: "Our young men, to the number of some 15,000, are serving with the colors …, and you will find their names among the list of killed or wounded on the battle fields of France."

Dorothy McKibben

In the lofty, hierarchical world of the Manhattan Project, Dorothy McKibben stuck up for the scientists and soldiers who didn't quite conform to the Army way. McKibben guarded the project's secrecy as she managed the tucked-away office in Santa Fe and the oversized egos on the Hill. Her job was to sign in new arrivals, arrange transportation and housing, and plan leisure time for the bosses. She was the versatile administrator who relieved the everyday pressures so Los Alamos scientists could concentrate on developing the atomic bomb. McKibben, a young widow who had moved with her son to Santa Fe for her health, stayed after the war and died in 1985 at 88.

Source: *109 East Palace* by Jennet Conant.

Dorothy McKibben. Photograph by Los Alamos Scientific Laboratory, courtesy Palace of the Governors Photo Archives (NMHM/DCA), #30187.

Timeline

1680: Pueblo Revolt drives Spanish out of Santa Fe.

1693: Spanish soldiers retake Santa Fe.

1822: Jemez massacre kills Navajo leaders before Mexican peace conference.

1846: U.S. Army enters Santa Fe and occupies New Mexico in Mexican-American War.

1862: Civil War armies engage at Glorieta Pass.

1886: Indian wars end in the Southwest.

1912: New Mexico becomes 47th state.

1918: 15,000 New Mexicans fight in World War I.

1942 – 1945: New Mexico fights World War II as soldiers endure Bataan Death March, Code Talkers help end war, and Los Alamos lab makes atomic bomb.

1952 – 1953: State guardsmen units deploy in Korea.

1959: New Mexico National Guard reorganizes.

1991: Guard's Desert Storm activation inspires patriotism.

2003: National Guard answers call for Iraq war.

Suggested Books

Cave, Dorothy. *Beyond Courage: One Regiment against Japan, 1941–1945*. Santa Fe: Sunstone Press, 2006.

Cave, Dorothy. *Four Trails to Valor: From Ancient Footprints to Modern Battlefields, A Journey of Four Peoples*. Santa Fe: Sunstone Press, 2007.

Clevenger, Steven. *America's First Warriors: Native Americans and Iraq*. Santa Fe: Museum of New Mexico Press, 2010.

Conant, Jennet. *109 East Palace: Robert Oppenheimer and the Secret City of Los Alamos*. New York: Simon & Schuster, 2005.

Edrington, Thomas S., and John Taylor. *The Battle of Glorieta Pass: A Gettysburg in the West, March 26–28, 1862*. Albuquerque: The University of New Mexico Press, 2006.

Flint, Richard. *No Settlement, No Conquest: A History of the Coronado Entrada*. Albuquerque: The University of New Mexico Press, 2008.

Fox, Stephen. *Uncivil Liberties: Italian Americans Under Siege During World War II*. Parkland: Universal Publishers/Upublish.com, 2002.

Grant, Blanche Chloe, ed. *Kit Carson's Own Story of His Life*. New Foreword by Marc Simmons. Santa Fe: Sunstone Press, 2007

Hunner, Jon. *Inventing Los Alamos: The Growth of an Atomic Community*. Norman: University of Oklahoma Press, 2007.

Inada, Lawson Fusao. *Only What We Could Carry: The Japanese American Internment Experience*. Berkeley: Heyday Books, 2000.

Jett, Daniel B., and Martha Shipman Andrews. *The Whole Damned World: New Mexico Aggies at War, 1941–1945: World War II Correspondence of Dean Daniel B. Jett.* Los Ranchos de Albuquerque: Published by New Mexico State University Library in collaboration with Rio Grande Books, 2009.

Knaut, Andrew L. *The Pueblo Revolt of 1680: Conquest and Resistance in Seventeenth-Century New Mexico.* Norman: University of Oklahoma Press, 1997.

Melzer, Richard. *Breakdown, How the Secret of the Atomic Bomb Was Stolen During World War II.* Santa Fe: Sunstone Press, 2000.

Reed, Judy. "Santa Fe in World War II, 1940–1947." *All Trails Lead to Santa Fe: An Anthology Commemorating the 400th Anniversary of the Founding of Santa Fe, New Mexico in 1610.* Santa Fe: Sunstone Press, 2010.

Rhodes, Richard. *The Making of the Atomic Bomb.* New York: Simon & Schuster, 1986.

Rogers, Everett M., and Nancy R. Bartlit. *Silent Voices of World War II: When Sons of the Land of Enchantment Met Sons of the Land of the Rising Sun.* Santa Fe: Sunstone Press, 2005.

Szasz, Ferenc Morton. *The Day the Sun Rose Twice: The Story of the Trinity Site Nuclear Explosion, July 16, 1945.* Albuquerque: The University of New Mexico Press, 1984.

Sides, Hampton. *Blood and Thunder: An Epic of the American West.* New York: Doubleday, 2006.

Simmons, Marc. *The Last Conquistador: Juan De Oñate and the Settling of the Far Southwest.* The Oklahoma western biographies, v. 2. Norman: University of Oklahoma Press, 1991.

Stanley, F. *The Civil War in New Mexico.* Santa Fe: Sunstone Press, 2011.

Townsend, Kenneth William. *World War II and the American Indian.* Albuquerque: The University of New Mexico Press, 2000.

Twitchell, Ralph Emerson. *The Military Occupation of the Territory of New Mexico, 1846–1851.* New Edition with Foreword by Richard Melzer. Santa Fe: Sunstone Press, 2007.

Suggested Websites
(active at time of publication)

Bataan Corregidor Memorial Foundation: www.bcmfofnm.org
Bataan story: www.reta.nmsu.edu/bataan/index2.html
New Mexico military history: www.drarchaeology.com/culthist/historic/battles.htm
State Army National Guard: www.nm.ngb.army.mil/

Family

A mariachi group from Guadalajara, Mexico, at Santa Fe Fiesta, 1938. Photograph courtesy Palace of the Governors Photo Archives (NMHM/DCA), #57772.

Life in a Lively Town: Celebrating Family and Community

by
Phaedra Haywood

Monica Sosaya Halford is an archetypal Santa Fe matriarch. Born in 1931 at old St. Vincent Hospital, she joined seven older siblings who grew up along Acequia Madre, Santa Fe's historic irrigation ditch. Acequia Madre Elementary School, home to several Halford murals, hadn't been built then. Present-day Sosaya Lane, named for her father, was a large open field.

"That was our playground," Halford said. "We used to dig fox holes there and pretend we were in the war. My sister learned to drive there."

Halford learned to swim in the Santa Fe River behind her family's summer cottage on Canyon Road. She attended Santa Fe High School when it was downtown. She was a regular at the famed Della's Shed, which doled out hot burgers on cold winter days for just 25 cents. "All of Santa Fe was my family," Halford said, remembering a girlhood crush cut short because the boy turned out to be a cousin. In those days, a boy interested in a date had to pass her mother's interrogation. At times, Halford remembered, the answers caused her mother to exclaim, "Oh dios, som primos"—oh lord, you are cousins.

Her Santa Fe roots began with an ancestor who rode with Don Diego de Vargas in 1693 on his mission of Spanish reconquest. But Halford is quintessentially Santa Fe not only because of her connection to the past but also because of her navigating nonstop changes that gripped Santa Fe before and during her time.

Monica Sosaya Halford, left, and her sister, Stella Montoya. Photograph by Jane Phillips.

The bonds of family and community have been strong in Santa Fe since it was founded in 1610. For generations, Halford's large family and others like it had changed slowly, even as the community's cultural identity continued to shift. Out of necessity, family was at the core of Santa Fe. Extended families were responsible for establishing the city of Santa Fe in the 1600s and 1700s. Over time, families spread out and built on to their homes as settlers survived on the frontier by relying on their large families to do grueling work and to provide mutual protection.

"Life was harsh here," said Santa Fe city historian José Garcia. "It was not for the weak."

A City "Transformed"

Although the rate of change seemed to accelerate in the World War II and postwar era, cultural upheaval had come to Santa Fe in the century before Halford's birth.

In 1846, U.S. troops fighting the Mexican-American War marched on Santa Fe and proclaimed everyone U.S. citizens, Garcia said. The war only added to the steady stream of Americans heading west on the Santa Fe Trail. The newcomers brought foreign ideas about race.

"From that day on, Santa Fe was transformed," Garcia said of the Army's arrival. "There were new laws, a new language, new people, new traditions and new objectives. Attitudes regarding Mexicans were brought here by the St. Louis crowd. Some people were happy to see new people coming in, some people were not. People tried to make distinctions between themselves and Mexicans."

Those outside attitudes also changed the way Santa Fe natives, descendants of Spanish settlers, thought of themselves. Upper-class Santa Feans, wary of being marginalized as people of a conquered land, stressed their ties to Spain as a way to put themselves on the equal footing with the European immigrants coming from the east, Garcia said.

Halford said she never cared much about being Spanish. In fact, she said, she wished for some Native American blood so she would be able to attend the Institute for American Indian Arts. But Halford's daughter Victoria Murphy remembers things differently. "Mom was very proud of her Spanish roots," Murphy said.

Change Comes for Women and Families

The makeup of the city wasn't the only thing undergoing massive changes while Halford was growing up. Residents of the once-isolated city, then fully engaged in trade with the east, were also exposed to new ideas, including some about gender roles. "I was bored in Santa Fe and my mother was very strict," she said. At 19, the daughter joined the U.S. Navy, thwarting her mother's attempts to steer her toward a clerical job in state government. She was stationed for four years in Hawaii. "I took my swimming lesson in Pearl Harbor," Halford said. "It was the best four years of my life."

Upon her return to Santa Fe, Halford married a newcomer, Richard Halford, an architect from Iowa. The couple began their own family in a house they bought around the corner from where she had grown up.

Life in the Halford home was much different than it had been in Monica Sosaya Halford's childhood home. While she grew up speaking both Spanish and English, her children spoke only English. She tried to teach them, instituting a Spanish-only rule at dinner time. But one night her husband asked her the Spanish word for carrots (*zanahorias*). She didn't know it. And that was the end of that.

Halford said her husband supported her artistic tendencies. A well-known santera, Halford also carved and did *colcha* (a traditional Spanish colonial style of embroidery) and mentored her grandchildren in the preservation of those arts.

Halford's husband did not demand that she cook. At holidays she didn't spend hours making tamales or bizcochitos as her mother had. When she did cook, Halford tended away from chile, posole and empanadaditas of her childhood and toward Midwestern meat and potatoes.

A family gathering at the home of Monica Sosaya Halford in October 2010. Photograph by Jane Phillips.

Halford's childhood Christmases included midnight Mass and the tradition of "mis Crismas," a ritual that saw children going door to door asking neighbors for treats. "That tradition left by the time we were in high school," Halford said. Even the big family dinners that commonly marked holidays fell by the wayside over time. "The kids started to want to do different things on Christmas," she said.

Halford and her siblings were required to do household chores. Cleaning the ashes from the woodburning stove and scattering them along the muddy lane was one of hers. With her children, things were different. "I tried to make them take responsibilities but it didn't work," she said. "They would sass me. The discipline is so different now. [When we were young] you would never dare talk back to your parents."

Races Mixed in Santa Fe

Halford was lucky to know her history. Many other Santa Feans did not. Santa Fe city historian José Garcia said he likes to provoke Santa Feans who claim to be Spanish by asking them to pinpoint their ancestral homes in Spain.

Garcia himself marked the third generation of his family to have been born near Pecos. He traced his roots to Zacatecas, Mexico, so he calls himself Mexican. Told they were Spanish and learning the Mexican connection, his four daughters were confused by an "identity problem," he said. "But I didn't have any answers for them," Garcia said. "I say, 'I am of multi-ethnic background, with ties to the ancient pueblos of the Rio Grande and the Andalusia area of Spain.'"

By the late 1900s, scholarly research and everyday observations were showing that the tricultural myth marketed to tourists in the mid-1920s— in which distinct Native Americans, Anglo-Saxons and Spaniards lived with equality side by side—was just that, a myth.

In reality, Santa Feans generally are people of mixed race.

For example Rebecca Scott Gonzales, a third-grade teacher at E.J. Martinez Elementary School, knows only that her father was born on the Ute reservation in Ignacio, Colorado, and her mother was Scottish, French and Choctaw. On one hand, her mother was listed on the membership roll of a federally recognized tribe. On another, she signed Gonzales up for the Daughters of the American Revolution, a nonprofit group with lineage-based membership. "Which is hysterical because I'm Spanish and Indian, two things they don't like very much," Gonzales said.

Gonzales said that even in the 1970s her father struggled with his cultural identity. "He tried to be more European," Gonzales said. "He anglicized everything. He even changed his name to Charles B. Gonsales. He didn't want me to learn Spanish that was not 'pure.' He would say, 'You're not Hispanic. You are not Latino. You are Spanish.'"

Gonzales said her mother, a woman who "couldn't even say tortilla," didn't want her daughter speaking Spanish at all.

Economic Divisions in Community

Valerie Martínez, poet laureate of Santa Fe from 2008 to 2010, left her hometown in the 1980s to live and study abroad. She returned a decade later and found a Santa Fe that was to her increasingly divided. "It seemed more segregated," Martinez said, who described herself as a "mixed blood person" with Hispanic, Navajo and Ohkay Owingeh roots. "When I was growing up everyone got along, or they didn't get along, but all the neighborhoods were mixed. Now I think that's starting to be less true of Santa Fe. And I think it's been divided a lot because of economics."

Martinez tried to erase those divisions via an art project and book she created called *Lines and Circles: A Celebration of Santa Fe Families.* For the project Martínez worked with three generations of 11 families, learning their stories and helping them create art and poetry. Martínez said racial diversity emerged as a defining issue. "We see now an influx of Mexican families," she said. "But the trouble between Mexican and Hispanic families, that blows my mind because a lot of the families don't know their own histories. We are having to face this kind of 'pure blood' thing. We have to face it because we have more and more of our citizens who intermarry and become more complex. We need to find ways to allow that to happen and rejoice in it and make sure there is tolerance."

Martínez said it's time for Santa Feans to invent new rituals akin to Zozobra and the Pet Parade. "I love those kind of secular things that bring people together. You see a lot of different people at those kind of events and I think it's because they are not laden with things they have to stand for and stand against."

Martínez also said she's bothered by the cultural one-upmanship of people competing for seniority based on how long their families have lived in the area. "I want someone to be able to say, 'I've been here for two years and I love this place,'" she said. "That should be as valuable."

Santa Fe, the People's Choice

Despite the economic divisions Martínez found upon her return—notably the high cost of living and lack of affordable housing—Santa Fe's identity as a small but cosmopolitan city surrounded by mountains remained attractive. Increasingly, people moved to Santa Fe by choice. Census figures showed that the city population grew 75 percent in less than 50 years, growing from 41,000 in 1970 to 72,000 in 2006, the most recent U.S. Census estimate.

Ramon Lovato said he moved from San Francisco to Santa Fe in 1990 at 34 years old with his wife and son for quality-of-life reasons. The family wanted good weather, nice restaurants, land and the country life. He and his wife wanted to send their son to a Waldorf School, something they couldn't afford in San Francisco. Lovato's son is now grown. Lovato and his wife have divorced, and he's moved out of the country home they bought near Eldorado. But he has no intention of leaving Santa Fe.

"I see no reason to leave," he said. "I have community here."

Santa Fe shows its festive side at the Historical Hysterical Parade each September during Fiesta. Photograph by Jane Phillips.

Arturo Vega moved to Santa Fe to find economic opportunity. His son translating, the 66-year baker and owner of Panaderia Zaragoza said in Spanish that he applied for legal immigration to the United States in 1981 for the sake of his children. When he was finally approved in 1993, he originally wanted to move to Nevada, but a brother who had already come to Santa Fe encouraged him to settle in the same place. Vega liked the fact that the city was not too big and was home to many people from Chihuahua. Vega said his bakery, which has been open 15 years, was the second Mexican-owned business in Santa Fe. And when he entered Santa Fe High School he was one of only 28 Mexican students. By graduation in 2002, Ivan Vega said, there were 60 or 70. Historian Garcia said it bothers him to hear his own "raza" disparage Mexicans. "The ones from Chihuahua could be your fifteenth cousins," he said.

Garcia said Santa Feans owe a debt of gratitude to Mexican immigrants for keeping Spanish alive in the city. "If it were not for the Mexican workers we have here, Spanish would not be heard in Santa Fe," Garcia said. "It would be a lost language. I'm grateful to them for that."

Family: Love and Honesty

Much as the long-ago settlers did, Santa Fe residents in 2010 also relied on tradition and faith to keep them going. In addition to being the home of the Cathedral Basilica of St. Francis of Assisi, the city also boasts a Buddhist stupa, a mosque, a Jewish temple and a Greek Orthodox church, to mention just a few of the dozens of places of worship in the city.

Santa Fe's many mouths also keep family traditions alive in a secular way, through their food, including some purely New Mexican dishes.

Gabe Gomez—a first generation American born in El Paso to Mexican parents and married to a woman from New Orleans—has incorporated green chile into the gumbo recipe he learned from his father-in-law.

Meanwhile, the Lovato family might celebrate holidays with Salvadoran tamales made with chicken, olives, raisins and capers, or New Mexican-style tamales made with pork and red chile. And seventh-generation Santa Fean Nicolasa Chavez, recalling a dish her grandmother from Ohio used to make at Christmas, still dreams about "the thing" in a dessert made of sponge cake, Jell-O—"red and green, of course"—and whipped cream.

Regardless of race, religion or ethnicity and regardless of the food one eats or the part of town one calls home, the people of Santa Fe still talk constantly about family.

"Family means friendship," said Halford's 10-year-old granddaughter, Sydney Halford. "Love, friendship and honesty, you have to be honest to your family and trustworthy. And you just need to love them."

Tamales are at the heart of a New Mexico tradition that brings families together before Christmas. Photograph by Natalie Guillén.

Tribal Membership Is Controversial Topic

by
Phaedra Haywood

I n 2009, the U.S. census estimated that American Indians composed about 3.5 percent of the population of Santa Fe County. A comparison to the number of enrolled tribal members listed on the website for the New Mexico Department of Indian Affairs showed an undercount of Native Americans. The state's number indicated that Native Americans composed between 15 and 19 percent of the county's population in 2000.

Regardless, Native Americans continue to play a significant role in many activities around the county, perhaps most notably by participating in the annual Indian Market, which draws thousands of visitors to Santa Fe and brings an estimated $100 million worth of spending into the city. Artists who wish to participate in the market must possess a Certificate of Indian Blood that authenticates membership of a federally recognized tribe.

John Torrez Nez, director of artist services for the market, said the blood-quantum requirement varies by tribe because it is up to each tribe to determine its own criteria. Nez said some tribes require members to be one-quarter Native American, while others have reduced the requirement as low as one-28th. "If a tribe claims you that's good enough for me," Nez said.

Artist Roxanne Swentzell, a member of Santa Clara Pueblo whose mother was Santa Clara and whose father was of German descent, said determining the qualifications has grown increasingly controversial as people intermarried. "I think it's a really hot topic myself," Swentzell said. "It's affecting so many of the people around here. There are people who are full-blood Pueblo Indians that are members of no tribe, because one tribe goes through the mother line and one goes through the father line and they miss out completely. Here at Santa Clara, when they started going through the father, women started having children out of wedlock because, when a woman has illegitimate children, the tribe acts as the father." Swentzell said she's heard some tribes are basing tribal membership on participation within the tribe.

"I like that route best because it's community-based," she said. "All these issues of membership and blood quantum get to be a distraction when I think the real issue about family is really about the state of community. How we are working together? It doesn't matter if you have blood quantum. It's if you are a real part of that place and those people."

Willa Cather's Bestseller Brings World to Santa Fe

by
Jason Strykowski

I t took a journalist to write one of New Mexico's most famed pieces of fictional literature. And, not surprisingly, Willa Cather focused on Santa Fe history. Cather was born in 1873 to a Virginia sheepherder who soon moved the family to Nebraska. The young Cather spent much of her youth and early career as a newspaper editor and writer, penning articles for numerous publications. She also wrote dozens of shorts stories before publishing her first novel in 1912.

Cather's next few books, including the classics *O Pioneers!* and *My Antonia,* turned her into one of America's most noted authors. One of her books, in fact, may even have inspired sections of F. Scott Fitzgerald's epochal *The Great Gatsby.*

Perhaps her most respected novel, *Death Comes for the Archbishop* grew out of Cather's fascination with New Mexico and the Southwest. Since childhood, Cather had devoured magazine articles on the Southwest, with its unique landscape and characters. In 1925, by then a tremendously successful writer, Cather visited New Mexico to research "her priests" and their homes.

Cather threw herself wholeheartedly into her reading on real-life Catholic luminaries Jean Baptiste Lamy, Antonio José Martinez and Joseph Machebeuf. Her research took her around the state as she visited Acoma, Taos, Alcalde, Abiquiú and the village of Lamy. In Santa Fe, she stayed at La

Fonda, just feet from the cathedral where the real Lamy once toiled. Even though she was still in the process of editing her last book, Cather returned to New Mexico a year later. This time she stayed with trendsetting New Mexican writer Mary Austin. Cather used Austin's New Mexico cabin as a writer's retreat before returning to the East Coast to finish the book in a surprisingly short period of time.

Willa Cather. Photograph by Nickolas Muray, courtesy Palace of the Governors Photo Archives (NMHM/DCA), #111734.

While writing, Cather took recorded history as mere suggestion, a dangerous decision in light of her use of real names. While she created fictitious pseudonyms for Lamy and Machebeuf, Martinez was represented in the novel under his actual name as was the pulp hero Kit Carson. Cather also based much of the novel on inaccurate reports tied to these men.

Even without fictionalization, Jean Baptiste Lamy's life story seemed the stuff of legend. A French-born and trained priest, Lamy traveled to the United States while still in his youth. A decade after his arrival, the Vatican, hoping to take advantage of the Treaty of Guadalupe Hidalgo, assigned Lamy to the newly created provisional diocese of New Mexico.

Lamy found numerous obstacles in Santa Fe. The clergy already installed in New Mexico refused to recognize the reorganization of the diocese or Lamy's leadership. Several priests butted heads with Lamy repeatedly over issues such as clerical lifestyles and the institution of tithes. Lamy also took on a larger cross-section of the New Mexican populace as he attempted to disband the Penitentes. Dying in 1888, Lamy never actually witnessed the partial completion of, perhaps, his greatest accomplishment—the cathedral that still stands in the center of Santa Fe.

A post card sent by Willa Cather from Santa Fe to a friend in the East. Photograph from *The Santa Fe New Mexican* archives.

The conflict and racial overtones in Lamy's history perfectly fueled Cather's imagination. His story was the tale of the Southwest in synecdoche. Through Lamy, Cather could explore the processes of cultural transformation, empire and colonization as New Mexico changed from a Mexican province to an American territory.

In the summer of 1927, the novel appeared in serial form. Knopf followed up that fall as it released *Death Comes for the Archbishop* in bound copy with a print run of 25,000 copies. Quickly, demand mounted for second and third editions of the book.

The book met not only with popular interest, but also with critical acclaim. The American Academy of Arts and Letters even presented Cather with the prestigious Howell's Medal for the best American novel. More distinctions soon followed as Cather received honorary degrees from Yale, Columbia, University of California, Berkeley and Princeton.

Cather succeeded *Death Comes for the Archbishop* with another historical novel. *Shadows on the Rock* took Cather from territorial New Mexico to colonial Quebec. *Shadows* found an admiring audience as well, netting Cather the Prix Femina Americana, a French literary honor.

Over the next 16 years, leading up to her death in 1947, Cather published two more novels and a compilation of short stories. Her final book, *The Old Beauty and the Others* was published just after her death.

Since its publication, *Death Comes for the Archbishop* has remained on the short list of classic American literature. *Time* magazine placed the book on its list of the 100 best English-language novels. The Modern Library ranks the book 61st on their catalog of 100 novels, only a dozen spots behind *The Women* by Cather's one-time acquaintance, D.H. Lawrence.

Santa Feans sing carols around a bonfire while they enjoy the Christmas Eve walk on Canyon Road. Photograph by Luis Sánchez Saturno.

Holiday Traditions Survive Generations

by
Robert Nott

When many people think of Christmas in Santa Fe, the image of a Christmas Eve walk up Canyon Road may immediately come to mind. But while that tradition is not even 40 years old (accounts vary as to exactly what year that event began in the 1970s), Santa Fe has been celebrating Christmas since 1610.

And while the classical music concerts, the ice sculpture on the Plaza, and the live nativity re-creations don't harken back to Spanish Colonial times, many current traditions trace their roots back to the late 1600s, when Santa Fe was founded. "Christmas here would have to be geared toward Christianity—it's almost unavoidable," said Susan Topp Weber, owner of Susan's Christmas Shop and author of the 2010 book *Christmas in Santa Fe*. "It's a unique city for a Christmas celebration, which is why people come here again and again every December for that flavor."

That flavor includes midnight Mass, Christmas Eve bonfires (which symbolize lighting the way for the Santo Niño, or Christ Child), and religious folk plays including Las Posadas, Los Pastores, and Los Tres Reyes.

Las Posadas—which is about Joseph and Mary's search for shelter in Bethlehem so she can give birth to the Baby Jesus—is still performed in Santa Fe before Christmas, with additional characters that the Spanish colonists did not conjure up for their original presentations: devils. In Santa Fe's version, these devils pop out of windows and doorways to chase Joseph and Mary away—to no avail.

John Flax, left, and Charles Gamble of Theater Grottesco in Santa Fe portray diablos for the holiday pageant Las Posadas. Photograph by Luis Sánchez Saturno.

In Weber's book, she notes that Anglo Christmas traditions—Christmas trees (perhaps piñon at first), stockings hung over the chimney with care, and even the stringing of lights (or candles)—arrived in Santa Fe in the 1820s, once the Santa Fe Trail opened up. Over time, of course, the three primary cultures here—Hispano, Native American, and Anglo—merged and mixed holiday traditions. "There's an interesting interweaving of the fabric of these three cultures here," Weber said, noting all the various events signifying the spiritual and the secular. "We still have the bonfires, the medieval plays, and Mass, but you've also got concerts, the ice sculpture, the (Gustave) Baumann marionettes, Santa Claus, Christmas at the Palace, the Pueblo dances, and even the Christmas train at the First National Bank."

That train first appeared before Christmas of 1954, Weber's book notes, when bank employees Don Van Soelen and Antonio Romero set up the first train. The exhibit has grown over time, and the not-so-distant sounds of the toy train's whistle pleases patrons of the bank. Christmas concerts performed by church congregations or locally based music groups take place in such revered halls as St. Francis Cathedral Basilica, the Loretto Chapel, San Miguel Mission, and Cristo Rey Catholic Church in the days leading up to Christmas.

A nativity scene graces the courtyard of La Fonda sometime between 1925 and 1945. Photograph by T. Harmon Parkhurst, courtesy Palace of the Governors Photo Archives (NMHM/DCA), #55657.

Likewise, *Nacimientos* (Nativities), which were not very common in New Mexico's colonial era, according to Weber, have become more widespread, often reflecting a regional feel or style. Cristo Rey Church displays a pueblo pottery nativity, while First Baptist Church stages a live outdoor nativity event, replete with shepherds, sheep, and donkey (as well as a live angel!).

And then, of course, on Christmas Eve (*La Noche Buena*), you can take in a concert, visit your church for services, and walk Canyon Road, where farolitos, luminarias, and bonfires still light the way, not only for the Christ Child, but for the thousands of visitors who take the walk.

Weber understands its importance in marketing Santa Fe as a Christmas city, but she's also seen that particular event get a little out of control. "It's more like Mardi Gras now—which is not what it was intended to be when it was started," she said.

Personalities: Families, Fiestas and Fun

by
Rob Dean

For 400 years, Santa Fe life has been, well, lively, thanks to people like these colorful few who represented their neighbors' many interests and talents.

Miguel de la Vega y Coca

In 1693 – 94, the waves of colonists arriving in Santa Fe included 16-year-old Miguel de la Vega y Coca and his wife, Manuela. They left a vivid record of colonial village life and joined settlers in building a village that, following Spanish custom, featured a palace, presidio and church ringing a plaza. Vega y Coca thrived in conditions that were ideal for farming and ranching—a river that ran full for irrigation, lush cottonwoods that shaded the banks, and fields that let sheep and crops flourish. Weavers, tinsmiths, carpenters and blacksmiths filled the homes with blankets, chandeliers, furniture and utensils. In time, the Vega y Cocas grew into an active family of eight daughters, and with each marriage Vega y Coca gained control of property that increased his holdings.

Source: *El Rancho de las Golondrinas* by Carmella Padilla.

Anne Cleland Howe

A descendant of English settlers who moved to post-Spanish colonial Florida, Anne Cleland Howe moved to Santa Fe in about 1850 with her husband, U.S. cavalry officer Marshall Howe. She was no quiet, secluded army wife, and that also was true in her life after Santa Fe. She died in Florida in 1893, but not before she worked there to start a hospital, orphanage and library association. In Santa Fe, Howe involved her young son in village life, making sure he learned Spanish and the skills of a horseman. Her commitment to education did not end with her son. In 1852, she opened the first nonsectarian school available to students regardless of ability to pay, a classroom that would closely fit today's definition of a public school.

Amado Chaves

When he died at 79 in 1930, Amado Chaves' obituary described a "live wire" who never lost interest in the affairs of Santa Fe, New Mexico or the world beyond. Chaves, a lawyer whose activism covered a wide range of community interests, was a legislator and a mayor. A prolific writer, he was an advocate for education, serving as the first superintendent of public instruction for New Mexico. Chaves bridged old and new. He said, "While we look about us and see the remains of a very ancient civilization, the world of mighty ages past, let us hold out our hands to accept of the new, with all the good it brings." Source: Office of the State Historian.

Brian Boru Dunne

One of the most eccentric characters in Santa Fe from statehood to the 1950s was Brian Boru Dunne. No one in town could fail to notice him. Hummingbird-like with a bony frame and sharp nose, Dunne wore a showy wide-brimmed hat with a silver band—famous locally for touching off a contest among people who claimed the hat after his death. He planted himself in the middle of the Santa Fe social scene, wrote a newspaper gossip column and hung out for years in the lobby doing ambush interviews of La Fonda guests. For years, Dunne, who died at 84 in 1962, wrote articles light in substance but heavy on sensation. Likewise, when he spoke, his dramatic delivery puffed up his empty rhetoric and made it seem profound. In 1913, Dunne famously testified before a legislative panel investigating corruption and ended up monopolizing the stage with his nonstop chatter that confounded and amused committee members and brought the meeting to an abrupt end.

Source: *My City Different* by Betty Bauer and *The Santa Fe New Mexican*.

Brian Boru Dunne, columnist and man about town, about 1955. Photograph by Tyler Dingee, courtesy Palace of the Governors Photo Archives (NMHM/DCA), #120361

Marion Hotopp, MD

In 1946, *Time* magazine stated that Santa Fe had the country's worst infant death rate. Three years earlier, Dr. Marion Hotopp had arrived in Santa Fe as a public health officer. Irritated because she thought the story distorted the facts, the outspoken and unyielding Hotopp used her anger to invigorate her work. In more than 20 years in Santa Fe public health, she was instrumental in improving the mortality rate of infants in rural areas by emphasizing the health and nutritional benefits of breastfeeding. She retired in 1967 and died in 1976.

Source: New Mexico Pediatric Society and *The Santa Fe New Mexican.*

Amalia Sena Sánchez

The first Fiesta queen of 1927 was an obvious choice, even though she felt unsuited for the role. Amalia Sena Sánchez belonged to a distinguished Santa Fe family of soldiers and public servants, but she also was a wife and mother who thought the queen ought to be a single woman. To Sena Sánchez, Fiesta meant beautiful parties, round-the-clock action at the elegant La Fonda and tables filled with food and refreshments and the Plaza. She and her children went all out for Fiesta. Her husband, Manuel, used to say, "I think I'm going to go someplace for fiestas because you're never home." Sena Sánchez's family name was forever associated with Sena Plaza, the one-time home on East Palace Avenue featuring 30-some rooms, a ballroom and a central courtyard. She died at 109 in 2002.

Source: *Turn Left at the Sleeping Dog* by Pen La Farge.

Amalia Sena Sánchez was the Fiesta queen in 1927.

Monte Chavez

In their heyday from the 1880s to 1950, Harvey hotels like La Fonda offered class and comfort to rail passengers. Harvey girls—wholesome, attractive young women between 18 and 30 who served restaurant guests—became known as the girls who civilized the West. Monte Chavez, who was born in 1911 and worked at La Fonda from 1929 to 1989, witnessed the Harvey-inspired boom in travel and tourism that hit Santa Fe. "We would all go out to dances and parties together," he said of the hotel staff, including the Harvey girls who were supposed to date only fellow employees. Some of the transplanted girls married lawyers, politicians and ranchers and became permanent Santa Fe residents. To Chavez, who died in 2004, La Fonda was a rowdy and informal place, memorable in no small part as the one Harvey hotel where the dignified "coat rule" couldn't survive.

Source: *The Harvey Girls* by Lesley Poling-Kempes.

Harvey girls at La Fonda and other hotels in the West served a growing number of tourists into the 1950s. Photograph from *The Santa Fe New Mexican* archives.

Pablita Velarde

From 1937 to 1943, Pablita Velarde documented traditional Pueblo life in 70 paintings done as a public-art project for Bandelier National Monument. Born in 1918 at Santa Clara, Velarde was sent at five years old to live and study at an Indian boarding school. The experience deepened her appreciation for her Native roots and led her to use art to depict her threatened culture. *Old Father Story Teller,* a book first published in 1960, created a lasting collection of her most prized paintings and her forefathers' most enduring stories. She died in 2006.

Pablita Velarde, an artist from Santa Clara Pueblo, about 1955. Photograph by Emmett P. Haddon, courtesy Palace of the Governors Photo Archives (NMHM/DCA), #151998.

Timeline

1610: Spanish establish Santa Fe.

1626: Santa Fe experiences Inquisition.

1821: Santa Fe Trail opens.

1865: Sisters of Charity offer medical care.

1868: Telegraph lines reach Santa Fe.

1880: Adolph Bandelier surveys Native ruins.

1881: Telephone service begins.

1900: Census puts city population at 5,603.

1902: Sunmount Sanatorium treats respiratory ailments.

1918: Worldwide influenza epidemic hits.

1919: City revives Fiesta and includes Spanish Market.

1927: Willa Cather publishes *Death Comes for the Archbishop*.

1929: Redone La Fonda reopens as a Harvey hotel.

1945: War veterans return home.

1946: Region's high infant mortality makes national news.

1948: Santa Fe Ski Basin installs chairlift.

1950: Population hits almost 28,000.

1972: La Familia community health center opens.

1973: De Vargas Center mall opens.

1981: National press makes Santa Fe a hot spot.

2000: Census counts population of 62,203.

Suggested Books

Aragon, Ray John de. *Padre Martínez and Bishop Lamy*. Santa Fe: Sunstone Press, 2006.

Aragon, Ray John de, translated from the Spanish. *Recollections of the Life of the Priest Don Antonio José Martínez* by Pedro Sánchez. Santa Fe: Sunstone Press, 2006.

Austin, Mary. *The American Rhythm, Studies and Reexpressions of American Songs*. Santa Fe: Sunstone Press, 2007.

Austin, Mary. *Earth Horizon*. Santa Fe: Sunstone Press, 2007.

Austin, Mary. *The Land of Journeys' Ending*. Santa Fe: Sunstone Press, 2007.

Austin, Mary. *The Land of Little Rain*. Santa Fe: Sunstone Press, 2007.

Bacigalupa, Drew. *Seven Carols, Seven Gifts: Christmas Stories for All Ages*. Santa Fe: Sunstone Press, 2007.

Chávez, Fray Angélico. *But Time and Chance, The Story of Padre Martínez of Taos, 1793–1867*. Santa Fe: Sunstone Press, 1981.

Bauer, Betty E. *My City Different: A Half-Century in Santa Fe*. Santa Fe: Sunstone Press, 2004.

Bustamante, Adrian. "Españoles, Castas, y Labradores: Santa Fe Society in the Eighteenth Century." *In Santa Fe: History of an Ancient City*, David Grant Noble, ed. Santa Fe: School for Advanced Research Press, 2008.

Ebinger, Virginia Nylander. *Aguinaldos: Christmas Customs, Music, and Foods of the Spanish-speaking Countries of the Americas*. Santa Fe: Sunstone Press, 2008.

Esquibel, Jose Antonio, and John B. Colligan. *The Spanish Recolonization of New Mexico: An Account of the Families Recruited at Mexico City in 1693*. Albuquerque: Hispanic Genealogical Research Center of New Mexico, 1999.

Frank, Lois Ellen. *Foods of the Southwest Indian Nations: Traditional & Contemporary Native American Recipes*. Berkeley: Ten Speed Press, 1991.

Gilbert, Fabiola Cabeza de Baca, and Gerri Chandler. *The Good Life: New Mexico Traditions and Food*. Santa Fe: Museum of New Mexico Press, 2005.

Jaramillo, Cleofas M. *Romance of a Little Village Girl*. Albuquerque: University of New Mexico Press, 2000.

La Farge, John Pen. *Turn Left at the Sleeping Dog: Scripting the Santa Fe Legend, 1920–1955*. Albuquerque: University of New Mexico Press, 2001.

La Farge, Oliver. *The Mother Ditch*. Santa Fe: Sunstone Press, 1983.

Laughlin, Ruth. *Caballeros: The Romance of Santa Fe and the Southwest*. Santa Fe: Sunstone Press, 2007.

Martínez, Valerie. *And They Called It Horizon, Santa Fe Poems*. Santa Fe: Sunstone Press, 2010.

Martínez, Valerie. *Lines and Circles, A Celebration of Santa Fe Families*. Santa Fe: Sunstone Press, 2010.

Massmann, Ann M., "Adelina 'Nina' Otero-Warren: A Spanish-American Cultural Broker." *Journal of the Southwest*, 2000.

Mitchell, Pablo. *Coyote Nation: Sexuality, Race, and Conquest in Modernizing New Mexico, 1880–1920*. Worlds of desire. Chicago: University Of Chicago Press, 2005.

Ortega, Pedro Ribera. *Christmas in Old Santa Fe*. Santa Fe: Sunstone Press, 1973.

Ortiz y Pino, Yolanda. *Original Native New Mexico Cooking*. Santa Fe: Sunstone Press, 1993.

Samora, Vangie. *Mujeres Valerosas: Meet the Extraordinary Women of the New Mexico Hispanic Women's Council*. Albuquerque: Hispanic Women's Council, 2006.

Reed, Maureen E. *A Woman's Place: Women Writing New Mexico*. Albuquerque: University of New Mexico Press, 2005.

Sando, Joe S. *Pueblo Profiles: Cultural Identity through Centuries of Change*. Santa Fe: Clear Light Publishers, 1998.

Simmons, Marc. *Charles F. Lummis, Author and Adventurer*. Santa Fe: Sunstone Press, 2008.

Twitchell, Ralph Emerson. *Old Santa Fe*. Santa Fe: Sunstone Press, 2007.

Udall, Stewart L. *The Forgotten Founders: Rethinking the History of the Old West*. Washington, DC: Island Press, 2002.

Underhill, Ruth Murray. *Life in the Pueblos.* Santa Fe: Ancient City Press, 1991.

Velarde, Pablita. *Old Father Story Teller.* Santa Fe: Clear Light Publishers, 1993.

Weber, David J. *Foreigners in Their Native Land: Historical Roots of the Mexican Americans.* Albuquerque: University of New Mexico Press, 2003.

Weber, Susan Topp. *Christmas in Santa Fe.* Layton: Gibbs Smith, 2010.

Whaley, Charlotte. *Nina Otero-Warren of Santa Fe.* Santa Fe: Sunstone Press, 2007.

Suggested websites
(active at time of publication)

Christus St. Vincent: www.stvin.org
Fiesta: www.media.museumofnewmexico.org/press_releases.
    php?action=detail&releaseID=67
New Mexico family services: www.cyfd.org/
Old Santa Fe Association: www.oldsantafe.org/

CONTRIBUTORS
(Information Current at Time of Publication)

Michael Abatemarco lives in Santa Fe and writes regularly for *Pasatiempo*, the arts and culture magazine of *The Santa Fe New Mexican*. He served as co-chair of Friends of Contemporary Art for the New Mexico Museum of Art.

Brian Barker has been the presentation editor for *The Santa Fe New Mexican* since 2005. He previously worked for *The Sporting News* in St. Louis and the *Press Democrat* in Santa Rosa, California.

Dennis Carroll is a freelance writer whose work has appeared in major newspapers and publications around the country including *The New York Times*, *The Christian Science Monitor* and *The Boston Globe*. Prior to moving to New Mexico in 2007, he was a speech writer in the Iowa governor's office.

Anne Constable joined *The Santa Fe New Mexican* in 2000 as an assistant city editor. Prior to that, she was a writer for the *Santa Fe Reporter* and a correspondent for *Time* magazine. She earned her undergraduate degree in publishing.

Rob Dean became the senior editor of *The Santa Fe New Mexican* in 1992. He previously worked at newspapers in Washington state and Montana. He earned undergraduate degrees in journalism, history and politics, and holds a master's degree in history.

Douglas Fairfield is a contributing writer to *Pasatiempo* and has lived in New Mexico since 1998. He has served on the faculties of colleges and universities in Michigan, Pennsylvania, and New Mexico, and is the former Curator of Art for the Albuquerque Museum of Art & History. He holds a master of fine arts degree and a doctorate in art history.

Julie Ann Grimm has covered local government in Santa Fe since 2003. Before that, she worked for The Associated Press in Albuquerque. She is a graduate of the University of Missouri School of Journalism.

Natalie Guillén joined *The Santa Fe New Mexican* as a photojournalist in 2005 after earning a degree at the University of Missouri School of Journalism. The daughter of a reporter, she grew up in the Seattle, Washington, area and has traveled and worked internationally. She organized photo training at three National Association of Hispanic Journalists conventions.

Phaedra Haywood has worked at *The Santa Fe New Mexican* since 1999. She currently covers county government. She was born in a cabin in the mountains near Ojo Sarco, and grew up in Santa Fe and rural Southern Colorado

Robin McKinney Martin is the owner of *The Santa Fe New Mexican, The Taos News* and the *Sangre de Cristo Chronicle*. She represents the second generation in her family newspaper business. She has been a newspaper publisher for more than 30 years. Her family has many connections with New Mexico history. Her great-grandfather on her father's side shipped on the Santa Fe Trail. Her grandfather on her mother's side brought the first herd of Aberdeen Angus cattle to the state. Her husband Meade's grandfather was the first president of the New Mexico Normal School in El Rito, New Mexico.

Sandra Baltazar Martínez has been with *The Santa Fe New Mexican* since 2008. She worked as a reporter for both English- and Spanish-language newspapers in California, where she completed her undergraduate degree. Martínez earned a master's in community journalism from the University of Alabama.

Staci Matlock joined *The Santa Fe New Mexican* as a reporter in 1999 and covers natural resources. She has worked as a reporter at *The Taos News*, as editor of an outdoor sports magazine in Tucson, and as publisher of a Spanish-English newspaper, *The Sonoran Journal*.

James McGrath Morris' latest book was the highly regarded *Pulitzer: A Life in Politics, Print, and Power*, published in 2010. His writing has appeared in numerous newspapers and magazines. He is a former teacher and newspaper reporter.

Clyde Mueller moved to Santa Fe in 1994, and became the director of photography for *The Santa Fe New Mexican*. He earned a bachelor's degree in integrated studies and has consulted in several Eastern European countries.

Kate Nash has worked for New Mexico newspapers since graduating from The University of New Mexico in 1999. She has degrees in journalism and Spanish, and covers government and politics for *The Santa Fe New Mexican*.

Robert Nott has written for *The Santa Fe New Mexican* since 1992. He's the author of three film books. A graduate of the American Academy of Dramatic Arts in New York City, he still finds time to keep busy as an actor and playwright.

Jane Phillips, an award-winning photojournalist and fine art photographer, has been with *The Santa Fe New Mexican* since 1995. Phillips earned her BFA from the School of Visual Arts in New York City. She worked at *New York Newsday*, *The New York Times*, *New York Post*, UPI and both the Maine and Santa Fe Photographic Workshops.

Bob Quick has been the business editor of *The Santa Fe New Mexican* for more than 20 years. He previously worked at the *Santa Fe Reporter*, *Bay City News* and other publications. As an English teacher in China from 1979 to 1981, he started a newsletter that was circulated throughout the country.

Luis Sánchez Saturno, originally from Caracas, Venezuela, joined *The Santa Fe New Mexican* in 2002. He graduated that year from Kent State University with a degree in mass communications. His work has appeared in *The New York Times* and *Sports Illustrated*. In 2004, he was nominated for the Pulitzer Prize for his work on heroin addicts in Rio Arriba County.

Tom Sharpe has worked as a journalist for more than 30 years, mostly in New Mexico. He also was a press secretary and speech writer for Governor Toney Anaya and director of communications for the National Council of La Raza in Washington, DC. He has a degree in magazine journalism from the University of Texas.

Jason Strykowski, in 2010, is a student in doctoral program in history at The University of New Mexico. His dissertation focuses on the development of skiing and outdoor recreation in the West. He earned his master's at UNM, concentrating his research on territorial New Mexico. He worked as a magazine writer and newspaper reporter.

Steve Terrell has worked for newspapers in Santa Fe for 30 years. He has been at *The Santa Fe New Mexican* since 1987, where he has covered politics, crime and government. His weekly music column "Terrell's Tune-up" has run for more than 21 years. He also writes two blogs.

Paul Weideman joined *The Santa Fe New Mexican* in 1997. He is a staff writer for *Pasatiempo* and editor of the monthly *Home\Santa Fe Real Estate Guide* magazine. He has bachelor's degrees in biology and editorial journalism, and previously worked for newspapers in Snoqualmie, Washington, and Los Alamos, New Mexico.

Study Guide

Santa Fe, Its 400th Year: Exploring The Past, Defining The Future is a starting point for deeper exploration of the history of Santa Fe and the diverse cultures that shaped it in the past and will shape it in the decades to come.

This study guide is a resource for students and teachers, and for readers who want to investigate more thoroughly the history of the city and surrounding area. The names, terms and study questions relate directly to the text of each chapter in this book.

Many of the study questions do not have right or wrong answers. They are instead springboards for exploration and discussion.

The publisher offers this guide to encourage dialogue in the classroom or in the living room.

Chapter 1
First Contact

Names to Know:

María Gertrudis Barceló, also known as Doña Tules
Susan Shelby Magoffin
Juan de Oñate
Pedro de Peralta
Estevan Rael-Gálvez

Terms to Know:

> San Gabriel
> Barrio de Analco
> Palace of the Governors
> Our Lady of Guadalupe Parish
> Somos un Pueblo Unidos

Study Questions:

- ☐ Why did Spanish conquistadors explore New Mexico?
- ☐ Did the Spanish meet resistance, and why?
- ☐ What is Santa Fe's relationship to Spain and to Mexico?
- ☐ What immigrant movement grew to become the region's largest in the 1990s and 2000s?
- ☐ Why do some contemporary scholars refer to the "mythical" racial identity of Northern New Mexico?

Chapter 2
Pathways

Names to Know:

> William Becknell
> N.B. Laughlin
> Mother Magdalen
> Miguel Antonio Otero Jr.
> José Leandro Perea
> Nina Otero-Warren
> Susan E. Wallace

Terms to Know:

> El Camino Real de Tierra Adentro
> Santa Fe Trail
> Atchison, Topeka and Santa Fe Railway
> Route 66
> New Mexico Rail Runner Express

Study Questions:

- ❏ What conditions did Spanish settlers find on the 1,700-mile journey on El Camino Real?
- ❏ What is the significance and relevance of the following statement? "They came and took away our religion, took away our language, took away our laws and our philosophical concepts."
- ❏ What new mode of transportation arrived in New Mexico in 1878, and how did it change Santa Fe?
- ❏ How did the1938 rerouting of U.S. Route 66 affect Santa Fe?
- ❏ What do transportation planners see as the most pressing issues beyond 2010?

Chapter 3
Storytelling

Names to Know:

Tom Chavéz
Nasario García
Enrique Salazar
Joe Sando
Marc Simmons

Terms to Know:

Story of La Llorona
La Voz del Pueblo
Santa Fe Poet Laureate
Poetry Slam
El Rancho de las Golondrinas

Study Questions:

- ❏ Why was the storytelling tradition valuable?
- ❏ What were some of the key developments that gave New Mexicans a reputation as keepers of a written record?
- ❏ What role did Lew Wallace, the author of *Ben-Hur: A Tale of the Christ,* play in Santa Fe and New Mexico?
- ❏ What was the first film made in New Mexico, and when was it made?
- ❏ What is the message of the Eagle Books series published in 2002?

Chapter 4
Faith

Names to Know:

    Fray Angélico Chávez
    Katharine Drexel
    Jean Baptiste Lamy
    Friar Isidro Ordoñez
    Robert Fortune Sanchez

Terms to Know:

    Franciscans
    Inquisition
    Interfaith Leadership Alliance
    Morada
    Pueblo Feast Days

Study Questions:

❏   What are some historical events or movements that show how the close connection between Spanish settlers and the Catholic Church influenced Santa Fe?

❏   In what way was that connection positive or negative?

❏   What led to the Penitente Brotherhood?

❏   When and why did the name of La Conquistadora change to Our Lady of Peace?

❏   What is the evidence in recent times of growing religious diversity?

Chapter 5
The Land

Names to Know:

    Phillip Bové
    Herman Montoya
    Reynaldo Romero
    Ernie Blake
    Diego de Vargas

Terms to Know:

    10th Mountain Division
    Acequia Madre
    Dale Ball Trail System
    Sangre de Cristo Water Co.
    Santa Fe Farmers Market

Study Questions:

    ❑ How long have people farmed the Santa Fe River basin?
    ❑ What area was known as the breadbasket of Santa Fe?
    ❑ What contribution did Fabiola Cabeza de Baca make to rural New Mexico?
    ❑ How did World War II influence the development of the western ski industry?
    ❑ What is the Sustainable Santa Fe Plan, and what is its goal?

Chapter 6
Rogues

Names of Know:

    Richard C de Baca
    Billy the Kid
    "Hoodoo Brown"
    Thomas B. Catron
    Klaus Fuchs

Terms to Know:

    Borrego murder cases
    Dodge City Gang
    Lincoln County War
    Prison Riot of 1980
    Santa Fe Ring

Study Questions:

    ❑ What, according to historian Michael J. Alarid, was the connection between the Anglo influx and a spike in crime in the territorial period?

    ❑ How did competition between railroads and the coming of the rail lines affect law and order?

    ❑ Who made up the Santa Fe Ring, and what did the Ring do?

    ❑ Do you agree that racial prejudice played a role in the convictions and executions of Thomas Johnson and Louis Young in the 1930s?

    ❑ What fueled the prison riot of 1980, and how did inmates demonstrate the depth of their unrest?

Chapter 7
Preserving Heritage

Names to Know:

    John Gaw Meem
    Popé
    José de Urrutia
    Feliciana Tapia Viarrial
    Donaciano Vigil

Terms to Know:

    Historic Design Review
    La Conquistadora
    Cornerstones
    Graham engravings
    Sociedad Folklórica

Study Questions:

    ❑ Why is San Miguel Mission a symbol of Santa Fe heritage?

    ❑ Why is Santa Fe often included in the same sentence with Quebec, Jamestown and St. Augustine?

    ❑ What circumstances led to the Pueblo Revolt and the Reconquest?

    ❑ What was the Tertio-Millennial celebration, and what did it say about Santa Fe's eagerness to celebrate its heritage?

    ❑ What acts of determination led in 1936 to federal recognition of Pojoaque Pueblo?

Chapter 8
Creativity

Names to Know:

T.C. Cannon
Charles Carrillo
Dorothy Dunn
Allan Houser
Maria Martinez
Georgia O'Keeffe

Terms to Know:

Los Cincos Pintores, the five painters
Spanish Colonial Arts Society
Institute of American Indian Arts
Museum of Fine Arts
SITE Santa Fe

Study Questions:

❏ What were the Santa Fe art colonies, and which artists belonged to which colonies?
❏ When did Indian Market begin, and what is its significance?
❏ What was the Studio School at Santa Fe Indian School?
❏ What factors helped make Santa Fe a center for artists?
❏ What is a santero?

Chapter 9
Learning

Names to Know:

Brother Botulph
John V. Conway
Edgar Lee Hewett
Estafanita Martinez
Pedro Bautista Pino

Terms to Know:

> Sisters of Loretto
> St. Michael's College
> St. Catherine Indian School
> Native Languages Preservation Act
> One-room school

Study Questions:

- ❏ When New Mexico's representative appealed in 1812 for money from the Spanish crown, what was his argument?
- ❏ What was the issue in 1884 when it took a citizens committee to reform school funding?
- ❏ What research institute took education out of the classroom and into the field for the study of archaeology?
- ❏ What do you think are the greatest changes in public education in the last three generations?
- ❏ What power-sharing innovation did school Superintendent Edward Ortiz try in 1989?

Chapter 10
Power

Names to Know:

> David Cargo
> Dennis Chavez
> George Gonzales
> Concha Ortiz y Pino de Kleven
> Miguel Trujillo

Terms to Know:

> Chimayó Tax Revolt
> Treaty of Guadalupe Hidalgo
> Land grants
> Personal politics
> Emerge New Mexico

Study Questions:

- ❑ What did Santa Fe authorities suspect when they detained explorer Zebulon Pike?
- ❑ Why did it take more than 60 years for New Mexico territory to become a state?
- ❑ In a political city, where the economy is based on politics and government, what are the challenges in balancing public and special interests?
- ❑ When did Native Americans win the right to vote in state elections, and what did it take for that to happen?
- ❑ What barriers do women face in electoral politics? Are those barriers coming down, or are they coming down fast enough?

Chapter 11
Warriors

Names to Know:

> Edward Canby
> Kit Carson
> Alexine, Ray and Refugio Chavez
> Dorothy McKibben
> Jose D. Sena

Terms to Know:

> Presidio
> Signal Corps
> Fort Union
> Rough Riders
> Bataan Death March

Study Questions:

- ❑ What were the immediate and long-term military, political and cultural impacts when the U.S. Army rode into Santa Fe in 1846?
- ❑ What made the campaign carried out by U.S. Army officers Kit Carson and James Carleton against Native Americans, the Navajo in particular, infamous?

❑ What did the Confederate Army want when it entered New Mexico in 1862?

❑ What is the special significance to Santa Fe of the 200th Coast Artillery that was stationed in the Philippines in the early days of World War II?

❑ On what basis does one choose between joining the National Guard or the regular military, and what choice would you make?

Chapter 12
Family

Names to Know:

> Willa Cather
> Amado Chaves
> Pedro Ribera Ortega
> Amalia Sena Sánchez
> Miguel de la Vega y Coca

Terms to Know:

> Sisters of Charity
> La Fonda
> Harvey Girls
> Sunmount Sanatorium
> Canyon Road Farolitos

Study Questions:

❑ What did Willa Cather's *Death Comes for the Archbishop* mean for Santa Fe?

❑ What lasting contribution did Pablita Velarde make in depicting and preserving Pueblo life?

❑ Who were Harvey Girls, what did they do at La Fonda, and what role did these women and the hotel play in the story of the modern West?

❑ How did Santa Fe Fiesta in the early-1900s compare to the event as it is a century later?

❑ What dubious distinction did *Time* magazine give Santa Fe in 1946, and what efforts corrected the problem?

INDEX

Prepared by Theresa A. Strottman

Page numbers in **bold** refer to illustrations.

LaVergne, TN USA
10 December 2010
208072LV00002B/79-400/P